# ETHICS IN SOCIAL RESEARCH

*Robert T. Bower*
*Priscilla de Gasparis*

# ETHICS IN
# SOCIAL RESEARCH

*Protecting the*
*Interests of*
*Human Subjects*

**PRAEGER PUBLISHERS**
**Praeger Special Studies**

New York • London • Sydney • Toronto

**Library of Congress Cataloging in Publication Data**

Bower, Robert T
  Ethics in social research.

  Bibliography: p.
  Includes indexes.
  1. Social science research—Moral and religious
aspects.  2. Ethics.  3. Privacy, Right of.
I. De Gasparis, Priscilla, joint author.  II. Title.
H62.B625            174'.9'3            78-19452
ISBN 0-03-046406-4

Some of the work upon which this publication is based was prepared under Contract
Numbers ADM-42-74-31 and 278-76-0084 (ER) with the National Institute of Mental
Health, Department of Health, Education and Welfare. Materials developed under
the contracts may be reproduced in whole or in part by the U.S. Government.

$SB/11245$  $/12.75.$  $8.79.$

PRAEGER PUBLISHERS, PRAEGER SPECIAL STUDIES
383 Madison Avenue, New York, N.Y., 10017, U.S.A.

Published in the United States of America in 1978
by Praeger Publishers,
A Division of Holt, Rinehart and Winston, CBS Inc.

89 038 987654321

© 1978 by Praeger Publishers

Printed in the United States of America

# *Preface*

The investigation resulting in this report benefited from the knowledge and experience of a task force comprised largely of representatives of social science disciplines. Chosen at the suggestion of their professional associations were M. Brewster Smith, American Psychological Association; Bernard Barber, American Sociological Association; James Carroll, American Political Science Association; George M. Foster, American Anthropological Association; Charles F. Cannell, American Statistical Association; and Irving Crespi, American Association for Public Opinion Research. Albert J. Reiss, Jr., whose name also appeared on the American Sociological Association list of suggested names and who had written cogently on the topic of the project, was added to the group, along with Albert Biderman, another author on professionalism and a representative of the Bureau of Social Science Research (BSSR).

The task force assembled for a two-day meeting in June 1975, along with representatives of several government agencies which were particularly concerned with the issues surrounding the protection of human subjects. Many of the themes that were developed at that meeting found their way into Chapters 1–6 of this book. A second meeting of the task force was held in February 1977 to consider the general conclusions and recommendations that might be offered our government sponsors and our other colleagues in social science research. That meeting was attended by everybody named above except George Foster, who was out of the country at the time, and Irving Crespi, who withdrew from participation for reasons of health. The American Association for Public Opinion Research suggested Mathew Hauck who agreed to join us as Crespi's replacement. At the meeting, a draft prepared by Bower was discussed and suggestions were made, leading to the Conclusions and Recommendations appearing as Chapter 7. That chapter, moderate though its statements may seem, should not be interpreted as a final and permanent agreement on the part of the task force members, let alone a conclusion as to the position that the professional groups they represent have or might adopt. Our report itself gives ample evidence of the divergence among men and women of scientific stature and integrity when dealing with matters of professional ethics. Chapter 7 can be seen only as a general consensus among a few who have tried in concert to treat some of the problems in conducting social research with fellow humans as the subjects of its investigations.

The report was coauthored by Robert T. Bower and Priscilla de Gasparis and reviewed by the study task force. Ms. de Gasparis also prepared the annotated bibliography with assistance from Tony Cantrick and Carol Greenhouse of BSSR and conducted the inquiries of the state of professional codes of ethics in their treatment of human subject protection (Appendix A) and of public concerns on the topic (Appendix B). Both of these appendix reports benefited from the editorial help of Albert Gollin. The whole long investigation, which was supported by the National Institute of Mental Health (NIMH), received invaluable assistance from Edward J. Flynn, Chief of the Institute's Applied Research Branch, and from Mitchell B. Balter, of its Psychopharmacology Research Branch.

# Contents

# ETHICS IN SOCIAL RESEARCH

# 1 / Introduction

The informal investigation that is summarized in this volume began with the title: "Protection of Human Subjects in Large-Scale Studies of Noninstitutionalized Normal Subjects." The referents of study have, specifically, been surveys and social experiments, with the purpose of exploring the particular problems such large-scale studies encounter in the use of normal people as research subjects, as distinct, primarily, from the problems of using subjects for experimentation in biomedical research. At the time we started, questions had been raised as to whether governmental regulations such as those the U.S. Department of Health, Education and Welfare (HEW) had issued could have equally viable application to both biomedical and social research, or whether some special set of regulations should be issued for the social research area. Since then, the creation of the Commission on the Protection of Human Subjects in Biomedical and Behavioral Research, with its congressional mandate to recommend means of control for research by agencies other than HEW, and the Privacy Protection Study Commission, enacted under the Privacy Act of 1974, with its mission to seek limits to the invasion of privacy in all sectors of the economy, have broadened the federal oversight of the issues and have added to the trend toward government regulation. Our hope for this study is that it will add some small increment to the discussion underway in social science and governmental circles about the wisdom of various actions that might be taken to promote the conduct of scientifically sound and ethical social research that protects the welfare of its human subjects.

In social science circles these discussions have intensified during the past few years, both in reaction to governmental initiatives and in response to the sort of professional concerns that have led to the promulgation of codes of ethics by professional associations. So far, not much in the way of consensus has emerged on most of the key issues being examined. Strong voices give reasoned arguments for extreme positions. At one pole is the view that inquiry should know no restrictions beyond the personal conscience of the inquirer. At the other pole is the position that extrascientific moral impera-tives require the adherence to externally imposed restrictions and the elimi-nation of any research practices that conflict with these extrascientific controls. In the territory between, where we have tried to set up camp, there is probably no spot safe from criticism from one side or the other, and it may be the better part of wisdom that we treat problems in this study, with little on solutions except at the very end where some procedural recommen-dations are offered.

The work on which we are reporting included a review of the litera-ture, a series of organized discussions at national and local professional association meetings, a review of professional codes of ethics, a special survey of the interests and activities of organized citizens' groups, and the deliberations of a task force, brought together in a two-day meeting to provide the perspectives of the disciplines of sociology, anthropology, pub-lic opinion research, political science, social statistics, and psychology, and to give its expert guidance to the inquiry. We had originally planned to limit our review to large-scale studies of the type suggested by the original project title, but so many of the ethical problems with which we are dealing cut across disciplinary lines in social science and appear in so many different types of research procedures that the separation proved too difficult to maintain. We have ended up eliminating from consideration only research dealing with special groups and presenting special issues, such as studies involving children, prisoners, and other institutional populations, and, of course, biomedical research.

After a brief history of recent developments, the chapters which follow discuss, in order, the risks which subjects of social research may encounter, the principle of informed consent, the weighing of risks and benefits, and the means by which control of social research may be exercised.

# 2 / *Historical Background*

A variety of explanations have been proposed by various authors to account for the phenomenon we presently witness: a rapidly increasing concern about the protection of the rights and welfare of human subjects in biomedical, behavioral, and social science research. These authors' views include both an emphasis on the civil rights movements (Barber 1973b) and a reference to the rapid post-World War II increase in public funding of research activities (Smith 1967; Sykes 1967). There is general agreement that, whatever the configuration of factors accounting for the present situation, the initial concern arose primarily in connection with biomedical research.

In considering what he calls "experimentation without restriction," Katz (1972) distinguishes among experimentation conducted before World War II, the Nazi war research which led up to the Nuremberg trials, and subsequent experimentation. The Nuremberg trials can be said to mark a watershed as far as reaction to experimenting on human beings is concerned. The Hippocratic Oath enjoins physicians not to do harm; yet there is ample evidence (see, for instance, Katz 1972: pp. 281–91) of risky, at times fatal, research being carried out on people without their consent or even their awareness in far more "normal" settings than the Nazi concentration camps. Nonetheless, it was outrage at the kinds of experiments performed by Nazi doctors on defenseless political and war prisoners, culminating in the Nuremberg trials, which served to make explicit for the first time, in the form of the Nuremberg Code, the ethical principles which ought to underlie biomedical research on human beings. The Nuremberg Code forms the basis for the Declaration of Helsinki, adopted by the World Medical Association in 1964, and the "Ethical Guidelines for Clinical Investigation" adopted by the American Medical Association in 1966. It is worth remembering, incidentally, that the position taken by the defense in the Nuremberg trials—

that the community ought to have precedence over the individual, "the welfare of the species overrides the welfare of the particular man" (Freund 1967)—was rejected.

Though the Nazi atrocities figure prominently, other factors contribute to our understanding. The point has been made that biomedical research tends to place the welfare of human subjects at risk, while social research tends to threaten the rights of its subjects. According to a commentator (Simmel 1968), the development of one particular right, namely that of privacy, can be traced back to the famous article establishing common-law jurisprudence in connection with privacy rights written by Warren and Brandeis in 1890, well before the Nuremberg Code. In any event, civil rights movements would appear to be a characteristic feature of the development of the Western world, perhaps in line with Sykes's formulation (1967) that our "ever more managed social order" has led to increasing concern with individual rights. While keeping in mind such broad systemic features, it is of particular utility in gaining an understanding of where we are now to trace the development of congressional and federal agency activity dealing with protecting the rights and welfare of human subjects and regulating the conduct of researchers.

According to Curran (1969) there was little law relevant to the research process before the 1960s. No specific federal or state statutes regulated any aspect of research and no legal actions were recorded except for some appellate court decisions and medical malpractice suits. Curran interprets the general legal position before the 1960s as one in which experiments on patients were conducted at the researcher's risk. A Michigan Supreme Court decision in 1935 marked an important step forward by sanctioning research so long as consent was in operation and the experimental procedure was not radically different from accepted practice—a decision thus interpretable as allowing research within reasonable bounds. It may have been the attempt to articulate these "reasonable bounds," as distinct from "arbitrary establishment of rules of conduct by the courts" (Curran 1969: 545), which prompted the recognition of a need to control and regulate research. There was also impetus from the findings of two survey research studies, one conducted by Welt in 1961 (see Katz 1972: 889) and a later one conducted by the Law-Medicine Research Institute at Boston University, indicating a general lack of ethical guidelines or even interest in establishing professional codes in the biomedical research world.

Prior to that period, the Food and Drug Administration in 1938 was given congressional authority to regulate drug investigation, but rarely used it. Because of Senator Kefauver's interest in the topic, and the thalidomide tragedy, the Kefauver-Harris Bill, the Drug Amendments of 1962, was passed. This bill contributed to the use of the principle of informed consent in investigating the effects of new drugs on people.

Beginning in 1946, grant applications for extramural research submitted to the U.S. Public Health Service (PHS) were subjected to a variety of review procedures. Ethical standards may have been implicit in these reviews, but such considerations were incidental to the major criteria of scientific merit and relevance. With the opening of the National Institutes of Health Clinical Research Center in 1953, however, concern with ethical standards moved into a central position primarily because of the use of "normal" volunteer subjects. The National Institutes of Health (NIH) issued a set of guidelines, "Group Considerations of Clinical Research Procedures Deviating from Accepted Medical Practice or Involving Unusual Hazard to Patients." In addition, an institute-wide clinical review committee was established to review questionable cases involving patients and all research projects involving normal volunteers. Consent was required for participation based on information presented to subjects "suited to their comprehension."

In the late 1950s an attempt was made by NIH to adopt the Nuremberg Code for both intramural and extramural research. The move failed "because of the difficulty of devising a single code that would cover with equal adequacy and flexibility the entire range of biomedical experimentation" (Frankel 1972: 14, quoting Chalkley). Despite this, events occurring between the late 1950s and the middle 1960s strengthened the belief that research involving human subjects required greater regulation and control. As already mentioned, the Boston University Law-Medicine Research Institute was unable to detect much activity in the research community directed toward developing ethical guidelines. Other factors fostering attention to the need for control included the increased public funds allocated to research which sharpened the need for public accountability: the Food and Drug Administration (FDA) activities which, prompted by Congress, resulted in mandatory subject consent for studies involving experimental drugs; specific instances of violation of ethical principles such as in the Jewish Chronic Disease Hospital case; growing concern at NIH about its legal responsibility regarding research; the World Medical Association's adoption of the Declaration of Helsinki; Congressman Gallagher's concern about invasion of privacy in 1965; and the generalized perception that in biomedical research manipulation was replacing observation. As a result, the National Health Advisory Council at a meeting in December 1965 resolved that PHS funding should be made contingent on prior review of a proposed research project by the investigator's institutional associates to assure an independent determination of the protection of the rights and welfare of the individual or individuals involved, of the appropriateness of the methods used to secure informed consent, and of the risks and potential medical benefits of the investigation (see Frankel 1972). Accordingly, in February 1966, the surgeon general issued the first official Policy and Procedure Order covering all PHS research and research training grant regulations and policy statements. This policy made PHS funding of each separate grant application contingent on an assurance that an institutional committee had reviewed the rights and welfare of the subjects involved, the appropriateness of the methods used to gain informed consent, and the risks and potential benefits of the proposed study.

Administrative difficulties of handling individual assurances led to a revision of the policy in July 1966. Single assurances accompanying separate grant applications could be replaced by general institutional assurances covering all subsequent applications from an institution. These assurances were required to stipulate compliance with the principles of the policy, describe the review committee, and outline the procedures adopted for surveillance of the research, the giving of advice, and the provisions for enforcement. All PHS grant applications involving human subjects were required to undergo review, and institutions were required to report changes in policy, in procedures, or in the composition of review committees.

In December 1966 a policy statement was issued with the aim of clarifying the position of the behavioral and social sciences vis-à-vis the new guidelines. This document affirmed that the guidelines in general applied to social research but acknowledged that some such studies "did not require the fully informed consent of the subject or even his knowledgeable participation" (see Frankel 1972: 36–37). Another policy revision in January 1967 made clear that despite the existence of institutional assurances, the PHS retained the responsibility for protecting the rights and welfare of subjects and would recommend disapproval of an application if the research was considered too hazardous.

In response to a PHS-NIH task force review report of the policy, another revision occurred in May 1969 and was issued in booklet form under the title, "Protection of the Individual as a Research Subject." The task force's major recommendation was that the policy be revised "to provide better understanding of the requirements" (Frankel 1972, quoting Confrey, p. 38). Confrey himself (1967), writing on PHS policy concerning grant-supported research with human beings, lists the various features of the policy as including institutional responsibility; independent review and surveillance of and advice on research projects; the need to take community norms into account during the review process; the possibility of designating separate review groups for particular areas; and the recognition that some behavioral research involves no personal risk but is still subject to the consideration of such matters as voluntary participation, confidentiality, and protection of subjects against misuse of findings. Furthermore, the policy was designed to reflect certain principles such as an avoidance of extreme positions; a recognition of the complementary roles of the granting agency, the grantee institution, and the individual researcher; and an appreciation of the diversity of institutional settings, types of research, subjects, and investigators. The revised policy reiterated the point that the grantee institution was responsible for the protection of human subjects. Its most important modification was the recognition that benefits to subjects could be other than medical, and that the new knowledge sought could be important enough to allow subjects to accept risk in the interest of the wider collectivity. It also described more closely what was meant by consent and reinstituted the requirement for certification that individual projects involving human subjects had been reviewed.

The next step in the evolution of policy statements concerning the protection of human subjects occurred in 1971 (first found in Chapter 1–40, "Protection of Human Subjects," HEW Grants Administrative Manual, April 1971, then issued in booklet form: *The Institutional Guide to DHEW Policy on Protection of Human Subjects,* December 1971). Two major changes can be noted. In the first place, the policy no longer applied only to PHS funding applications but to all HEW grant and contract activities involving human subjects. In the second place, the requirements for obtaining informed consent were given in considerably greater detail:

> Informed consent is the agreement obtained from a subject or from his authorized representative, to the subject's participation in any activity.
> The basic elements of informed consent are:
> 1. A fair explanation of the procedures to be followed, including an identification of those which are experimental;
> 2. A description of the attendant discomforts and risks;
> 3. A description of the benefits to be expected;
> 4. A disclosure of appropriate alternative procedures that would be advantageous for the subject;
> 5. An offer to answer any enquiries concerning the procedures;
> 6. An instruction that the subject is free to withdraw his consent and to discontinue participation in the project or activity at any time.
> In addition, the agreement, written or oral, entered into by the subject, should include no exculpatory language through which the subject is made to waive, or appear to waive, any of his legal rights, or to release the institution or its agents from liability for negligence *(The Institutional Guide to DHEW Policy on Protection of Human Subjects.)*

The policy required informed-consent procedures to be fully documented. Three forms of documentation were provided, two requiring the signature of the subject or the subject's authorized representative, the third form allowing for modification of the two "primary procedures" but warning that granting of permission to use modified procedures imposes additional responsibility upon the review committee and the institution to establish that the risk to any subject is minimum, that use of either of the primary procedures for obtaining informed consent would surely invalidate objectives of considerable immediate importance, and that any reasonable alternative means for attaining these objectives would be less advantageous to the subject.

This brings us to the most recent wave of activities within HEW concerning protection of human subjects. In October 1973 the department issued a new proposed general policy, which was then published in final form on May 30, 1974, to become effective July 1, 1974. It noted that the department was working on special policies dealing with prisoners, children, fetuses and abortuses, and with the institutionalized mentally disabled; that it was considering policies dealing specifically with candidates for psychosurgery or sterilization, and for subjects used in social science research; and that programs administered by the Office of Education (OE) and the National Institute of Education (NIE) were exempted until the policy was adopted or implemented through regulations issued by these agencies. The most notable change was the elevation of the policy to the status of federal regulation. A number of other changes from the 1971 policy can be noted too. The regulations define "subject at risk" as

any individual who may be exposed to the possibility of injury, including physical, psychological, or social injury, as a consequence of participation as a subject in any research, development, or related activity which departs from the application of those established and accepted methods necessary to meet his needs, or which increases the ordinary risks of daily life, including the recognized risks inherent in a chosen occupation or field of service (*Federal Register* 39, no. 105 [May 30, 1974]: 18917).

The term "informed consent" is more specifically defined as "the knowing consent of an individual or his legally authorized representative, so situated as to be able to exercise free power of choice without undue inducement or any element of force, fraud, deceit, duress, or other form of constraint or coercion." The "basic elements" of informed consent remain as they were in the 1971 policy. Institutional review committees (called "institutional ethical review boards" in the technical amendments to the policy published in March 1975) are required to determine whether "legally effective informed consent" will be obtained, although the regulations, again as in 1971, continue to allow modification of this requirement provided a committee's rationale for permitting such modification is carefully documented. The regulations break new ground by prescribing the composition of institutional review boards: there must be at least five members of varying professional background, including at least one person from outside the institution.

In November 1973 draft rules for research on children, prisoners, and the mentally infirm were published, followed in August 1974 by additional proposed rule making governing research on the fetus, the abortus, pregnant women, in vitro fertilization, prisoners, and the institutionalized mentally disabled. NIE requirements for award and administration of grants for educational research, including the protection of subjects, were issued in November 1974. As a result of the Buckley Amendments (see below), proposed rules for protecting the privacy rights of students and parents were issued by HEW in January 1975, and a notice of proposed joint rule making on the confidentiality of alcohol and drug abuse patient records by HEW and the Special Action Office for Drug Abuse Prevention (SAODAP) appeared in the *Federal Register* of May 9, 1975.

On the congressional side, the single most important piece of legislation dealing with this issue passed recently is the National Research Act, initiated by Senator Edward Kennedy, and signed into law (PL 93–348) as an amendment to the Public Health Service Act. Title II of the act established a National Commission for the Protection of Human Subjects of Biomedical and Behavioral Science Research with the mandate to conduct a comprehensive investigation of the basic ethical principles which should underlie such research and to develop guidelines for assuring greater congruity between the ethical principles and the actual conduct of research. In addition, the commission is required to undertake a wide-ranging study of the ethical, social, and legal implications of advances in biomedical and behavioral science and technology. The act also provides for making the commission's recommendations applicable to all federal agencies, for establishing a national advisory council to watch over the protection of subjects after the demise of the commission, and for the establishment of institutional review boards and an ethical guidance program within HEW.

The National Research Act is not the only piece of legislation signed into law recently which pertains either directly or indirectly to the conduct of social research. PL 93–380, the Education Amendments of 1974, better known as the Buckley Amendments, is designed to protect the rights and privacy of parents and students by granting to students (or their parents if the students are under 18) the right of access to official records directly related to them and by prohibiting, with some exceptions, the release of personally identifiable information about students to anyone else without the written consent of students or their parents. In addition, all instructional material used in connection with any research or experimentation program must be available to parents of children engaged in such a program. An amendment to the Buckley provisions (PL 93–568) defines "official school record" and exempts certain confidential letters and personal financial information from the provisions of the law. It also adds some exceptions to the requirement of obtaining informed consent from parents or students before data transmittal to third parties is permitted—mainly in the case of other educational institutions and state or federal agencies including organizations concerned with predictive tests and improving instruction, provided the data are not personally identifiable, the purpose for their use is known, and they are destroyed after completion of the study.

A final piece of important legislation considered is the Privacy Act of 1974 (PL 93–579). In general this act requires federal agencies to identify their record-keeping systems annually, establishes minimum standards for all systems to regulate the data accumulation process as well as its security and use, permits individuals access to their own records and allows them to challenge the accuracy of the data therein, provides administrative and judicial machinery for oversight, and establishes the seven-member Privacy Protection Study Commission to examine the privacy issues further and consider their solutions in the private sector. With respect to the crucial issue of informed consent, the act provides that unless an individual gives her or his consent, no agency may disclose records except under specified conditions or for purposes expressly provided for in the bill. The latter include disclosures to officers within the same agency who need the records for their work, pursuant to "routine use"—that is, use compatible with the purposes for which the records were collected following public notice and comment on the type of routine use; releases to the Bureau of the Census to perform its statutory functions, to the National Archives when preservation is warranted, to other agencies in connection with law enforcement activities, to committees of Congress with jurisdiction, to the comptroller general or pursuant to court order; disclosure when the health and safety of the individual is involved; and releases required by the Freedom of Information Act for statistical purposes, provided the information is not in personally identifiable form.

The research community's reaction to the Privacy Act is somewhat ambiguous due in part to the unclear wording of the act (the Office of Management and Budget, given responsibility for oversight, has issued a 114-page document of guidelines for implementation and other agencies have followed suit). Hulett (1975), after careful consideration of the Privacy Act for the adequate protection of the rights of informants as well as for its effects on the furtherance of knowledge, suggests that it needs further amendment. He feels that specific laws applying to particular agencies are necessary because agencies' needs, activities, and requirements are so different. Another important issue he sees needing resolution is the relationship between the right to privacy, the knowledge needed for compulsory legal processes, and the provisions of the Freedom of Information Act. A satisfactory balance needs to be struck between protecting confidentiality and sharing identifiable statistics and data for research purposes; and the position of contractors and other extramural researchers should be clarified. Bryant and Hansen (1976) view valid statistics as having great social utility and criticize the lack of clear distinction between administrative and statistical records. The authors are not aware of a single instance in which the use of records for statistical purposes has been of detriment to an individual, and they argue that the concept of invasion of privacy is irrelevant to statistical studies when such information is not released in personally identifiable form. If legislators are indeed seriously concerned with invasions of privacy, a better solution, they feel, would be provided by according legal protection to the maintenance of data confidentiality.

# 3 / Risks

The treatment of risks in this chapter is organized around six forbidding terms that are frequently used in the writings and discussions of the ethical problems in protecting the subjects of social research: coercion, or the exercise of undue pressure to induce a subject to participate when he would rather not; deception, or misleading the subject on what the study is all about; invasion of privacy, or intrusion into matters that the subject would rather keep to himself; breach of confidentiality, or permitting information about individual subjects to be passed on to others; stress, or the psychological difficulties that participation in a study might cause; and collective risks, or the harm a study might cause to others beyond the individual subject himself. The terms are by no means mutually exclusive. In a hypothetical instance, a particularly unfortunate subject could be coerced into a study through a deceptively misleading description he was given, to find himself involved in procedures which invade his privacy and cause him stress, partly because the information he provided was not kept confidential and partly because he saw the results of the research as risky to the interests of the collectivity to which he belonged.

The multiplicity of conceivable psychological and social injuries is just one of the problems in talking about risks in social research. Another is the possibility of creating some dire image of an ethically corrupt social science which places the rights and welfare of the public in jeopardy through its manipulative malfeasance. The image-building starts with the use of the ominous terms above and continues as one tries to find, or imagine, as many ills as possible in order to see what it is, if anything, that needs a cure. In fact, it is difficult to find much evidence of undeniable outright harm caused to the subjects of social research. Where abuses have been alleged they have also been debated by reasonable persons on both sides. Some of the risks discussed in this section are matters of serious ethical concern to social scientists and to others who may have a role in the setting of standards for the conduct of social research; others are much like the normal risks of everyday life.

The consideration of risks to subjects of social research is sufficiently multidimensional and controversial in its own right to at least try to separate it from the area of ethical concern surrounding research in the biomedical area, though the two tend to be linked in legal and ethical discussions of researchers' responsibilities and limitations, as well as in federal laws and regulations. Most significant at present is their joint treatment in the HEW regulations and in their combined consideration under the mandate of the Commission on the Protection of Human Subjects in Biomedical and Behavioral Research. The attitude of the social science practitioners toward this marriage, as one hears it discussed among social science groups, is ambivalent. It seems a more natural alliance on an interprofessional level for those involved in such endeavors as medical sociology or clinical research in psychology than for those whose research does not bring them into medical institutional settings or into working relationships with medical researchers. As a matter of self-interested strategy in handling the public policy problems of human subject protection, a case can be made for an alliance with a profession that is better established and more prestigious in the public eye; but at the same time, there are sufficient differences in the nature of the risks to subjects in the two areas at least to raise questions about the continued viability of the union.

In most social science studies—particularly the large-scale studies we are focusing on—people's behavior and attitudes are measured insofar as possible under the normal conditions of everyday life. The investigator tries to avoid, or limit, the introduction of exogenous elements that might produce artifacts affecting the response to his inquiry if the naturalness of the setting were altered. At an extreme in avoiding the artifacts is the study based entirely on unperceived or covert observation; more frequent are the studies that require overt personal contact by data collectors in as natural a social and physical setting as circumstances will allow. In considering the role of such data collectors, social scientists worry not only about any attitudinal predilections that might come across to respondents, but also about any characteristics the data collectors may seem to possess that might affect responses, such as their position of authority which the respondent might feel compelled to respect. The investigator, says most social science in theory and practice, should try to maintain an equal-status position with the subject. It is perhaps not a semantic accident that the word "subject" is more apt to be found in medical research where in most cases a hierarchical role relationship between investigator-cum-doctor and subject-cum-patient is inevitable, and that in social research the traditional term for someone under investigation is hierarchically neutral—"respondent," "participant," "interviewee," "informant." Similarly, social scientists—unlike biomedical investigators—typically gather data (there are exceptions) where the subjects would normally find themselves in the course of their daily activities: at home, on the campus, at work, at the shopping center, or on the streetcorner—places in which they would have no particular reason to feel defenseless or infer that they should relinquish their rights before the authority of a researcher. In addition, medical research tends to deal in technical substance and procedures phrased in esoteric language, further reducing the control that the average subject might feel he exercises in the research process and giving more emphasis to the authority of the investigator. The procedures of social research, generally, are more easily explained in common language.

This is not to say that the differences between the two research areas are clear-cut and absolute. Much social experimentation takes place in laboratories, even with researchers in white coats; and much medical research, in epidemiology for instance, takes place in everyday settings with investigators in mufti. Furthermore, even the most participatory of social research may not completely escape an element of real or imagined hierarchical difference between researcher and subject. Kelman (1972), for instance, sees a sufficient power differential between the social scientist and his subject— especially when social scientists deal mostly with underprivileged groups— to conclude that some of the solutions to ethical problems in research lie in attempts to redress the power imbalance in the conduct of social studies. Kelman might nevertheless agree to a substantial difference in this respect between the two research areas.

Beyond the obvious fact that the major risks for subjects of biomedical research are usually of a physiological nature and rarely so in social research, the differences in role relationships between investigator and subject in the two areas result in distinctions in the ways risks may be perceived. In respect to the concept of privacy, for instance, the same inquiries into a subject's personal behavior and activities that could seem quite legitimate in a biomedical research setting, pervaded as it is by the tradition of the doctor's authority and legally sustained assumptions of confidentiality, can be considered "invasions of privacy" when asked by social scientists for equally valid research purposes. Not surprisingly, possible invasions of privacy are considered to be among the major risks to which subjects of social research may be exposed, while such considerations are infrequently raised in biomedical studies. On the other hand, the more egalitarian nature of social research participation puts its subjects in a reasonable position to maintain their autonomy and allows them a sense of control over what they will say and how they will act during the course of an inquiry; by and large, they are far from defenseless. There would appear to us to be enough of a difference between the two areas to treat social science as a separate category with its distinct problems in the discussion of risks which follows.

## COERCION

If social scientists could conduct their studies with only self-initiated volunteers as subjects, there would be little cause for concern about coercion as an ethical issue. But as Rosenthal and Rosnow (1975:199) point out in their review of the available evidence dealing with the nature and status of volunteering subjects, "the ethical dilemma results from the likelihood that fully informed voluntarism, while it may satisfy the moral concern of researchers, may be contraindicated for the scientific concern in many cases; and experimenters must weigh the social ethic against the scientific ethic in deciding which violation would constitute the greater moral danger.

Most modern social research calls for particular, designated subjects who must somehow be enticed to participate in the study. True, before World War II there was a tendency at least in public opinion studies to rely on sheer numbers, however recruited, from whatever available lists, with little concern about the proportion who participated as long as there were enough of them. Since those early days, the application of probability sampling principles to survey research has left virtually all large-scale social science studies dependent on the participation of those members of the public whom the social scientist selects in accordance with his research—individuals chosen because of their roles in a community, membership in a group, their particular social or economic characteristics, or because they fall by chance into a sample of some large population. This need for purposeful selection in social studies, accompanied by the requirement that a high proportion of the designated subjects actually participate, leads to the quite understandable attempt to induce people to participate as well as to the potential for ethical abuse by undue persuasion or other forms of coercion.

Coercion could, theoretically, take several different forms: the payment of extravagant gifts or stipends, the undue use of authority, threats concerning the consequences of nonparticipation, or excessive persuasion. The payment of something in the form of gifts or stipends to subjects is not at all infrequent in social research. Students may be paid for their participation in campus experiments; in marketing research respondents may be offered a gift (a pair of stockings, a book); in large-scale mail surveys those who send back their questionnaire may be promised a summary of the findings of the study; interviewees, especially when the interview is long or carried out in several sessions, may be paid for their time. But it is unlikely that such inducements frequently would be found to be excessive. Social research is not generally the recipient of lavish funding and most studies can be carried out successfully without any payment at all to the subjects. In a rare instance involving a special population, there is a report of inmates of an Illinois prison making a maximum of $1.35 per day in the very few prison industry jobs that are available who were offered $50 a month for participation in an experimental study. Normally, among the noninstitutionalized public, payments made to subjects are apt to be on the order of $5 to a respondent for car fare and time to come in for an interview, or minimum wage payments to students participating in a psychological experiment.

Though the use of gifts and stipends has sometimes been seen as a means of coercing subjects to submit to procedures that they might otherwise choose to avoid, it might with equal propriety be viewed as fair payment for subjects' time and inconvenience in performing their indispensable roles in the research (Vargus 1971). It is an equally appropriate ethical question to ask whether it is unfair *not* to pay respondents, and the social scientist could be in a more tenable ethical position if it were normal practice to pay all participants in research for their contributions. In some cases, researchers have decided to do just that because of pressures from community groups in areas where research is taking place, particularly in low-income urban areas blessed with alert indigenous leadership. These decisions do not necessarily follow from the ethical consideration of the investigator, but rather are responses to what members of the community consider appropriate in the circumstance.

An extreme case of the use of authority to gain cooperation in research is provided by the U.S. Decennial Census, where participation is required by the authority of law. In normal social research, which lacks such legal buttressing, the use of authority takes more subtle forms, ranging from the not-so-subtle erstwhile practice in the military of ordering troops to report for tests, through professors requesting students to fill out questionnaires, down to the mere speculative possibility that the dress or manner or academic status of an interviewer will lead to the attribution of an authority that does not exist. The main problem for the social scientist stems from the linkage in the minds of people and in much of real life between status and authority and the distinct likelihood that status clues provided by the researcher in the form of titles (psychologist, anthropologist) or appearance (business suit and tie) or speech (sounds upper-class) or any other form will encourage the subject to assume that the investigator possesses some authority to require his participation.

The use of outright threats in social research, if it occurs at all, is at least rare enough to go unnoticed in the literature. Unduly persuasive techniques are probably more likely, and they are probably more frequently used when subjects, for whatever reasons, wish to withdraw from further participation than when they are initially recruited. Though standard ethics policies, and current HEW regulations, require that subjects be informed of their freedom to discontinue participation at any time without prejudice, Menges (1973) points out the difficulty in achieving the severance if it spoils random assignment conditions or if it disrupts a previous relationship, for example, between teacher and student. It would be unreasonable to suppose that a researcher would not do his best to ensure the continued validity of the research, but there appears to be no firm evidence that the efforts extend into severe forms of duress.

## DECEPTION

The subjects of social studies may be misled in a number of ways: by a misstatement of the purposes of a study or the uses that will be made of its results, by disguise of the variables being measured, by a misleading description of the study's procedures, or by misinformation about its sponsorship. Such deviations from the full truth, which can range from outright lies to mild and ambiguous forms of dissembling, have their scientific purposes. Stated most broadly, they may serve to keep from the subject's awareness elements that are exogenous to the variables under study but which might modify behavior or influence reaction to inquiries if they were known to the subject. A host of social scientists have noted the propensity on the part of people to modify their behavior if they know what it is that is under scrutiny or measurement. How can you study fear as normally experienced if you tell the subjects you are doing so and permit them to prepare for the shock? How can you probe the extent of obedience if subjects are aware of what you are doing and can decide ahead of time how obedient they wish to appear in an experimental situation? If you say you are working for the Anti-Defamation League, may not respondents temper their expressions of prejudice? Or can you find out how hospitable people are to strangers if the stranger identifies himself as a social science researcher studying hospitality?

In their various forms, deception and disguise in social research are assumed to be quite frequent, although no quantitative studies are to be found to support the assumption, except in the case of psychological experimentation. In that area, Stricker (1967) provides the published finding that 19.3 percent of the studies reported in four psychological journals in 1964 used deception; we know that there are other types of research as well in which the subject is misled as a standard scientific practice. Before-and-after studies of mass media productions, or of propaganda material, typically disguise the nature of the study in the "before" measurement so as not to produce undue attention to the stimulus that will follow. Studies of attitudes toward particular social and political issues (for example, U.S. foreign policy, welfare reform, desegregation) often begin in the guise of much more general surveys, so that the salience of the issue under study, in comparison with other issues, may be measured before the respondent's full attention is focused on the main issue. The more reliable studies of vote intention, when supported by political parties or candidates, dissemble about sponsorship lest "compliance bias" set in. This is to say nothing about a whole area of research involving unobtrusive measures (to be discussed later) where the fact of the research itself tends to be hidden.

These uses of deception have been subjected in recent years to increasing criticism in social science circles. Mead (1969), for instance, argues that complete truthfulness about the purposes of research is the only viable approach and that the use of deception denigrates the subject, has deleterious effects on the investigator, and may invalidate the experiment because of the human propensity for picking up multiple subtle cues. Baumrind (1972) dislikes deception in psychological experimentation, particularly insofar as it deprives others of their freedom of choice. Seeman (1969) sees the dilemmas surrounding the use of deception in terms of public policy as related to the Supreme Court Miranda and Escobedo decisions that the government is obliged to respect the dignity and integrity of its citizens and that the individual is entitled to remain silent unless freely choosing to do otherwise; and he feels that the best ethical position vis-a-vis deception is probably that bad means cannot lead to a good end. Warwick (1975) adds that if deception is justified on the advancement-of-knowledge argument it may be equally justified in protecting the presidency or in preserving national security, even in circumstances where such ends may be against the broader public interest. The very frequency with which deception is used in social research has led some scholars to fear that it is becoming a research norm. For instance, Kelman (1966), who acknowledges that some problems can be investigated only if deception is employed, is nonetheless concerned about its automatic use without sufficient weighing of the pros and cons. Stricker (1967) notes that deception has become such a well-regarded methodological device that it may be incorporated in research design solely for prestige purposes. Beyond that, there is some concern that widespread duplicity in social science research, especially in studies among college students, may contribute to a general moral climate in society of cynicism and distrust.

Some investigation that has been carried out on the subjects of psychological research has tended to confirm the widespread nature of deceptive practices and also illustrates some of the methodological difficulties deception may cause. Stricker and Messick (1967), for instance, report finding a high incidence of suspicion on the part of research subjects concerning experimental deception, a surprising finding since their subjects were of high-school age and presumably more naive than average subjects. In a general evaluation of research incorporating deception written with Jackson (1969), they point out that the efficacy of deception is rarely measured, a grave methodological neglect since it is not known how suspiciousness affects the experimental findings. Bonacich (1970) reports being confronted with subjects who, because of past experience with research incorporating deception in its design, do not believe what they are told under any circumstances. Consequently, she calls on researchers to stop polluting the natural resource of behavioral and social scientists, namely subjects. Fillenbaum (1966), in an effort to study the effect of prior deception on subsequent experimental performance, found that about one-half to one-third of the subjects were suspicious to begin with, a proportion that was slightly increased after exposure to a mildly deceptive experiment. These findings suggest that not only researchers but also subjects may be starting to see deception in laboratory research as the norm.

As would be expected, there are those who feel that some of the critics go too far in their moral condemnation of deceptive research practices. Gergen (1973), for instance, says that "we speak blithely of deception without taking into account that this is a highly pejorative term for actions that almost all people would endorse under other rubrics." He was referring to the use of deception in everyday life; certainly the point may be made in passing that fooling others is not unique to social research—dissembling in personal intercourse, so as not to offend the sensitivities of others, is a part of common courtesy; misstatement of available options is accepted as standard in diplomacy; and purposeful deception is an agreeable strategy in the games we play from hide-and-seek to gin rummy.

## PRIVACY

The social scientist as invader of personal privacy is also being discussed with increasing vigor in professional circles. Social researchers appear to approach the research subject in at least three different guises. Like a blind date, not uninvited but also not to be embraced on first meeting, he may prove embarrassing in the demands he makes or the topics he insists on discussing and, furthermore, may be hard to get rid of. Or, as welcomed quest, he may later turn out to be a tattle-tale who spills to others the intimacies that have been confided. Or, he may spy on the subject, by entering the house garbed as a friend or by peeking from behind a bush in the garden. We will discuss the second two manifestations later in the contexts of confidentiality and unobtrusive measures and consider here the invasions of privacy that can take place during the "blind date" of the data collection process, after some thoughts on the concept of privacy.

In the history of U.S. law relating to privacy, a starting point is an 1890 *Harvard Law Review* article by Warren and Brandeis, entitled "The Right to Privacy," which propounded a right to be left alone and provided a basis for subsequent legal activities designed to protect this right. Prosser (1960) identified four somewhat distinctive kinds of invasions of privacy as recognized by U.S. courts. The first concerns unwarranted intrusion upon a person's solitude or private concerns and is illustrated by such violations as eavesdropping, wiretapping, and public surveillance. The second, a category specifically addressed by Warren and Brandeis, deals with the public disclosure of embarrassing private facts about individuals. The third type concerns false publicity including impersonation and forgery. Prosser's fourth category can be considered the most proprietary since it is concerned with false appropriation by individual A to his or her own advantage of individual B's name or likeness. Developments in the legal domain subsequent to Prosser's work have primarily served to sharpen further the legal concept of privacy and to delineate the extent and means by which the right to privacy can be protected by the law. Beaney (1966:254), for instance, defines the right to privacy as

> the legally recognized freedom or power of an individual (group, association, class) to determine the extent to which another individual (group, association, class, or government) may (a) obtain or make use of his ideas, writings, name, or other indica of identity, or (b) obtain or reveal information about him, or those for whom he is personally responsible, or (c) intrude physically or in more subtle ways into his life space and his chosen activities.

According to Beaney, examination of the record makes clear that the Supreme Court tends to uphold individual privacy against unreasonable governmental intrusion. He acknowledges that there are a variety of nonjudicial means of protecting privacy such as legislation at federal as well as state levels and administrative decrees.

For Street (1970), another legal scholar who has addressed the relationship between privacy and the law, the essential component of privacy is the right to be left alone, with protection against offensive intrusion and unreasonable publicity, including the passing of information to third parties. Both Beaney and Street emphasize the interrelationship between legal developments and public opinion in connection with the protection of privacy. As Street puts it, lawyers cannot provide answers unaided but need to be guided by public opinion, especially in regard to how much interference with privacy the public will tolerate. While acknowledging that principles of privacy have been established in the United States through the work of Prosser and Warren and Brandeis, Street is skeptical of their general impact and does not believe that self-controlling institutional arrangements are sufficient to guard against infringements on privacy.

Social scientists joining in the discussion have defined privacy as "the right of the individual to decide for himself how much of his life—his thoughts, emotions and the facts that are personal to him—he will share with others" (Frankel 1975). Riecken and Boruch (1974) see invasion of privacy occurring "when a researcher intrudes on the physical isolation or private activities or beliefs of a research subject or group." For Shils (1966), privacy can exist only within an interactive, communicative framework. Essentially it involves control over information—what goes to whom—of which voluntarism is an important component. Altman (1975) defines privacy as "the selective control of access to the self or to one's group."

For Simmel (1968:482) the right to privacy "asserts the sacredness of the person," and he suggests that "perhaps the dominant reason for privacy, namely the desire to be insulated from observation, is intimately related to motives of avoiding criticism, punishment, or the discomfort of feeling inhibited."

Ruebhausen and Brim (1966), in their article on the relationship between privacy and behavioral science research, point out that recognition of the claim to private personality is relatively recent. Although they see the claim conflicting with other valued rights, such as that of an informed and effective government, law enforcement, and the free dissemination of information, they state that it is nonetheless a "moral imperative" of our times. For them privacy has two aspects: the right to be left alone and the right to share and communicate. "Both of these conflicting needs, in mutually supportive interaction, are essential to the well-being of individuals and institutions, and any definition of privacy, or of private personality, must reflect this plastic duality: sharing and concealment" (p. 426). They point out that since persons live in communities, the right to privacy can never be absolute—often it must be set aside to satisfy the community's needs.

The social and cultural relativity of the concept of privacy suggested in some of these discussions has been highlighted by others. Jack Elinson of Columbia University, in a talk given at a 1975 National Academy of Sciences seminar on drug abuse, pointed to anthropological work in suggesting that privacy does not necessarily lead to benign human relations and should be accepted as a "moral imperative" only with caution. "Nice" people who get along well with others seem to be found as frequently, or more frequently, in open, nonprivate societies as in circumspect ones. He went on to suggest that within our own society we lack good empirical information on how much value people place on privacy, that it may be a particularly beloved concept for the intellectual middle class from whose ranks social scientists and social science policy makers are drawn, and that the research subjects most concerned about privacy are apt to be social deviants—for example, street criminals or wealthy tax evaders who really have something to hide.

Studies of public opinion tend to support the conception of privacy as a social variable subject to rapid change over time. In the short history of survey research, there is evidence of change either in the definition of what people (subjects) consider to be private or in researchers' assumptions about subjects' sense of privacy. The work of Kinsey et al. demonstrated that many people showed a more willing response to questions about their sexual behavior than was previously thought possible. Frankel (1976) tells of the market researchers' reluctance to include questions on feminine hygiene in interview studies until it was tried some 20 years ago and respondents were found to be most cooperative. On the other hand, the field abounds with tales of questions (for example, family income) that are encountering increasing difficulty.

The ambiguities surrounding privacy as a concept and the lack of information about its content (what is it that people, or most people, consider to be private?) make it extremely difficult if not impossible to decide what data may be and may not be collected about subjects on purely a priori grounds. Nevertheless, attempts have been made. Conrad (1967) reports on a survey in the Office of Education of some 50 projects using 109 instruments with more than 5,300 items of which 10 were found by the reviewers to be "objectionable." The study followed unfavorable publicity in the mid 1960s about items included in school-administered psychological tests that evoked congressional response and a variety of reactions in the social scientific community (see the *American Psychologist*, November 1965 and May 1966). It is understandable that most social scientists are not enthusiastic about making ad hoc judgments about precluding entire areas from investigation. Their reluctance arises not only because the empirical data for the judgments do not exist in usable forms but more significantly because of a realization that among the most important things to study for a better understanding of human relations are precisely those aspects of attitudes, actions, and interpersonal behavior that are most "private."

Bennett (1967) takes issue with those who claim that privacy is an inalienable right. For him, making a public outcry over "rights" and "privacy" unnecessarily hinders intelligent discussion of the real issue, the management of communication. Privacy can be incompatible with the peaceful coexistence of communities because our social system depends on an exchange of information for cooperation. The moral imperative, therefore, is to encourage communication while respecting personal confidence, not to invoke blindly a right to privacy. Before claims to privacy are asserted, Bennett suggests, we need to analyze the situation in terms of how damaging the revelation might be to the person involved, how many others might be harmed, and the importance of the revelation to the general welfare. The results of such an analysis could then be a basis for "a rational assessment of the values at issue." Essentially, Bennett calls for something like a risk-benefit assessment for settling thorny issues arising from conflict between an individual's right to privacy and society's need to know.

Sears (1968), also questioning the thesis of privacy as an overriding value, ends an article dealing with educational research in apocalyptic summary: "The blunt fact is that, unless our scientific understanding of man can be brought to a far higher plane within the next couple of decades than it has been in the last couple of millenia, there will be no one left whose privacy can be defended."

## BREACHES OF CONFIDENTIALITY

The guarantee of anonymity to subjects has long been taken for granted as an indispensable condition in social research; it is the commonly held assumption in the profession, just as it is in medicine, law, and journalism, that people will tell a truer tale and act with less inhibition if they believe that what they say or do will be held in the strictest confidence. This scientific rationale, combined with the ethical principle that one respects the privacy of research subjects, has created uniform agreement among social scientists that confidentiality should be preserved by every possible means to protect the interests of both social science and the subjects of its research. The codes of ethics of professional associations, insofar as they deal with human subject protection at all, treat the preservation of confidentiality as an ethical principle. In the case of one of the earlier codes—that of the American Association of Public Opinion Research (AAPOR)—the statement is an all but unqualified one: "We shall protect the anonymity of every respondent, unless the respondent waives such anonymity for specified uses. In addition, we shall hold as privileged and confidential all information that tends to identify the respondent" (AAPOR, *Code of Professional Ethics and Practices*).

As social research has become more pervasive in American society, and as vested commercial and other interest groups have become more aware of the uses to which data collected in studies might be put, the threat to such confidentiality principles has increased—for example, from automobile manufacturers who would like the names of people with old cars so that they may know where to sell the new ones, from political candidates who would like to know who is for or against them so that they may better solicit contributions, or from agencies sponsoring evaluation research that may wish to know of any malfeasance among program participants so that corrective action can be taken against them. It is safe to say that professional social scientists have little difficulty in taking a strong stand against any breaches of confidentiality that arise out of attempts by a researcher to gain some advantage with a sponsor or with other private parties who would like access to privileged information. Unlike some of the other issues we are discussing, the principle of keeping a promise of anonymity to a subject in such circumstances is uncontroversial, and the reputation of any social researcher known to break the rule would suffer. However, despite such professional frowns and despite the fact that abuses of privileged information have not been well documented in the literature, that they have and may continue to occur is not questioned by social researchers: indeed, it is their assumed existence that has stimulated such unequivocal pronouncements as that of the AAPOR Code quoted above.

Threats to confidentiality from courts and other governmental bodies that can issue subpoenas for information about individuals from the records of studies designed for other purposes create far greater difficulty to social science and have received much more attention in the literature. Kershaw (1972), for instance, in his discussion of the New Jersey Income Maintenance experiment, notes several attempts to issue subpoenas by a variety of agents, including two welfare departments, the General Accounting Office, and the Senate Finance Committee. Feuillan (1974) cites several other cases in demonstrating the lack of protection afforded to social science data. In *United States v. Doe* (460 F. 2d 328; 1972), the U.S. Court of Appeals for the First Circuit decided against Professor Samuel Popkin of Harvard, who had refused to divulge confidential information collected from his research subjects before a federal grand jury looking into the Pentagon Papers case, claiming a First Amendment privilege to keep his sources secret. (The Supreme Court subsequently refused to review the decision.) A second case involved a guarantee of confidentiality of interview data made by a New York State commission looking into the Attica prison riot. This guarantee was not honored by the same state's attorney general. The New York courts blocked the attorney general's efforts on the basis of a contravening public policy—the policy of the state to live up to its promises. As Feuillan points out, however, such a "public policy" escape is not easily generalized to situations in other states or to most social science research. A Syracuse University project (Carroll and Knerr 1976), sponsored by the Council of Social Science Associations and supported by the Russell Sage Foundation, has compiled information on other cases involving threats to confidentiality by subpoena in the course of its data compilation.

There are certain standard procedures in social research, many of them adopted long before researchers had subpoenas in mind, which offer subjects some protection against legal recourse to information collected about them in large-scale studies. The removal and destruction of identifying "face-sheet" information is a standard practice where survey research studies do not require a second contact with respondents. Random response schemes in data collection have been devised that permit analysis of aggregated data without anyone being able to discover how an individual answered a question (Boruch 1971). Protecting data by placing it in data banks in foreign countries has been used (for example, the student files of the American Council on Education) to insure the immunity of the data to legal process.

Such procedural safeguards are not foolproof nor do they cover the circumstances of all social research. More recently, attention has been given to legislative and judicial solutions. Legislators may grant certain privileges to researchers carrying out work funded by a particular statute, as exemplified by provisions of the National Drug Abuse Prevention and Control Act of 1970 which permits the secretary of HEW to grant testimonial privilege to researchers looking into drug use. A similar provision has been enacted for alcohol research in the Comprehensive Alcohol, Alcoholism Prevention, Treatment, and Rehabilitation Act; and the Omnibus Crime Control and Safe Streets Act of 1968 provided immunity from legal process for research information collected by the Law Enforcement Assistance Administration. Such privileges could be written into other acts if legislators feel that the social value of the research overrides the protection offered to society by its ability to discover individuals who may be breaking the law.

Despite the setback (from the standpoint of the confidentiality principle) of the Popkin decision, others have proposed the promotion of state and federal statutes that would grant to social researchers a broad testimonial privilege similar to that enjoyed by doctors and lawyers (Feuillan 1974; Committee on Federal Evaluation Research 1975). It is recognized that such a privilege would have its limitations (indeed, doctors' and lawyers' privileges are not unlimited). Most social scientists would probably not feel that information revealing an intent to commit murder or child abuse, a contagious disease, or severe psychiatric problems—accidentally acquired in the course of a study not designed to deal with such subjects—should remain privileged, even though a blanket promise of confidentiality was tendered. In any case, it seems unlikely that legislators would accept a privilege so broad that it would protect severely antisocial conditions from disclosure, particularly if those conditions were not themselves under study. Nejelski and Lerman (1971) have proposed a model shield statute that would grant a privilege against subpoenas for social researchers except when a waiver is obtained from the subject for release of the information and a finding is made by the subpoena-issuing body that the information is both relevant to the case and unobtainable elsewhere. Such a means of protecting the subjects' confidentiality in sensitive areas is high on the agenda for social research, but so far the prospects have not been good for an early solution.

## STRESS

Stress is a word found frequently in psychological literature where it often means a harmful psychological disturbance such as anxiety, shock, horror, fear, or the more ominous-sounding term of the HEW regulations, "psychological injury." Here we are taking the liberty of broadening the meaning to include some other sorts of harm to an individual's mental equilibrium that may be identified as possible consequences of research participation, such as loss of self-esteem, generation of self-doubt, and even the unhappy reactions which subjects may experience in studies that inadvertently get people annoyed, worried, embarrassed, or just plain bored.

Stuart Cook, in a chapter on ethical issues prepared for the third edition of *Research Methods in Social Relations* (Cook 1976), concentrates on the more serious side of the spectrum in his discussion of stressful situations in the research process. Drawing his illustrations largely from social psychological experiments, Cook notes the horror created in studies designed to produce emotional reactions by showing pictures of concentration-camp victims or persons who have drowned; and the threats to sexual identity in a study of attitude change in which subjects were given the false information that they displayed signs of homosexuality. Cook also discusses studies that expose research subjects to preplanned failure, as in some educational achievement experiments; to fear, as in studies on reactions to emergency situations; and to emotional shock, for example, a driver-reaction study with a realistic dummy thrust in the path of the participating motorist.

Cook further notes four topic areas where subjects may be induced to act in ways that would diminish their self-respect: situations in which subjects may yield to dishonest inclinations (for example, agree to participate in a conjectured burglary) in the course of investigations of the nature and determinants of honesty; studies in which subjects are led to believe that apparent harm is done to others, such as in Milgram's experiments on obedience; studies that tamper with subjects' views by exposing them to group pressures, such as in the Asch conformity experiments; and, with the application of unobtrusive measures, studies in which many of the unwitting subjects fail to give help to others when it is needed, for example, to a planted epileptic faking a seizure or a man with a cane falling on a subway floor.

It is characteristic of the types of research exemplified above that the stress-producing situation is deliberately inserted in the study design as a dependent or independent variable; and much of the ethical controversy has centered around studies in which the element of stress was not an accidental or unanticipated consequence of research participation. Milgram's work has been widely discussed as an example of excess, but it is instructive to take his own views into account. In response to Baumrind's (1964) criticisms of his work on obedience, Milgram (1964) notes that a follow-up questionnaire administered not long after the experiment indicated that only 1.3 percent of the subjects were sorry they took part in the study, 15 percent described their feelings as neutral, and 84 percent were glad. A further follow-up conducted a year later found no sign of long-term injury, and thus, in Milgram's judgment, the participants were not exposed to harm.

Ring, Wallston, and Corey (1970) conducted a Milgram-type obedience experiment with the express purpose of establishing the extent to which various modes of debriefing allay the experiment-induced tension of subjects. According to the authors, many of the subjects were upset by the experiment, but they regarded it as a positive experience and did not regret participating. A follow-up interview was taken with 20 of the original 57 subjects and "failed to disclose any serious effects." On the other hand, 15 percent of these subjects did say that in retrospect they regretted having taken part in the experiment.

A proactive attempt to assess stress is found in Farr and Seaver (1975), who presented 86 introductory psychology students with descriptions of threats of varying severity that might figure as experimental treatments. The subjects were asked to rate the threats on a scale of 1 to 5. The procedures were designed to represent several different areas of psychological research and a variety of stress-arousing situations. On the basis of the findings, the authors suggest that procedures which were rated greater than 3—a moderate amount of tension and stress—should be used with caution and impose serious responsibilities on researchers to protect the welfare of their subjects. Of the 15 procedures presented, the following had ratings higher than 3:

Give a five minute speech on a current topic to a group of other students.
Your two-man team competes against another for a $10 prize. Although your partner did well, your team loses due to your troubles with the game.
The experimenter tells you that a test you took in the experiment indicates that you have latent homosexual tendencies.
When recalling a long test of words you were to learn, another subject received a painful shock for each mistake you made.
Sit in a small room for ten minutes with the thing you are most afraid of.

Before leaving the general topic of stress, as we have loosely defined it, a word should be said about its occasional, and usually inadvertent, emergence in social research other than psychological experimentation. The social scientist pursuing such areas as adolescent-parent relations within families, police-community interactions, courtship behavior in a society, effects of a social program on its participants, public reactions to social issues, or whatever, would under normal circumstances try to avoid the introduction of stress-producing elements to his inquiry for fear of losing the cooperation of the subjects, and to make sure that his findings will not be distorted by reactions to the stress that was produced rather than to the variable under investigation. Stimuli that might produce such reactions as anxiety, fear, or annoyance are to be avoided. Stress thus tends to occur only accidentally in much of social research. The possibility of its occurrence is indirectly addressed in procedural manuals for data collectors, where attention is given to respect for the dignity, feelings, and well-being of respondents, and abounds in professional anecdotes: the woman in an attitude survey about heroin addiction, obviously very distressed, explains that her son is an addict; the subject in a social experiment designed to test ways of rehabilitating ex-prisoners is upset and depressed by the demands put on him by the project's efforts to find him a job; the polite, well-educated, and informed respondent, caught in the sample's mesh, is grievously annoyed at wasting time answering the interviewer's intellectually demeaning questions. Reliable information does not appear to be available on the frequency of such accidents in social research or the harm that occurs when they do happen. One would assume that occurrence of accidental stress varies by topic and by the characteristics and life circumstances of respondents, but there is very little evidence for investigators to use in making a priori ethical judgments.

## COLLECTIVE AND SOCIAL INJURY

The concept of social injury which is found (undefined) in the HEW guidelines could presumably have three different meanings.

First, it could refer to some actual harm occurring to an individual subject in his relations to others as a result of his participation in a research project. A dramatic example is given by Appell (1974) in which he refers to Cora Du Bois's account in the reprinted version of *People of Alor*, of the experiences of informants with whom she worked before World War II. To quote Appell: "During the war they claimed to the Japanese that they were under the protection of an American, and as a result, they were publicly executed." In a less dramatic and more up-to-date case of the use of the concept in this first sense, one finds the decisions of a U.S. District Court in Pennsylvania (364 F Supp. 915, 1973) which enjoined a drug-abuse study among public school children, designed to identify prospects for a prevention program, on several grounds, including the possibility that the study could offer "opportunities for a child to suffer insurmountable harm from a labeling such as 'drug abuser' at an age when the cruelty of other children is at an extreme." In both cases the harm comes when preservation of anonymity fails.

A second meaning a social injury might apply to a situation is where a subject, who wished to protect and promote the interests of the group to which he belonged, or of some other group, feels that his right to serve his own social goals has been abridged in the research because he lacked suffi-cient information about the uses that could be made of the information he provided; in effect, he was deprived of his rights because of an inadequacy of informed consent procedures. Under both of these definitions the focus is on jeopardy to the individual subject, thus corresponding both to the guidelines that have been formulated in government agencies and to the emphasis in U.S. law on protection of the rights that adhere to individual citizens.

The idea of collectively held rights of groups, organizations, or institu-tions is at the center of a third possible meaning of social injury: that the interests of collectivities might risk some future setback as a result of a research study. The idea of group risk has only recently emerged as a consideration in the specific context of the protection of research subjects in the course of an investigation, although an ethical concern for research effects on collectivities extends back at least as far as Robert Lynd's *Knowl-edge for What?* in the early 1940s. Lynd saw the proper role of social science as directed to the solution of social problems, with research justified mainly by the contribution it can make to the betterment of the condition of the poor and underprivileged. Over the subsequent 30 or 40 years, the theme of moral responsibility for research results and the uses to which they may be put—beneficial or detrimental to the interest of subgroups in the popula-tion—has continued as a part of the general ethical debate in social science research. The so-called Moynihan Report came under attack, not on the basis of the research procedures used in the studies that Moynihan collected and interpreted, but because of the depiction of the black family which critics felt was damaging to the image of blacks in the United States and potentially detrimental to their interests through effects the research might have on public policies affecting blacks. Concern about the potential benefit or harm to groups resulting from research results and their interpretations is particularly relevant in sociology because of its claims as a field interested in the collective aspects of human behavior. Biderman and Crawford (1968) and Reiss (1973) have commented on the strange neglect of attention to the rights of collectivities in a discipline that spends so much effort in the study of organized groups. Also, the standard use in quantitative social research (even that which is not focused on particular groups) of group characteris-tics—age, sex, race, marital status, income, and so on—as explanatory vari-ables is apt to lead to the presentation of research results in ways that are ideally suited to the identification of intergroup differences and the drawing of comparisons that may seem invidious with respect to one group or favorable for another.

Another link between the social scientist's concern for population sub-groups and the protection of subjects is found in some of the discussions of the relative powerlessness of minority-group members and people at lower socioeconomic levels in society when confronted by the research process. Kelman (1972), for instance, sees members of disadvantaged groups as more readily available as research subjects "precisely because of their power deficiency. Investigators can induce them more easily to participate in research that members of more powerful groups would find objectionable and more securely expect them to put up with procedures that higher status subjects would challenge." He adds certain groups in institutions to the list of power deficients: institutionalized children, hospital patients, army recruits, grade school pupils, and college sophomores. Galliher (1973) also refers to the "general agreement" that some classes of subjects need protection (for example, the poor), but he further argues that attempts to protect some groups through professional codes of ethics also involve the protection of others who are less needy: the well-entrenched and powerful. In a somewhat dissident view, Vargus (1971) feels that low-income and powerless citizens are beginning to resist their "guinea-pig" roles in research where the benefits to them are not clear, and Josephson (1970) reports on a concrete case of organized resistance in a low-income area to a Columbia University School of Public Health study. Similar resistance was encountered in a District of Columbia public health survey, leading to a negotiation for payment to subjects. Several authors have written of the need to overcome potential resistance in community research by such means as soliciting opinion and ideas for the research from community members (Rippey 1970), by provision of services to the community (Vargus 1971), or by some relaxation of scientific rigor and placing more emphasis on participant observation techniques (Le Compte 1970). Government initiatives, such as that of the Department of Housing and Urban Development's Model Cities Program, have led to the incorporation of low-income community members in research staffs, partly justified as a fair trade-off for community participation in the research.

The collective interests of less-privileged groups have apparently become a significant part of the debate over human subjects' protection in research, particularly among sociologists, and even more difficult questions are raised here than in dealing with the problems of individual respondents. Adequate protection of group interests would appear to involve not only the assurance that such interests are adequately protected in the formulation of the research (and who is to speak for the group?), but that they are preserved in the uses to which the research results are put (and who can predict?). These are thorny problems for which agreeable solutions have yet to be devised.

Similar problems arise in attempts to respond ethically to the collective interests of other units such as societies, communities, institutions, and organizations. Anthropologists, for instance, recognize a responsibility for collectivities in which they work by stating, in the American Anthropological

Association *Statement on Ethics,* their "obligation to reflect on the foreseeable repercussions of research and publication on the general population being studied." The economist Rivlin (1974), in her discussion of social experimentation, has suggested a situation in which a whole town or housing market may be damaged by a large-scale social experiment which tries out rent subsidies for some and results in higher rents for all; and another in which the introduction of educational vouchering may destroy the local public school system.

## RISKS AND RESEARCH METHODS

In the above attempt to cut across disciplines and methodologies in discussing possible risks for social research subjects, it remains evident that some modes of research have acquired their own rather distinct sets of ethical problems. The intensive, long-lasting field investigations of whole societies that are undertaken by anthropologists and some sociologists raise concerns, particularly about collective risks and the possibility of socially harmful disruptions in interpersonal relations. On the other hand, when psychologists write about the ethical problems of experimentation, they tend to concentrate on the issues of deception and stress. Three other modes of research that carry their own ethical impedimenta are discussed here, by way of summary: large scale social surveys as they have been carried out, with increasing frequency, over the past 40 years; large controlled field experimentation with social programs, a more recent development; and "unobtrusive measures," a time-hallowed tradition in social data collection now laboring under a new title.

### Social Surveys

Most sample surveys of the general population may be relatively free from some of the risks under discussion such as purposefully induced stress or outright deception, but they have certain structural features that could create the potential for other types of ethical abuse. In the typical large study, the investigator assigns responsibility to the field director, who passes assignments down to local field supervisors (often scattered in distant locations), who issue directions to interviewers, who sally forth to contact the designated respondents, reporting back only to the local supervisor. Control in such cases is generally exercised through written instructions: the questionnaire itself, directions as to what must be said to respondents in requesting their cooperation, and, often, a telephone number respondents may call to register complaints or to request further information. After the fact, the interviewer's performance may be checked by another contact with the respondent—often by telephone and usually by the local supervisor—but the decentralized process does not permit the sort of immediate control over the investigator-subject interaction that is possible, for instance, in research conducted in a laboratory setting. This relative lack of immediate control, along with the demands which studies put on interviewers to elicit and retain the cooperation of respondents, leads to concerns about the possibility of ethical abuse in the form of overly assiduous inducement to participate, or a reluctance to permit the respondent to terminate the inquiry, or the insensitivity of an interviewer when confronted with an emotionally disturbed respondent leading to further inadvertent stress, or the disclosure of what was said in an interview to a third party. If widespread abuses of this sort exist at the local data-collection level, they seem to have escaped documentation in the literature on research ethics (although the breach of confidentiality by some commercial research organizations that have provided lists of respondents' names to companies for subsequent sales solicitations has been noted, as has the unethical use of surveys as a guise for a sales pitch at the doorstep). It may be that such abuses are too infrequent in fact to deserve much notice in print, and it is indeed possible that the more successful interviewers have found that the best policy for completing the assignment and keeping their jobs is an unaggressive, respectful demeanor and adherence to the ethics of privacy.

Researchers have paid considerably more attention to problems of protecting the confidentiality that is typically promised in the conduct of a survey from the subsequent threats posed by subpoena, as discussed above. Some protection is possible in many one-time surveys that do not require the collection of identifying information beyond an address or a telephone number preserved temporarily for the purpose of validation—information that can be easily removed and destroyed soon after it is collected. On highly sensitive topics where even these means seem inadequate, random response techniques might be used to remove all possibility of personal identification, although at considerable cost to efficiency. Survey researchers using the panel design, which involves repeated interviews with the same subjects, are not so fortunate, since the identifying information must be kept until the last wave of interviews is completed and the results are coded and matched by individual case. The use of matching by code numbers with identifying data locked up in files or shipping the data off to foreign countries are only partial solutions.

Two alternatives to personal interviews in social surveys are worth discussing. First, telephone interviews are used with increasing frequency for the collection of social data because they are inexpensive and quick; and they also offer fewer risks for the average respondent than personal interviews. A respondent may be annoyed at having his dinner or television watching interrupted and may be further disturbed by the sorts of questions asked, but it is easier for him to protect himself if we can assume that hanging up a phone on a voice is easier than shutting the door on a face. With random digit dialing, one runs the risk of offending some respondents whose phones are unlisted to avoid such intrusions, but the procedure permits interviews to proceed without knowledge of such identifying information as name or address. Secondly, mailed questionnaires offer the respondent even better opportunities to decide not to participate. He can withdraw by simply not filling out and returning the questionnaire, and he has the advantage of being able to inspect all the questions before he decides to participate. The exercise of that option by so many potential respondents, however, creates the methodological problem of low return rates, and some of the attempts to reduce the problem have raised ethical eyebrows. Response rates can be increased if nonresponders are sent second or third copies of the questionnaire with further requests for cooperation. Tricks have been devised to identify the responders and nonresponders even when confidentiality is ostensibly being preserved by not asking for a signature on the questionnaire. The address on the envelope provided to return the questionnaire gives a room number, a different one for each respondent, or the identifying information is coded in invisible ink. Then only the delinquent need get the second mailing. Confidentiality is not necessarily breached by such procedures since the identifying data can still be destroyed, but the deception involved is obvious and such tricks are both destructive to honorable relationships and scientifically unnecessary. Alternatives, such as asking the respondent to send off a separate postcard to say he has sent back his questionnaire, serve the purpose just as well without the ethical drawbacks.

## Social Experiments

The large-scale social experiments that have come into prominence during the past decade bring with them a set of ethical issues somewhat different from those found in the social survey area, in part because of the dual role of their subjects as participants in the program that is being tested and the test that is being conducted. As Riecken and Boruch (1974) point out: "It is difficult to separate the ethical problems of a proposed social program from the ethical problems of an experimental evaluation of this progam if only because the evaluation involves a controlled trial of the program itself." The discussions of ethical problems in both the above-quoted work and in the more recently published Brookings report, *Ethical and Legal Issues in Social Experimentation* (Rivlin and Timpane 1975) combine both program issues and research issues. Riecken and Boruch mention, for instance, the unanticipated side effects that programs of social intervention may produce such as disruption of previously stable family relations, creating disadvantages to some of the participants even though the program is designed to be generally beneficial, and the particular vulnerability of social interventions to the charge of "manipulation," especially if the research appears to disregard the preferences of people it is designed to serve. Both works refer to the short-lived boon that participants in programs may enjoy and the subsequent letdown when the program is terminated or phased out.

Another issue in social experimentation associates that branch of social research closely with a biomedical research concern: how to justify the denial of a treatment (or a program) to others than those selected as members of the experimental group when the treatment (or program) is thought to be beneficial. For example, in a recently completed BSSR study designed to test techniques for rehabilitation, ex-inmates of federal prisons were randomly divided into four groups: one receiving a weekly payment comparable to unemployment compensation, a second given special job placement assistance, a third getting both, and the fourth getting nothing. In effect, the control group was denied treatments that were assumed to be beneficial to the subjects in their readjustment to life outside of prison and that would certainly be seen (at least the money part) as advantageous by the ex-prisoners. The problem of inequitable distribution of benefits has led to suggestions for modification of the experimental designs so that control groups can get at least some benefits from their participation in the experiments (Zeisel 1970; Rivlin and Timpane 1975).

The potential collective risks associated with social experiments have been noted, particularly in Rivlin (1974), and Rivlin and Timpane (1975)—risks to institutions, such as school systems, that could be threatened by educational vouchering trials, or risks to groups in the area surrounding an experiment that could be threatened by the indirect economic effects on the community of a large-scale program of economic intervention on behalf of the test population. Again, as Schultze points out in Rivlin and Timpane (1975), social experiments have most of the characteristics, particularly those creating collective risks, of the social programs that are carried out without prior test and without the professional involvement of social science researchers. That observation hardly relieves the social scientist of ethical responsibility when he becomes involved in the design and execution of an experiment, but it does point up the new difficulty for the researcher in protecting the welfare of subjects over whose fate he has only limited control.

## Unobtrusive Measures

The use of unobtrusive data collection methods, such as observation of public or private behavior, disguised recording of conversation by microphones or of behavior by hidden cameras, and gathering of information about people from such available repositories as trash cans, public archives, newspaper files, and Who's Who, became popular in social science circles before the current wave of concern about ethical issues (Sechrest 1975). The methodological strength of the procedures lies in their circumvention of the artifacts created by direct interaction of researcher and subject, such as respondents' error in self-reporting or distortions created by reactions to the interviewer or the interview situation. By the same token, such measures avoid some of the risks that are associated with overt data collection, such as undue coercion to participate, embarrassment caused by sensitive questions in an interview, or impositions on time. Except where worrisome scenes are enacted so that reactions can be unobtrusively observed, the problem of research-created stress is also avoided. Problems of confidentiality, too, are side-stepped in many unobtrusive studies that do not involve the collection of identifying information about the subjects.

The most strenuous objections to studies involving unobtrusive measures come under the heading of invasion of privacy, with privacy defined as the individual's right to decide what of himself he will expose, to whom, and in what circumstances. Purists would say that the inviolable right is clearly denied when the subject does not know he is being observed by the researcher; but that is a position with which both researcher and subject may disagree. People who are observed in public places, it can be argued, are already exercising their right to decide how they will behave in front of others, the presence of a social scientist among the others being of little consequence. In more private settings—the cocktail party, the factory workroom, the union meeting, the men's room—subjects would be expected to alter their behavior to the setting, and the intrusion of the unidentified researcher raises more serious questions of infringement of right to privacy. It still could be that the subject would not feel any unconscionable infringement of his rights through the observations of an objective social scientist bound by principles of confidentiality; it is another area in which we lack data on the point of view of the public-cum-subject.

Along with the invasion of privacy, the ethical problem of deception also may be raised in discussing unobtrusive measurement. In studies using pure observation, the deception is in the complete concealment of the researcher's presence. More covert dissemblance is involved in the participant observation studies where the researcher takes an active part in the proceedings in a clearly noninvestigatory guise. In such a guise the researcher, it is feared, might actively entrap the subject into the expression of attitudes, or confessions of sins, or displays of behavior that he would otherwise withhold. Such studies have proved to be particularly useful for the investigation of deviant behavior, but the brave researcher that undertakes them nowadays can expect the vocal opposition of many of his peers on the grounds of deception and invasion of privacy; and a substantial burden is put on him to protect the confidentiality of his data, even though his use of observational procedures may get the applause of others who find his unobtrusive techniques ethically superior because of their very unobtrusiveness.

# 4 / *Informed Consent*

Informed consent, as a principle, enjoys general acceptance among the authors of works on professional ethics. Baumrind (1972) holds it to be the most important of ethical dicta and also the one most commonly violated —she expresses outrage at acts which rob others of their freedom of choice. Edsall (1969) finds that the individual exercise of free judgment is the most important concept underlying the emphasis on informed consent. Through its use, she holds, the right to volunteer is also honored; difficulties, however, occur in establishing criteria for what constitutes "informed" and "consent." Wolfensberg (1967) is another who sees informed consent as a key issue but he goes on to point out that the ability to be informed is a continuous rather than a categorical variable. Beecher (1966) and Calabresi (1969), while agreeing on the central importance of the principle, do not agree that by itself it constitutes sufficient safeguard for protecting the rights and welfare of human experimental subjects. Beecher maintains that the ethical reliability of the investigator provides an even better safeguard; Calabresi also calls for group screening procedures and establishment of compensation funds for those who still suffer injury as a result of research, despite all possible safeguards.

The Department of Health, Education and Welfare has led the way in the formulation of the principle of informed consent into a set of procedures to be applied to individual studies involving human subjects. Rather explicitly, the regulations require that the "basic elements necessary for consent" include a fair description of the research procedures, their purposes, and identification of those which are experimental; a description of the discomforts, risks, and benefits which can be expected; disclosure of other appropriate procedures which may be better for the subject; an offer to answer any questions concerning the research; and the instruction that the subject may change his mind at any time and withdraw from the research "without prejudice."

Some of the phrases ("identification of any procedures which are experimental," "alternative prodecures that might be advantageous") seem inappropriate or at least ambiguous in application to most social research and more in accord with the biomedical model—a problem that could be resolved only by a very flexible interpretation of that language. A more important matter may be the elements that are missed when dealing with the subjects of social research. Reiss (1973), for instance, in discussing the nature of the contract to be drawn between social researcher and subject, includes in rephrased version all but one of the HEW basic elements for informed consent and adds suggestions for other statements, covering as possible risks "social harm, particularly for organizations as a consequence of evaluation or change experiments; for both subjects and organizations the conditions for disclosure of identity must be stated; and the fact that the investigator cannot legally guarantee the identity or privacy of sources of information *must* be stated." He also includes:

> A statement of the form in which the data are to be kept or stored, particularly for information on private matters.
> A statement providing full identity of investigators, those who acquire the information, and any relevant auspices for the inquiry.
> A statement of whether any deception is involved in the inquiry and the conditions for disclosure of deception when practiced.
> A statement of the ends to which the results of inquiry will be put, including:
> any use by others than those directly attached to the inquiry; the nature and form of any publication, including steps taken to protect the integrity of private matters in any public use of information.

With Reiss's additions, the informed-consent elements would appear to cover all manner of risk that could occur in social research. In application, however, the list might require a procedure so extensive as to hinder its acceptance for many forms of research studies, as Reiss recognizes. This and other problems are discussed below.

## SCIENTIFIC QUESTIONS

Many authors have noted the conflict that exists in much of social research between the principle of informed consent and the validity of research findings. In a theme similar to that raised in connection with the use of deception, it is pointed out that preknowledge can interfere with the results obtained (Corwin and Nagi 1972), that information can exacerbate interactive effects (Menges 1973), and that informed-consent procedures can lead to biased sampling and distorted results (Ruebhausen and Brim 1966). One of the questions that has received some research attention is the extent to which information may reduce willingness to participate. In studying potential participation in various types of psychological experiments, for instance, Berscheid et al. (1973) found that the highest level of likely participation in "stressful" experiments was to be expected when only the "cover story" or rationale was presented. For nonstressful experiments varying the amount of prior information did not influence the potential subjects' likelihood of participation.

The types of methodological difficulties presented by informed-consent procedures vary considerably by type of research. Studies using unobtrusive measures designed to eliminate the reactive responses created by the known presence of a researcher could not be conducted at all if consent were required before anyone becomes a subject. An alternative, consent at the end of the data collection, is possible in some studies among restricted groups where individuals can be identified and approached, but it would still leave out observation studies of unidentified populations, such as passers-by on the sidewalk.

The dissemblance used in social psychological experimentation to disguise the nature of variables under study obviously runs counter to informed-consent procedures that require prior disclosure free of any element of deceit and full explanation of study procedures and their purposes. The ex-post explanation (a usual practice) can restore honorable relations between researcher and subjects. A difficult problem still remains where initial explanations disguised the known possibility of some form of stress in order to avoid influencing subjects' reactions. Harm may be mitigated in debriefing, but study procedures may be seen as running counter to the purposes of the informed-consent doctrine.

The conflict between ethical and scientific objectives created by informed-consent procedures does not exist solely for observation studies and psychological experiments. The attitude researcher who wishes to avoid a "response set" may, for instance, disguise the full content of the questionnaire he is using. The correct information about sponsorship of a study may be omitted in order to avoid "compliance bias" or to limit effects that stem from elements extraneous to the content of the inquiry. For all social survey researchers, probably the greatest fear is the loss of respondents and a consequent decrease in the sample's reliability if the informed-consent procedures are too long, too elaborate, or too ominous. There is only one study known to the authors that provides any data on the actual effects of informed consent procedures on survey outcomes. Singer (1977) reports on a National Opinion Research Center sample interviewing study in which she varied (for subsamples) the amount of information provided to the respon-

dents, the assurance or lack of assurance of confidentiality, and the requirement of signatures on the consent forms. The results indicated that
signatures had a slight chilling effect and reduced the willingness of people
to be interviewed and that the assurance of confidentiality produced better
response to sensitive questions about respondents' behavior.

Another problem, of what to tell the control group, comes up in any
study where control groups are used but particularly cogently in social
experiments that incorporate beneficial treatments for experimental groups.
How much should control-group members know about the total study, and
how would full knowledge affect their willingness to participate or their
reaction to their own situation when they know that they are denied benefits
others are getting? The difficulty in finding a scientifically viable and ethically proper answer to this question is exacerbated by the general control-
group problem of "contamination" of control-group members through
contact with experimental-group members who might affect their reactions.

## SUBJECTS' UNDERSTANDING

Menges (1973) asks how informed consent can be obtained where the
proposed investigation is too complex for easy comprehension; and in a
similar vein, Parsons (1969) writes of the difficulty posed by the "competence gap," that is, the extent to which laypersons or people who do not have
particular expertise in a certain area are able to understand and comprehend
the subtleties of the information given them concerning research in order
that they may make an informed choice whether or not to participate.
Brown (in Rivlin and Timpane 1975) is particularly concerned about the
"competence gap" in social experiments that include large numbers of low-
income, less-educated participants.

The extent to which comprehension actually presents a serious problem
in social research has not yet been subjected to systematic investigation, and
it has only recently been touched in biomedical research. Some lack of
understanding on the part of hospitalized research subjects may be behind
the findings of Gray's study (1974, 1975) in which he found that despite the
existence of informed-consent forms, 39 percent of the subjects he interviewed became aware only from talking to him that they were participating
in a research project. A majority of those who knew they were participating
did not understand certain vital aspects of the research. Furthermore, despite the existence of signed informed-consent forms, four subjects (8 percent) were unwilling participants.

In social science one can imagine circumstances in which problems of
understanding may well occur. For instance, the conditions under which
confidentiality might be breached, as well as the likelihood that it would be,

could be difficult to explain adequately to respondents and could present important ethical elements in some social research studies. Such contingencies are not easy to get across, particularly to subjects who are unsophisticated with regard to such matters as legal process and computer data storage. Similarly, speculations about long-range consequences of research participation, for example, in the social risk area, could cause problems of understanding for people who are used to thinking in short-term perspectives. There is also the problem that, when a full-blown statement is used, crucial points may be missed by the respondent. Finally, long and comprehensive statements could seem so formidable to the subjects that they could conclude that consent would involve a far more dangerous undertaking than is the case.

## INVESTIGATOR'S UNDERSTANDING

One of the major problems confronting the social scientist in presenting a fair and accurate statement to prospective respondents (particularly if all the elements both in the HEW regulations and additional elements of particular relevance to social research, such as those suggested by Reiss, are to be covered) is the distinct possibility that he himself may not have the information that would be desired before he begins the investigation. Take, for example, some of the risks that a subject might be imagined to encounter during the data-collection process. Whether it is more coercive of participation if the identity of the powerful government agency sponsoring this study is stated, or more coercive (as well as deceptive) if that fact is omitted, may be anybody's guess, and is debatable both on points of abstract ethics and on assumptions of participants' subjective reactions. Often the social scientist can only speculate on what parts of his inquiry may be invasions of privacy that should be called to all the subjects' attention before the study starts, if privacy is defined as each individual's right to decide what he will reveal. Similarly, what in a survey or an experiment may turn out to be emotionally upsetting to some subjects or annoying to others may simply not be known sufficiently in advance to give due warning in informed-consent statements. Even when stress is suspected, its magnitude may be underestimated—Milgram (1964) tells us that he did not guess in his obedience experiments that some of his subjects would become as obedient to the requirement that they cause pain to others as they turned out to be.

The possibility of assessing the long-range consequences of social research participation, so that realistic estimates concerning them can be incorporated in informed-consent procedures, is even more problematic. If it is considered that stress might be experienced or self-esteem lowered in an experiment, how transient or long-lasting is the condition? What problems of readjustment could be encountered following the completion of a large-scale social experiment involving economic intervention? When dealing with the area of collective risks to a group under investigation, can it be made clear ahead of time how the data will be analyzed, what the analysis will show, how, where, and when it will be published, and what subsequent interpretation may be made of it that could benefit or harm collectivities.

When it is impossible for informed consent to cover such questions, either because of the lack of research findings to provide the necessary assessments or because the researcher cannot exercise control over the uses of his findings short of suppression, some efforts may be in order to protect the interests of subjects beyond the introductory remarks at the first encounter. The decision of the Cook Committee established by the American Psychological Association to look into the protection of human subjects was to deal with less-than-immediate problems by less-than-immediate solutions. They incorporated as an ethical principle a responsibility for researchers to continue their attention to subjects' welfare after the completion of the data-collection procedures. This suggests a direction, beyond informed consent, for further consideration by other social scientist groups.

## FORM AND CONTENT

Questions on how much information should be provided subjects and what should be emphasized, as seen from the subject's point of view, have recently received attention by psychological researchers interested in the effect of prior information on experimental results. Epstein, Suedfeld, and Silverstein (1973), for example, report on the results of studies focusing on the subjects' expectations concerning their own and the experimenter's behavior within the laboratory setting. Subjects were asked questions concerning the kind of information experimenters should supply to prospective candidates for research. More than half (55 percent) of the subjects wished to be given a description of the experiment and an explanation of their task in it, 38 percent wished to be forewarned of any danger, 29 percent desired information about the length, time, and place of the experiment, and 24 percent wanted to know about the purpose of the experiment. A much smaller number wished to be informed about the expected results (7 percent) and what the data would be used for (6 percent). In response to another question about withdrawal from the experimental situation, one-third thought withdrawal is justified when the experiment involves invasion of privacy, pain, discomfort, embarrassment, or degradation; and about one-fourth when the experiment involves deception or insufficient information. A second study, designed to measure subjects' expectations concerning the likelihood of a variety of negative occurrences within experimental situations, however, found that 70 to 85 percent of the subjects do *not* expect to be told the purpose of the experiment.

As such studies are carried out in other areas of social research, we may develop a better understanding of the public's view of what information is desirable as a condition for participation in research. Eleanor Singer's (1977) study of the effects of informed-consent procedures on reponses to a survey does not deal directly with attitudes toward those procedures, but it is a step in the direction of finding out how our subjects feel about our problems. By and large, in efforts to assess public acceptability of the content and comprehensiveness of informed-consent procedures, we are currently operating with no more than assumptions based on the success and failure of past research in recruiting and retaining subjects.

Some more specific problems emerge as social scientists try to adapt the forms prescribed by the HEW regulations for documenting informed consent, that is, a written statement embodying all the elements to be read and signed by subjects; an oral statement, with written summary to be signed and witnessed; or a "modification" of the above, which may be used only if risk-benefit requirements are met to justify it.

At risk of belaboring the obvious, we may point out some of the difficulties in applying signed consent procedures to many types of social research studies. In telephone surveys using random samples, there is no sane way to acquire signatures ahead of time and only the most dubious possibilities for getting them after the interview. Mail surveys, when designed to preserve the anonymity of respondents by not requiring signatures, would have to open the door to breaches of confidentiality if consent signatures were required. A similar difficulty occurs in personal interview sample surveys that often do not require knowledge of the respondent's name even by the interviewer; signatures would add a chink in the armor devised to protect the subject's anonymity. In long-lasting anthropological investigations signatures would be impossible if the study is conducted in illiterate societies or communities and awkward, to say the least, in other circumstances if the study involves a wide variety of semihumanistic, semiscientific procedures and stresses the slow, informal, and cumulative amassing of data. Signatures may be more feasible than elsewhere in psychological experiments and in large-scale social experiments in which the subjects are identified in advance and are under observation throughout the course of the study.

In almost all types of social research one would expect some concern about the "chilling effect" of required signatures (Singer 1977). The signing of a document could suggest to subjects that they are signing away or transferring rights to the researcher, a conception probably more congenial to biomedical research in which the subject-patient might assume he is placing some of his autonomy in the hands of the researcher-doctor. The contract that most social science study directors would have in mind does not include the transfer of autonomy; it is more like a mutual agreement for cooperation among nonadversarial equals.

Almost any modifications of the informed-consent requirements not involving subjects' signatures would be more in accordance with the procedures that have developed in the conduct of social studies and with the role-relationships involved in social research; and it is safe to say that social scientists tend to opt for the third form in the HEW regulations. But even without subjects' signatures there are still problems with the appropriate procedures for achieving informed consent. A suggestion has been made by Reiss (1973) that an "investigator's guarantee," signed by the researcher and left with the respondent, might have value in protecting the subjects' rights and enhancing their opportunities to protest if the guaranteed conditions are not met. Such a document has the virtue of preserving anonymity in studies because the identity of the respondent need not be recorded. It seems a particularly appropriate procedure in social survey work and, in fact, has already been used in some studies.

Despite all the problems associated with content, extensiveness, and procedures when using informed consent in social science studies, there are two elements that can be incorporated which provide essential protection to the respondent in the bargain he strikes with the researcher, without great damage to the scientific purity of the investigation: the assertion that the subject's initial participation is indeed voluntary, unrequired, and granted or not granted with impunity; and that his participation may be withdrawn at any juncture, freely, completely, and without embarrassing consequences. In studies where there are no scientific concerns to inhibit the fullest of disclosure, obviously a lot more can be said, limited only by the subject's tolerance for such emanations. When tangible risks can be identified in studies where the fullest of disclosure would be counterproductive to the validity of the work, there are still ways out of the dilemma with the exercise of reasoned judgment. As has been suggested by Barber (1975), there are cases where a less-than-complete, honest but ambiguous statement is appropriate. Such statements could be accompanied by an added emphasis on the elements of voluntary participation and free withdrawal mentioned above, or by a promise for fuller disclosure at the end of the inquiry. There are probably a variety of other solutions to meet the requirements of particular studies.

# 5 / Weighing Risks and Benefits

The conduct of social research is replete with ethical dilemmas caused by the confrontation of conflicting values. The scientific ethic of reliability and validity vies with a social ethic of respect for subjects' rights and dignity. The long-range contribution that social research may make to human understanding may be weighed against its possible contribution to an aura of manipulation and distrust. The hope that social investigations will be used to formulate more benign social policies is coupled with fears about their use to the disadvantage of some social groups. And, to take a formulation from the HEW regulations, risks that subjects may encounter by participating in research must be weighed against the benefits they might receive.

## BENEFITS TO SUBJECTS

The benefits to the individual participants in social research have never received much attention or notice in the literature; apparently social scientists are not given to proclamations about the lesser virtues of their work. But there are some personal benefits that subjects may receive, that should not be completely ignored in the risk-benefit equation. Generally in survey research, for instance, respondents are found to have received satisfaction from the encounter with the interviewer. A study conducted by the Survey Research Center showed that most of the respondents to an interview study on savings accounts, when recontacted by mail afterward, said they found the study interesting, were favorably disposed toward being interviewed again, and liked the interviewer as a person (Lansing, Ginsburg, and Braaten 1961). One would expect that such personal benefits would vary with the topics of the inquiry and the characteristics of individual respondents. The

44

retired widower might welcome an interruption which a busy businessman would deplore; but the abiding myth, at least in survey research circles, is that most people seem to enjoy the experience and interviewers have greater difficulty in disengagement from overly effusive respondents than in rejection by the uninterested. Similar satisfaction with the experience has been recorded in other types of social research as well. Note has been taken above of more expressions of pleasure than distress from ex-subjects of psychological experimentation (Milgram 1964), and the experience of anthropologists suggests that they are more likely than not to be welcomed back to the communities they have previously studied.

Aside from the pleasure of the occasion, one may assume there is some further personal gratification to be derived from participating in research as part of the social and political process of democratic decision making. Public opinion surveys, for example, offer subjects the opportunity to express their views about politicians and social issues between election years. In a recent survey published in *Current Opinion* in 1975, George Gallup found that 37 percent of the adult public feel that polls serve a useful or beneficial purpose, 31 percent feel they give the citizen a chance to be heard, and 29 percent expressed other positive attitudes. Only 1 percent voiced the opinion that public opinion polls constitute an invasion of or infringement on privacy.

The participant in a social experiment could also have reason to feel that what he is doing is important in the formulation of social policy. It has been suggested, indeed, that voluntary cooperation with and participation in research should be a part of the citizenship obligations of all responsible persons (Mead 1969; Parsons 1969). The extent to which citizens who find themselves in the role of subjects in social research feel a congenial sense of participation in the social process is not known on the basis of any hard data, but it seems a likely enough circumstance to weigh on the side of personal benefit in the equation.

It is also not beyond imagination that subjects may learn something as a result of their participation in some social research studies. Certainly one hopes that is the case in research carried out in academic settings where playing the role of respondents may be part of the social science curriculum. But even where the education of subjects is not intended, some learning may take place if the topic of the study is thought-provoking, if it induces introspection, or if it stimulates new ideas or activities. In a small political science study a few years ago, people who had been interviewed about their political preferences were found to participate more in subsequent elections than those who had not—apparently the study achieved one of the purposes for which civics courses are taught in U.S. high schools (Kraut and McConahay 1973). It has been suggested that even in areas that are considered high risk, for instance in studies that might create self-doubt or diminish self-esteem, there may be the countervailing benefit of self-knowledge (Gergen 1973).

## SOCIAL VALUE OF SOCIAL RESEARCH

Scientific inquiry in the pursuit of knowledge is a value expressed both in its own right and in opposition to control or regulation of scientific enterprise. Glass (1965), for instance, sees as the "third commandment" of an ethical basis of science a "fearlessness in the defense of intellectual freedom, for science cannot prosper where there is constraint upon daring thinking, where society dictates what experiments may be conducted, or where the statement of one's conclusions may lead to loss of livelihood, imprisonment, or even death." Spinrad (1970: 235), writing of few years later, expresses a similar point of view where he states: "A society which limits the academics' area of inquiry and expression is hurting itself by reducing its potential for knowledge."

Proponents of scientific freedom as an immutable value can find in history convincing examples of knowledge retarded by the shackling of science—the tribulations of Galileo or the prohibition placed on the human dissection in medieval Europe (Reynolds 1972)—but in some prestigious circles the argument appears to be losing some of its force. Edsall (1975) reports that one of the major recommendations of the American Association for the Advancement of Science's committee on scientific freedom and responsibility is that these two issues—scientific freedom and responsibility —are inseparable and that it should be recognized that freedom is an acquired and not an inalienable right. Petersen (1972) makes a similar point with respect to academic freedom by pointing out that this too is not an absolute right but rather an institutional norm which like others should be weighed to find the ratio most conducive to promoting social welfare. According to Vaughan (1967), the norm of unrestricted freedom of scientific inquiry is based on the value that knowledge is better than ignorance, a viewpoint which generally argues that a scientific end justifies any means, neglecting the fact that the scientific set of values and norms is not paramount but only one of many value sets constituting the social fabric. The whole matter remains under active debate as a recent editorial in *Science* (September 19, 1975) and letters to the editor of the same journal (see *Science*, October 24, 1975) testify. Some interesting counterarguments appear. One was put forward by Erikson (1968) who, in partial refutation of Denzin's (1968) assertion that the social science professions have considerably less power and authority than the established professions, pointed out that those professions, notably law, religion, and medicine, have free license only when they are serving the personal needs of their clients, not when they are conducting research. Another is found in a letter to the editor by Garb (*Science,* November 28, 1975: 834), arguing that "the real issue is not freedom to do research, since few areas of research are prohibited by law, but freedom to use tax-payer funds to conduct research that the tax-payer may not need or want, or may even oppose."

In addition to the value of scientific freedom, whether seen in its pure or its conditional form, the more mundane argument may be made on the benefit side of the equation that social science has proven itself in the practical crucible of utility if we consider its use in innumerable areas of public and private decision making. We have the frequently cited examples of the use of social research by the military during World War II, leading among other things to the plans adopted for demobilization, and Kenneth Clark's research incorporated in Thurgood Marshall's brief leading to the 1954 Supreme Court decision in the Brown case. To those may be added the uses to which social research findings have been put in decisions on such wide-ranging matters as how to run a political campaign, formulate a social program, select a jury, change an education curriculum, choose a TV series, train military recruits, organize a public campaign, rehabilitate ex-drug addicts, and so forth. The claim that might have seemed rather dubious a few generations ago may now be made quite convincingly: that applied social research has established its usefulness in the affairs of modern society. The prevailing model for resolution of the ethical conundrum is a scale that weighs the risks to subjects against the benefits of research with the decision to conduct a study or not dependent on how the lever tips. As a general scheme for ethical judgments in situations short of apodictic moral absolutes, it is hard to argue with the proposition that all factors should be intelligently considered in reaching decisions. Some problems remain, however, in the simple application of the model to much of social science research.

One can identify and describe, at least in speculative terms, the benefits that participation in research may bring to subjects or to the society in which they live, just as one may identify many of the risks that subjects may encounter. If only such risks and benefits were calculable in some form of measurement, in the model of an economic cost-benefit analysis, for example, the problem of ethical judgment—of deciding on reasonable and generally acceptable grounds whether to say yea or nay to a proposed bit of research—might be solved by the application of the quantitative calculus. But the risks of social research are often not only incalculable but quite unknown—they often emerge accidentally in the course of the work and are identified after the fact as "unanticipated consequences." Many types of potential danger discussed in a previous chapter are only dangerous if so defined by the subjects themselves—an "invasion of privacy" depends on what a subject considers to be private, and "coercion" may vary more with the subject's sense of freedom to resist than with any actions taken by the investigator. Not enough is known to make sufficiently good predictions on subjective reactions to these elements in a study to properly weigh them in the cost-benefit equation. The judgments about risks that can be made ahead of time tend to be either based upon untested assumptions about subjects' feelings on the matter or based upon the investigator's (or the review committee's) own sense of right and wrong, such as a judgment that unobtrusive observation ipso facto violates basic rights and is unethical. In the later case, there is no need for the scale.

The weighing of the benefits of social research in relation to risks of harm is even more confounding as a procedure. The benefits to individual subjects resulting from their research participation tend to be in the nature of unmeasured surmises, as suggested previously. The more frequently proposed counterweight to risks in the equation is the benefits to society (or to science and through it to society) that accrue through the conduct of scientific social research. Societal benefits may be more firmly grounded in the accumulated evidence of effective application of social research findings, but how does one go about comparing the risk of harm to individuals, and the long-range benefits to the collectivity, with anything like the precision which the risk/benefit formula implies? Smith (1976) says it can't be done, though he does not reject the idea of considering individual risks and societal benefits within the broad framework of ethical judgment.

The simple scale model of risk-benefit assessment, if used for decisions to approve or reject a proposed study, also fails to conform with some of the procedural circumstances in which many social studies are carried out. Only rarely does a social study, at the time it is first proposed, lend itself to the full assessment of risks and benefits or to the formulation of procedures to assure that all angles have been covered in full ethical review so that its subjects will receive maximum protection. In a typical case, the rationale of the study, the general content of the data to be collected, and the broad outlines of the design would be known in advance and described in a proposal prepared for ethical review and submission to a potential sponsor; usually, the questionnaire is still to be constructed and pretested, the sample remains to be drawn, the coding and data processing need to be organized, and the analysis remains to be planned in detail. Even the steps between inception and contact with the first subject may require months of preliminary work and the making of many decisions about procedures that affect the treatment of the study's subjects; and in large-scale research, subsequent decisions may be made over the course of several years.

The need for sequential assessment of risks may be illustrated by outlining the procedure of a large-scale evaluation study of a social program involving data collection from program records and the conduct of surveys among the client population. An initial ethical review when the study is first proposed would deal only with the broad purposes and general outline of the research; a second review might deal with any problems raised by the questions to be asked in the survey and the nature of the informed-consent statements to be made to the subjects; unanticipated occurrences during the interview, such as anxieties raised in the minds of respondents, might call for another review during the course of the pretest and the survey in order to consider possible "debriefing" procedures; as the data processing is initiated, questions may be raised about the coding of responses given in interviews that identify subjects, about the security of procedures that match interview records with file information on respondents, or about disaggregation of data that might permit individuals or program administrative units to be identified; when the data are reported, questions may still remain as to whether the interests of subjects are adequately protected if, for instance, quotations used to illustrate the text could be traced by knowledgeable readers to their sources or if administrative units requiring anonymity are too thinly disguised—for example, "the political science faculty of a Connecticut Ivy League College"; finally, the conscientious social scientist and his ethics committee may be concerned about subsequent uses of the data which have been collected with the promise that no harm would come to the subjects' social group as the result of their participation in the research.

Another deficiency of the simple risk-benefit assessment model, according to some scholars, is that it is not well adapted to the participatory nature of most social science research. In companion pieces in *Daedalus* (Spring 1969), Margaret Mead and Talcott Parsons discuss the collaborative nature of social research with Mead viewing the collaboration as a description of current anthropological practice and Parsons as a prescription for general conduct of the affairs of social science. Mead (1969), for instance, sees rules governing experimentation as a means for controlling experts and, thus, to some extent, as a denial of trust. For her, the solution to preventing ethical violations does not lie in a cost-benefit assessment, but rather in a research model in which the subject also serves as collaborator. From this perspective, participation in research can be viewed as responsible citizenship activity, especially when public funds are involved, on the assumption that the use of public money implies public support. In a similar vein, Parsons (1969) characterizes the relationship between subject and professional as one of solidarity. In contrast to the usual market relationship where payment follows receipt of specific benefits, "solidary" relationships are more akin to marriage where the "for better or worse" principle operates rather than the quid pro quo principle. The participatory approach to the dilemma, if carried to the extreme assumption that the subject is equally knowledgeable in all circumstances, could border on ethical irresponsibility in cases where the investigator does have a clearer view of where he is leading his participants. But it is still appealing because of the dignity it grants the subject and because of the possibility that many of those gaps in understanding of what may be subjectively described as undesirable for the participants in research may be filled by the participants themselves as the research evolves.

Social research is such a mixed bag of procedures that there is probably no one prescriptive or proscriptive package that could be used across the board in assessing ethical issues and reaching agreeable solutions. The types of risks that subjects may encounter vary with the types of studies being conducted and with the specific content of the inquiry; equally, we may assume that the benefits that individuals or society may derive depend on such variable factors as the importance of the study, how well it is carried out, and who pays attention to the results. The participatory model may be particularly well suited to field work in anthropology and to exploratory attitude research in sociology or social psychology; the risk-benefit model may fit a little better in areas of psychological experimentation where the psychologist is the only good judge of expected risks. Only the absolutists are able to say across the board that everything should be permitted so as not to restrict the advancement of knowledge or that some types of research should be proscribed because they may infringe on basic rights. The gray area in between is occupied by case-by-case judgments of researchers and the review committees to which they are increasingly accountable. One hopes for judgments made by reasonable men and women, sensitive both to the conflicting values that pervade the field of ethics and to the possibility of risks that stem from the various types of data social scientists collect and the procedures they use in collecting them.

# 6 / *Regulation of Social Research*

The three major forms of research control—self-regulation, regulation by professional associations, and governmental control—while analytically separable, are inextricably linked with one another in practice and can perhaps best be seen as operating at three different levels. At the level of the actual day-to-day conduct of research, the onus for protecting the rights and welfare of human subjects falls on the individual researcher or, since in this era of "big science" individuals rarely work alone, on the team of researchers. Professional associations set standards of professional conduct to which individual practitioners are supposed to adhere and in that way impinge on individual conceptions of appropriate professional behavior. Finally, government not only funds much of the kinds of large-scale research we have been talking about but also represents the interests of the public, with regulatory initiatives that tend to evoke reactions, cooperative and otherwise, from both researchers and their professional associations.

## SELF AND COLLEAGUE CONTROL

Within the context of biomedical research, the wise, responsible, humane physician is often seen as the best protector of the rights and welfare of human subjects. To the extent that Western conceptions of morality are heavily individualistic, the physician's counterpart, a conscientious social science investigator, would seem an appropriate guardian of the subjects of social science research, so long as such an individual is in a position to effect protection. As mentioned earlier, however, social research is largely a team effort. A project director may have the best interests of his respondents at

51

heart, but he himself is rarely in actual contact with the respondents, though he does, of course, have influence over the research team members working for him and can warn them against infringing on the rights of subjects. While he is responsible for the conduct of those working under him, protecting the rights and welfare of research participants must often devolve upon others than himself. Beyond the practical necessity of colleagues' cooperation in most social research enterprises, the very conception of independent scholarly responsibility comes into question when the scholar's self-interest is permitted full rein and when he is in a position to affect the lives of large numbers of human subjects. So the development of informal or formal mechanisms of peer review would appear to be necessary to meet both the practical problems of common purpose among cooperating investigators in organized large-scale research and the ethical concerns about individual self-interest that might create a less-than-optimum situation for the protection of subjects.

## REVIEW COMMITTEES

Informal committees with various titles and composition have been reviewing the ethics of social research projects for as long as anyone can remember—departmental dissertation committees at universities, policy boards in nonprofit organizations, outside advisory committees to larger studies sponsored by foundations or government agencies, or, most frequently, members of a project team getting together from time to time to discuss the progress and problems of their work. Such traditional mechanisms, though lacking the explicit, formal mandate and prescribed procedures of latter-day human subject protection committees, probably still served the purposes of providing attention to subjects' interests when conscientious questions arose, and of the socialization of new researchers in whatever ethical values were *au courant*.

The formalization and wide adoption of institutional review boards (IRBs), established to concentrate exclusively on ethical matters, has undoubtedly come about as a result of HEW regulations and, as with other parts of the regulations, may have their origins in biomedical research. The standing review committee form is probably particularly congenial to a collegial administrative mechanism in a training hospital setting with its tendency toward specialized committees, but it is not entirely foreign to the circumstances of organized, large-scale, social research conducted by institutions. Most of the opposition to HEW's committee review regulations has hinged on substantive elements prescribed for the committees' consideration and the procedures laid down for their operation, rather than on the regulations' insistence on review committees per se. As we have noted previously, there are serious questions in social research about the nature and extent of any harm or injury that could be caused, the possibility of assessing risk with any degree of accuracy, the nature of the information to include in informed-consent statements, and the feasibility of written consent forms; but few questions have been raised about the advisability of committees of peers to consider such matters.

The use of the institutional review committee as a device to deal specifically with ethical problems in the treatment of research subjects is a recent phenomenon, and until recently we have had no research results on its effectiveness in social research. In the medical area, Barber et al. (1973) found discrepancies between purpose and performance in the operation of IRB review of biomedical research projects. Similar research by Gray (1974, 1975 a, b) confirmed the Barber finding that most committees are relatively permissive and that "the absence of effective monitoring procedures and lack of feedback from research subjects limits the impact of the review procedures on the actual conduct of research" (Gray 1975a: 318). Melmon et al. (1970) provide a description of the activities of the San Francisco Medical Center Review Committee during its first two years of operation in which it rejected 17 proposals out of 340 reviewed involving human subjects: seven, because the committee was unable to assess the risk-benefit ratio; eight, because of the absence of adequate precautions; and two, because the level of risk incurred was judged unacceptable.

This committee dealt only with biomedical research; bridging the social area is a new study conducted by the Survey Research Center at the University of Michigan (Cooke and Tannenbaum 1977) looking into the operations of IRB's which handled both biomedical and behavioral studies. The study has produced a vast amount of data on the composition and procedures employed by committees, not all of which, unfortunately, is yet tabulated to show the views of the behavioral science review board members and investigators separately from those of their biomedical colleagues. Among the data, however, emerges the interesting finding that the behavioral scientists tend to take a more favorable view toward the review process. For example, when the study's respondents were asked, in respect to the hypothetical borderline case of a researcher "doing a paper on the development of institutional policy in which he wishes to interview administrators in the institution," whether such an exercise should be brought before a human subjects review committee, 43 percent of the behavioral scientists said it should compared to 25 percent of the biomedical IRB members. Despite the grumblings one finds in this study and at large concerning the difficulties encountered by researchers in working with formal peer committees, the process appears to be working with a fairly wide, but by no means universal, acceptance.

## PROFESSIONAL ASSOCIATIONS

Students of professionalization have noted several distinct characteristics of established professions which set them apart from other occupational groups. For instance, professions seek to maintain control of the content of their work, and they strive to preempt the mechanisms of its regulation and control, often with the connivance of government. Additional characteristics include the tendency toward indoctrination of new members, formal training in a body of abstract and often esoteric knowledge, and their possession of what Parsons refers to as a "service ideology" being best understood by contrast with the commercial interests that motivate non-professional occupational groups. Most of these criteria, mustered to define professions, seem more applicable to older ones such as law or medicine than to the social sciences. Laymen are wont to join in the control over the content of some social science inquiries—as clients with their own ideas of how the study should be done or as instant researchers themselves; public opinion research is an area where such incursions are not infrequent. Social scientists also have not quite yet attained the positions of influence they would need to assure governmental assistance in protecting their autonomy. Social scientists frequently, indeed, find themselves involved in struggles to prevent the passage of federal or state laws that would impose undesirable control. Only the psychologists have achieved any success, through their efforts toward certification and licensing, in initiating legislation which benefits the public by protecting it from untrained practitioners, but which also helps psychologists maintain professional control over their practice.

The tendency of professions to maintain autonomy in the conduct of their work, insofar as that tendency is predicated on a model of professional knowledge as esoteric knowledge, also does not apply to the social sciences as neatly as it may to law or medicine. But this is not to say that social scientists embarked on research can be seen as lacking in the familiarity with relevant theoretical developments and the substantive knowledge that is gained through professional training and experience, or that such theoretical and substantive knowledge is necessarily any easier to acquire than the knowledge in other professional spheres. Biomedical knowledge is usually considered too complex for the layman to comprehend, but even in the case of social science, the risks and benefits of a research study may be more apparent to the professionals working in that area than to the people recruited at home, in the workplace, or in college who are called upon to participate as subjects. To the extent that such a competence gap exists, one would expect social scientists to insist on some control over the regulation of the work, using the knowledge they possess to assess ethical considerations and correct violations.

Many of the professional associations have for some time been actively engaged in the promulgation of codes of ethics which include consideration of research subjects, and there appears to have been an accelerated movement in that direction recently (see Appendix A). It is likely that if concern with ethical principles increases within the wider society, notably within the federal government, the movement will gain greater force. Such codes, however, are not universally seen as a panacea to all the problems involved in the protection of the rights and welfare of subjects. A serious objection to codes of ethics is made by those who see their prime purpose as that of protecting the profession instead of the public. According to this view, a code of ethics is little more than a public-relations document, designed to allay the public's fears, and has little real substantive content (Roth 1969). Related to this is the observation (Wolfensberg 1967) that even when there is substance, it is not always based, as it should be, on clearly stated ethical principles. And when the ethical principles are clearly stated, there remains the translation problem from general principles to specific instances (Barber 1967). One hears the view that inflexible reliance on codes of ethics can prove perilous because of the idiosyncratic features of specific instances; some feel that a better safeguard is provided by the responsible researcher who consults with his colleagues when faced with a difficult decision.

The extent to which a code of ethics is not merely a public-relations document, and the extent to which it incorporates matters of real substance, depends in large measure on how well it captures and molds the informed thinking of those who are supposed to subscribe to the code on appropriate ethical principles and on how firmly the principles should be enforced. And this brings us to a real problem: the lack of consensus in the social science research community about how the professional associations should guide the conduct of research involving human subjects. The American Psychological Association (APA) has been the most thorough and systematic in developing an ethical code which best reflects the position of the majority of its members. Yet disagreement and dispute about the code's contents remain, both because it is too restrictive and because it is too lax. Gergen (1973) may be cited as one of many who took the former view. In responding to an early draft version of the code, he expressed his objection to premature and overly absolutistic codification of ethical principles. First, he argued, more research is needed to find out how much research participants are actually concerned with ethical issues, and second, it should be remembered that concepts such as "harm" show considerable cultural variability—self-doubt, for instance, in some ethical systems is a virtue. As a result, he would rather have the APA use advisory statements than ethical principles. In contrast stands Baumrind (1971, 1972, 1975), who has consistently criticized APA's code for not being restrictive enough. She objects particularly to the code's adherence to conventional standards, its risk-benefit approach, its qualifications of the principle of informed consent, and its failure to deal adequately with the problem of experimental manipulation and deception. She feels that the activities of social or behavioral scientists and the values they promulgate are more important than the products of the behavioral science enterprises. Wallwork (1975) argues that the method used by the APA to formulate its code of ethics, "democratic group discussion and agreement," satisfies the social-contract basis of Kohlberg's fifth state of moral development, but he agrees with Baumrind's criticism of the code's reliance on risk-benefit assessment and its failure to emphasize sufficiently the importance of informed consent. He would like to see the code place more emphasis on substantive rights.

While the American Psychological Association presents an interesting case because of its extensive prior collection of critical incidents and consultation with members in arriving at its code of ethics, it is also instructive to look at viewpoints expressed during the American Sociological Association's (ASA) development of a code of ethics, since the ASA includes among its members many researchers experienced in large-scale research, the particular focus of our inquiry. For Becker (1964), ethical codes tend to be either equivocal or vague. In preference to working toward establishing a code and in recognition of the lack of underlying consensus on the appropriate and important ethical principles which ought to be incorporated in such a document, he proposed that the ASA sponsor a symposium on the ethical problems characteristically facing sociologists. Writing in the same year, Freidson (1964) asserted that debate is better than artificial delineation of issues. He raised the question of whether sociologists are primarily practitioners or whether they are primarily scholars and scientists. If the former, a code of ethics, state licensing, and enforcement mechanisms are needed; if the latter, no ethical code is necessary. Five years later, Schuler (1969), writing within the context of the Camelot project, for which U.S. social scientists were recruited to conduct military-sponsored research on social change in foreign countries, urged the ASA to move more rapidly in formulating a generally acceptable code of ethics, in part because of the necessity he saw for securing the independence of scholarly research from governmental control. Friedrichs (1970) commented that the code of ethics proposed by the ASA in 1968 would lead to further divisiveness in a discipline already torn between adopting "system" or "conflict" as its basic frame of reference and engaged in critical reexamination of its previously presumed value neutrality. He noted the irony of a professedly value-free discipline attempting to codify ethics on an empirical basis and expressed his criticism of approaches to ethics which view persons as means, not ends: sociology's emphasis ought to be on rationalizing and humanizing our common social existence. Hofmann (1972) writes that most sociologists agree that maintaining the trust of subjects is important and that sociologists are accountable for their own activities. He holds that ultimate ends can some-times justify ethically questionable methods, and whether research is legiti-mate has to be decided on a case-by-case basis. On the other hand, the importance of subject trust and professional accountability means that social scientists cannot follow a purely scientific ethos. He holds that they must discard the notion that the goal of science is knowledge and must rather focus on creating a good society with the well-being of persons as its most important aim. Galliher (1973), like Hofmann, sees a case-by-case approach as the most viable means for settling ethical dilemmas. As a substantive suggestion, he would have the ASA's code modified to permit unhampered research on publicly accountable behavior, and he would have harm to subjects, including that resulting from the violation of data confidentiality, calculated on an individual cost versus societal benefit basis by professionals.

## GOVERNMENT CONTROL

Government control of research reaches back more than a decade. As noted in Chapter 2, guidelines for the protection of human subjects first promulgated by the Public Health Service and confined to research funded by it later became applicable to research funded by any subdivision of HEW and have now taken on the force of regulations. The National Commission for the Protection of Human Subjects is currently considering the advisabil-ity of regulating *all* research involving human subjects.

Since government concern with the conduct of research first arose with specific reference to biomedical research in the agency sponsoring the bulk of that research, the Public Health Service, it is instructive to take a detailed look at the reasoning underlying policy statements issued by that agency. Confrey's (1968) work is of particular interest in this regard since at that time he was the director of the Division of Research Grants, National Institutes of Health, of the Public Health Service. According to Confrey, the 1966 policy was designed to incorporate the notions that federal control should avoid extremes; that the complementarity of roles between the granting agency, the grantee institution, and the investigator should be reflected; that the diversity of institutional settings and types of research, subjects, and investigators should be recognized; and that the traditional concept of a grant as "a form of financial assistance to an institution on behalf of an investigator so that he may pursue a problem in which he is interested and which coincides with an area of biomedical research relating to a national objective" should be retained. Many of the features of the policy described by Confrey are still in force now ten years later. These include the policy's emphasis on the grantee institution as the locus of responsibility; its require-ment that research proposals receive independent review by a committee of the institution; that institutions establish mechanisms providing for surveillance of funded research and for advice and consultation to researchers confronting ethical dilemmas; and that grantee institutions have on file at NIH their general assurance of compliance with the policy and conduct research in accordance with the laws and norms of the local community.

In describing his agency's experiences with the policy, Confrey discusses some typical questions asked by grantee institutions. The question why the PHS did not leave the responsibility for the ethical conduct of research to the relevant professional associations is particularly interesting when considering problems of control and regulation. Confrey (1967: 131) asserts that there are two aspects to this problem, namely:

> the formulation of ethical codes and the formulation of administrative standards for implementation of the codes. Under the principle of complementary roles, the Service expects professional societies to continue their efforts at devising and refining such codes. The Government as well as other components of society will benefit from these endeavors. Until such a time as these codes are widely adopted and their objectives realized, the Service will continue its primary role of highlighting problems and requiring—albeit in general terms—administrative steps necessary to minimize such problems.

The implications of this are clear: The development of substantive ethical principles was to be primarily the task of professional associations with the government focusing on administrative procedures. But Confrey's remarks can also be interpreted as justifying the need for government intervention in "highlighting problems" and taking steps to "minimize such problems" precisely because of the failure of professional associations to regulate their own research activities.

Frankel's (1972) analysis of PHS policy on research involving human subjects between 1966 and 1969, with an afterword devoted to the 1972 revisions, identified five basic underlying values used as guides:

protecting subjects from harm and exposing them to risk only with their consent;
keeping government interference to a minimum;
maintaining cooperation between the PHS, the grantee institution, and the individual investigator;
retaining the diversity of scientific research;
permitting maximum freedom to the search for knowledge.

On the basis of Confrey's and Frankel's analyses, the policy makers cannot be accused of being wholly insensitive to the needs and concerns of the research community, at least not during the early stages of the development of policy for protecting the rights and welfare of human subjects. Nevertheless, recent developments such as the change in the policy's status from that of guidelines to regulations, and greater specification of terms such as "at risk," have tended to make the policy more restrictive. In addition, the establishment of the National Commission for the Protection of Human Subjects in Biomedical and Behavioral Science Research can be taken as another indicator of increased governmental concern that research involving human subjects be governmentally monitored.

Perhaps the most immediately apparent reason for these new developments is that the earlier policy was seen as inadequate. Testifying before the House Subcommittee on Health hearings in connection with the Protection of Human Subjects Act, Barber (1973) declared himself in favor of the proposed legislation on grounds that the biomedical professions had amply demonstrated their inability to control their own conduct ethically, that existing safeguards were either insufficient or not well implemented, and that certain areas are too sensitive and important to be placed only under professional control and therefore need governmental oversight. Barber, although acknowledging that the nature of risk in social research is milder than in biomedical research, has consistently exhorted the social science research community to respond with reason to controls emanating from the government, and he has warned social researchers against repeating the mistake made by biomedical researchers in their claim that their activities are too innocuous to warrant regulation.

Other more general explanations of the government's increasing involvement with the conduct of research take into account not only its overall regulatory function—which means it plays a legitimate role in taking responsibility for subjects involved in research it sponsors—but also its accountability in light of the vast amount of public monies expended on biomedical, behavioral, and social research. Using a broader historical perspective, Romano (1974) sees the principles governing experimentation with human beings evolving over time toward greater crystallization—in medicine, for instance, informal guidelines developed over the centuries have changed toward a civilly enforced body of legal and administrative regulations to control research projects and the use of human subjects—and it is not surprising that government intervention tends toward sharper policy focus or greater restrictiveness.

The response by social scientists to the more recent HEW regulations has, predictably, been mixed. In *Footnotes* (1975) the newsletter of the American Sociological Association, there was a report on the "general fear" that the full force of these restrictive regulations would be applied to social research, an unfair and unnecessary development because social research is mainly harmless and does not place respondents at risk. Other objections have been expressed in papers read at professional meetings. Ellis (1974), for example, alleges that research in general has a negative public image, that behavioral science in particular excites public suspicion because its products are so intangible, and that the regulations have the undesirable consequence of reinforcing these negative attitudes. Ellis furthermore objects to the rule that research should benefit participants—although individual human rights deserve protection, the right of mankind to acquire knowledge should not be overlooked; everyone should be obliged to participate since ultimately research will benefit all. Bowers (1974) asks whether the regulations will result in the social sciences ceasing their move toward empiricism and veering instead toward the more humanistically oriented pole. He also comments on the tension which restricting the fact-finding function of social research will place on it as the finder of solutions to pressing social problems. Bowers's fear that the major impact of the regulations will be evasion and "white-collar crime" is also found in Fox (1974), who mentions, as a specific example of the unanticipated and unintended consequences of well-meant legislation, the weakening of self-regulation by professionals. She notes that the regulations tend to make explicit "the non-contractual elements of contract."

The objections, both substantive and procedural, voiced by professional social scientists to governmental control as manifested in the regulations, suffer from the absence of empirical data that one would like to have available before making judgments. It is, in fact, a thread through this book that insufficient research has been conducted to provide the requisite information to the social scientist or to the agency that would regulate his work or to provide them with a reasonable groundwork of knowledge for their decisions on the application of ethical principles.

# 7 / *Summary and Conclusions*

This study began with the mandate to examine the ethical problems in the use of human subjects in large-scale social research studies among normal adult populations, for the purpose of providing information that could be helpful in formulating regulations for human subject protection in the social research enterprise. The work involved an extensive literature review, the examination of professional codes of ethics, an informal study of organized citizen concern about the topic, discussions with social scientists at professional association conferences and meetings of a task force of expert advisors from various social science disciplines.

We see our effort as a small step in a continuing process of solution-seeking and adjustment of interests among the social scientists in their work settings and their professional associations, and among the public through its representatives in Congress, the administration agencies, and the press. On both sides, the degree of attention and the pace of activity have been increasing rapidly during the past several years. In social science, more and more books are being written and articles published in professional journals, courses on professional ethics are emerging as part of social science curricula at universities, sessions are finding their way into programs at professional conferences, and codes of ethics are being adopted for the first time or undergoing revision by professional associations. On the public side, the HEW initiatives toward regulation of human subject protection during the 1960s have been followed in the 1970s by such legislation as the National Research Act, the Buckley Educational Amendments, the Privacy Act, and the Freedom of Information Act, all with provisions affecting in one way or another the manner in which social research may have access to its subjects or the ways it shall act to protect their interests.

There is nothing in what we have examined to suggest that this bustle has resulted from major new sins committed by social scientists in their treatment of human subjects, or from old sins newly detected. Within the social science fraternity itself there is general acceptance of the proposition that evidence of cases of actual harm occurring to a normal adult citizen because of his research participation is hard to come by. There have been no recent major scandals to excite the national press, and in our informal inquiry among organized citizen groups we had difficulty in uncovering even much evidence of interest. The reconsideration of social science research ethics which we have seen appears to have arisen in part as a reaction to the emergence of government regulation and in part from professional social science initiative consonant with the new national concerns about individual rights, most dramatically exemplified by the civil rights movement of the 1960s in which many social scientists themselves played a role. And on the government side, the regulation of human subject protection in social research seems not to have been stimulated by fears about the shenanigans of social scientists or the plight of their respondents, but rather to have been pulled along as an appendage to the regulations for the protection of biomedical research subjects who were seen to be at risk of quite tangible physical harm, with an added impetus given to the movement by the new public concern about privacy.

Despite the scattering of empirical studies on ethical issues that have been noted in the book, there is still insufficient research and systematic accumulation of experience to illuminate many of the problems in human subject protection and to provide better grounds for sound judgments on the potential effects of proposed study procedures. To give some examples:

Many of the risks for subjects that have been discussed as particularly relevant in the conduct of social research are the risks of unfortunate and in most cases unintended subjective reactions to the research procedures or study topics—perceived by subjects as invasions of privacy, for example, or seen to cause embarrassment or other forms of stress (as that term has been loosely defined in Chapter 3), or a concern that a subject may have about the effects of his participation on the lot of a collectivity with which he identifies. The investigator, as he starts his study, may be armed with nothing more than hunches about such reactions. In the area of social psychology, a number of studies have been conducted dealing with reactions of experimental subjects and potential subjects to the experimental situation, but in other areas of social research, beyond some tidbits in published studies, very little is available that would inform a researcher or an ethical review committee about the negative effects that a proposed study might have. On an allied point, we have no good empirical data on what efforts to gain the participation of research subjects the latter would consider to be coercive

—that is, what would cause them to participate "against their better judgment."

We do know something about the effectiveness of informed-consent procedures in the biomedical area, through works such as those of Barber and Gray. The study by Eleanor Singer (1977) and the National Opinion Research Center provides helpful information on how the use of various informed-consent models affects the conduct of social surveys. These are good starts, but one suspects that more will remain to be discovered about the amount of information the average subject needs in order that he may feel sufficiently informed and the sorts of information he feels to be most essential to his decision to participate.

As the peer review process becomes increasingly formalized through the institution of human subject protection committees, several problems emerge. A review committee whose composition does not include experts in social science methodology may have difficulty in assessing any viable alterations to the procedures that are proposed, while a committee with expertise concentrated in one area could be too receptive to a colleague's proposal. The role that outside representatives of the larger community may play on a committee needs some concentrated investigation. Despite the recent work of Cooke and Tannenbaum (1977), there is more we need to know about the effect of committee composition on the review process and the dynamics of decision making in project reviews.

The protection of subjects' anonymity is of great concern to social scientists. Insofar as the possibility of subpoena is the threat, the solution lies with legislatures and courts, but there are some other areas where researchers may take a hand. Ways in which aggregated data may be produced without the possibility of any individual's answers to specific questions being determined, such as those suggested by Boruch and others, might be further developed. It would be of interest also to know how much people (or most people) care whether certain sorts of information that they reveal get passed on to others; it is possible that some topics could be investigated as well without as with promises of anonymity.

The reader of the previous chapters will see the difficulty in formulating conclusions or recommendations that would represent anything like a consensus of a social science viewpoint on the topics under discussion. Men and women of equal experience and probity give articulate expression to diametrically opposed views even on such initial questions as whether any appreciable risks of harm exist for the subject-participants in social research, or what responsibility there is for anybody to do anything about it if potential harm should be discernible. Among those who see a problem, its features take most any form, and for those who seek a solution, its direction lies down any number of paths. The assumption should not be made that our concluding remarks necessarily represent generally held views in the social science community, let alone the views of any professional association. The statements that follow were prepared after discussion with the members of the study Task Force, identified in the Preface, in an attempt to summarize major points of agreement among that small group of scholars.

## SOME CONCLUSIONS

1. The *ideal* model for the conduct of social research investigations—sometimes referred to as the "participatory" model—is one in which subject and investigator are seen as equal partners in a mutually advantageous effort. It is a model that emphasizes the rights of respondents in decision making before and during the research process, that deemphasizes status differences between researcher and researched, and that accentuates the application of general societal norms of interpersonal relations to the procedures of research. Much social research raises no significant barrier to the application of this model. For example, sample surveys of the general noninstitutional-ized adult public, or studies of such occupational groups as teachers, doctors, bankers, housewives, policemen, or lawyers, can be conducted without any diminution of the respondents' sense of freedom to refuse or discontinue their participation, or to demand whatever information they wish about the research. In anthropological field work, to take another example, the partner relationship between investigator and informants tends to be emphasized in establishing rapport with another cultural group and to be preserved as a matter of necessity. If all social science research could be made to fit the ideal model, there would be little left for ethical concern, but there are studies that prescribe less than equality in the interchange of information, others where the investigator is in a better position to make judgments about risks than the respondent-subject, and still others in which the subjects may feel disadvantaged in the full exercise of their rights because of their own status and the assumed superior authority of the research. Equal-status participation still remains as a goal for the conduct of social research, even though not fully achieved in practice. Furthermore, the model distinguishes social research to a degree, from the biomedical research to which it is wedded in current regulations, since the latter raises higher barriers of status disequilibrium and disparity in knowledge.

2. The assessment of pro's and con's, a necessary process in any intelligent decision making, is inevitable in ethical evaluation of research procedures, whether required by legislation or not. In most of social research, however, the assessment of both the risk of harm and of the potential of benefits is limited by a lack of knowledge on which to base judgments. However much may be assumed about what harms and what benefits the

subjects and potential subjects would themselves see as important to them, very little is actually known about these matters. Some possible harms, such as the subpoena of data on an individual who has committed or witnessed a crime, and some possible benefits, such as the improvement of a welfare program as a result of a social experiment, may be tangible enough to weigh unequivocally in the balance, but most of the factors that must be considered are intangible and subjective. The risk-benefit formulation is particularly difficult to apply in ethical review when risks to individuals are compared to benefits to society, as frequently has been proposed, since societal benefits are at least as much the province of national politics as of research ethics. Though harm-benefit assessment should remain part of the process of ethical review, it is better in current circumstances to put a bit more of the emphasis on informed-consent procedures, which stress the decision-making rights of the subject, than on the harm-benefit calculations, which place more of the responsibility on the investigator and his peers.

3. Social science employs a variety of data-collection methods in the investigation of a wide range of topics. Each of the major methods used, such as laboratory experimentation, social experiments, intensive field investigations, social surveys, and unobtrusive observations, is apt to produce its own set of problems in protecting the welfare of research subjects. Similarly, the topics of inquiry may vary from those that are perceived by individual subjects as embarrassingly sensitive invasions of privacy or potentially dangerous, at one extreme, to those that are quite harmless and personally enjoyable, on the other. Given such a range, it would appear that:

Only a limited set of minimal rules can apply across all social science projects, without inviting too much latitude for some or too stringent requirements for others.

The procedures used in ethical review should emphasize and facilitate a case-by-case consideration of individual projects.

Assessments of projects on a case-by-case basis require expertise in the methods of social inquiry as well as general reasonableness and intelligence.

4. The suggestion for only minimal prescription for across-the-board application does not imply any conclusion that all the problems to be solved are trivial, harmless though much in social research may be. It is, rather, a recognition that some of the more difficult problems need their own treatment after they have been given full and separate consideration. For instance, the various unobtrusive measures that have been used by themselves and as adjuncts to other data collection methods deserve more careful examination before conclusions are reached about the ethics of their use in different forms, on different subjects, and in different places. The use of deception,

most notable in social psychological experimentation but found in other areas as well, can have either well-founded or flimsy scientific justification, and departures from truth can vary in form from outright lies to the mildest of dissemblance. There are circumstances in which deception could well be considered outside the pale and others where it would cause but the mildest of ethical qualms. At the other end of the scientific spectrum, anthropological and ethnographic studies may find difficulty in following even quite lenient prespecified requirements, for instance in respect to informed-consent procedures, due to the slow and varied processes of gaining acceptance in communities and the ambiguities in identifying a "subject." At the same time, anthropology, more than some other disciplines, must address itself to the problem of protection against collective harm. We suggest that special problem areas in social science such as these be given separate treatment with a view to the establishment (not necessarily by government regulation) of reasonable guidelines for protection of research subjects and limits defining acceptable practices.

5. Some form of peer review is desirable in any research involving human subjects, whether or not supported by a sponsor who requires an accounting, and however unthreatening to his subjects the research proposer may feel his inquiry to be. Such peer review is already normal in social research, at least as an element of informal collegial cooperation and interchange of views. It is particularly prevalent in the case of large-scale studies that involve teams of researchers and advisors. If more structured peer review procedures are formulated in a reasonable manner, they need not be considered as more than an extension of good research planning practice. The sorts of committees or boards (institutional review boards, research ethics committees, human subjects committees) that have been established at universities and research institutions can constitute appropriate forums for review and guidance on ethical procedures in social research studies involving human subjects. We support the use of institutional boards for review of social science studies. The recommendations that follow have to do with the appropriate composition, procedures, and responsibilities of such boards when dealing with social science studies.

## SOME RECOMMENDATIONS

1. *Dissemination of information:* In addition to the research suggested by the comments above, we feel the need for a mechanism to keep social science investigators and the institutional committees that review their work abreast of the developments in human subject protection. At the present time, the hundreds of IRB's at universities and other institutions would

appear to be operating in isolation from one another. Except to the extent they may be guided by HEW regulations, they are independently developing policies and procedures with little exchange of lessons learned from their experiences gained through dealing with the ethical problems of social science studies. Specifically, we recommend the promotion of a journal or newsletter, directed to review committees and investigators, that would provide the following sorts of information:

Case accounts of IRB deliberations and decisions in the review of problematic social science projects.

Summaries of proposed and enacted legislation and regulations that affect human subject protection.

Summaries of the conclusions of new research as it becomes available.

Reports on the activities of social science professional associations, such as reports of ethics committees and adoptions or changes in codes of ethics.

Notice of pertinent official hearings and summaries of their findings.

Interim statements and conclusions of special study commissions, such as the Commission on Protection of Human Subjects in Biomedical and Behavioral Research and the Privacy Protection Study Commission.

An appropriate model for such a reporting system is the specialized "case law reporter" which is found in numerous variations in the legal profession, for example, the *Family Law Reporter,* put out by the Bureau of National Affairs, *Amicus,* published by the National Center for Law and the Handicapped, the *Weekly Report* of the Community Nutrition Institute, and the *Washington Weekly Newsletter* of the National Senior Citizens Law Center, to mention some proximate examples.

2. *Peer Review:* The most important function of an IRB is to protect the human subjects by preventing the conduct of research in ways that would be deleterious to their individual welfare. This is a function that should be carried out with full consideration also of the rights of researchers in a free society and of the contributions that social research can make to an understanding of the human condition. The composition of an IRB should be such as to permit it to meet those requirements to a reasonable degree within the limits imposed by the size and resources of the institution.

For the review of social science projects, several of the reviewers on a committee should be social scientists and at least one reviewer should be familiar with the alternative procedures that can be used to obtain data in the particular area of social science investigation of the project.

The rules under which IRB's operate (as established by the institution or by government regulation) should be flexible enough to permit the use of temporary members or consultants, or the formation of subcommittees, to meet the need of social science project review where the regular committee lacks the requisite experience.

When identifiable groups exist that can represent the interests of the respondents of a study, members should be asked to join in the review as advisors on procedures, particularly in cases where the subjects themselves are members of groups that would appear to be in any way inhibited in exercising their rights as research participants.

3. *Informed Consent:* It is important in all informed-consent procedures that emphasis be placed on the voluntary nature of participation in social research studies and, specifically, on the rights of participants to refuse participation and to suspend or terminate their participation at any time during the data-collection process.

In other respects, informed-consent procedures, and the content of informed-consent statements and guarantees made to respondents, may vary by project so as to permit consideration of such factors as the assessed degree of risk to subjects (considering both frequency and seriousness), potential benefits to subjects and society, and the vulnerability of subjects to circumstances in which the exercise of their rights to consent or withhold consent might be diminished.

The information given about the nature of the study and the procedures involving the participant's cooperation should include elements that might be assumed to affect the willingness of the participant to become involved in the study. When there are risks of harm to participants inherent in the research effort and when the risks are beyond the normal hazards of life, a description of the risks should be provided along with a statement on the procedures that will be adopted, if any, to minimize the risks.

At the time of first contact with participants, consent may be obtained in a variety of forms, such as signatures on written statements, explicit oral agreements, or conventional signs of willingness to proceed, as appropriate to the circumstance of the study. An investigator and his committee should be guided in the form of consent adopted mainly by the consideration of the best means of protecting the interests of respondents.

4. *Procedural Matters:* Requirements for documentation of compliance with human subject protection regulations in social research studies should be flexible so as to permit adjustment to the particular circumstances of the studies. A requirement of signed consent forms, for example, could be appropriate in some social studies, could render others impossible, and in some cases might increase the risks to subjects. The appropriate specific means of documentation can be best judged by the review committee.

A system of sequential review is desirable in many social studies. The IRB should determine at its first review meeting on a proposed study whether subjects will be at risk of harm, and if harm is determined to be a realistic possibility, what subsequent reviews are required—for instance, upon completion of the study instruments and the formulation of the informed-consent statements; during a pretest phase when effects of the procedures can be more clearly appreciated; after data collection has been completed in a situation where that process could be seen as potentially producing harmful effects requiring remedial action; or to review a draft report or data file if questions of possible identifiability of persons or institutions can be anticipated.

The committees that are increasingly called upon to review social science studies should consider the advisability of periodic audits by outsiders of their policies and procedures and of the consequences of their decisions. Such audits would establish an element of accountability in committee operations and could perform a constructive function through recommendations to the committees and the institutions they are serving.

5. *Task Force Comments:* Three of the Task Force members added statements qualifying their endorsement of these recommendations. George Foster agrees that the conclusions and recommendations above are appropriate for the conduct of the types of large-scale social research on which the report focuses. He does not feel, however, that the formal review process through IRBs and the informed-consent procedures as formulated can apply to traditional anthropological research without inviting dishonesty in statements of research intentions or crippling restrictions on the conduct of field investigations. Bernard Barber accepts the recommendations and adds the suggestion that there should be some appeal mechanism from the decisions of IRB's through a supralocal review agency, to be used in extreme cases of local differences. Albert Reiss, Jr., also concurring in the recommendations as written, points out that there are special problems of consent in research on organizations and that there may be circumstances in which informed consent is not applicable, such as in social observation studies.

# APPENDIX A/ *Ethical codes of professional associations*

The development of a formal code of ethics can be taken as a significant indicator of a profession's willingness to assume at least some measure of responsibility for regulating the conduct of its members. Such codes can, of course, vary widely in their scope of concerns and degree of explicitness, expecially in their treatment of ethical conduct in research involving human subjects. Even where written codes exist, the standards or principles adduced may be difficult to apply in concrete circumstances; procedures and powers of enforcement may be quite limited. Where no code exists, it seems fair to infer that little claim can be made of self-regulation by an organized profession, although individual members may nonetheless feel bound by some transcending standards of appropriate conduct. Thus, analytically, existence of a formal code can perhaps best be seen as a necessary but not sufficient condition of effective professional self-regulation.

We sought to gain some orienting information on the extent and character of self-regulation, especially as embodied in formal codes, by means of a survey of professional associations as well as scientific societies initially selected as likely to include social researchers among their members. A number of medical, allied health, and legal associations were also surveyed in order to provide some comparative data from professional sectors for which ethical questions in both research and practice have long been prominent.

Associations have been classified into broad types by their responses to our request for copies of "existing codes or ethical statements." It was sometimes difficult to classify an association, based on information made available to us, as to its type or the nature of its code or set of standards. It should be understood, therefore, that an element of discretion is inevitably involved in the judgments made.

## ASSOCIATIONS WITH CODES OF ETHICS

We found 39 associations with codes of ethics that can be classified according to whether or not they contain materials explicitly dealing with the protection of human subjects in research. Twenty-one gave some explicit recognition of problems in this area, either in the codes of ethics supplied to us (17) or by means of a letter or document related to current federal regulatory policies or legislative initiatives (4). The former have been further subdivided into behavioral and social science associations and biomedical and related associations. Eight associations made specific reference to endorsement of or subscription to the ethical code of other associations. Another ten associations have codes of professional ethics that do not, however, deal explicitly or directly with the protection of human subjects in research. Each of these five sets of associations will be listed, with accompanying comments drawn from or based upon the materials supplied.

### Associations Involved with Social and Behavioral Science Research

#### American Anthropological Association

"Principles of Professional Responsibility" (adopted 1971). There are six principles, the first of which governs "relations with those studied," while the rest deal with responsibilities toward the public, the discipline, students, sponsors, and governments. The first principle identifies responsibility toward those studied as paramount: "The anthropologist must do everything within his power to protect their physical, social and psychological welfare and to honor their dignity and privacy." It goes on to specify the obligations which relationships based on trust incur; the need to inform respondents of the aims of the investigation; the informants' right to anonymity and confidentiality; the obligation to reflect on foreseeable repercussions of research and publication on the population being studied, and to communicate the anticipated consequences of the research. It warns against exploitation of informants and proscribes secret reports of research findings. Finally, it prescribes cooperation with members of the host society and recognition of social and cultural pluralism.

#### American Association for Public Opinion Research

"Code of Professional Ethics and Practices" (1960). Aside from general principles governing the conduct of professional practice and relationships to the public, and clients or sponsors, AAPOR, under its "principles of professional responsibility in our dealings with people," specifically states:

"We shall protect the anonymity of every respondent. We shall hold as privileged and confidential all information which tends to identify the respondent."

## American Marketing Association

Respondents' anonymity will be protected and research information will be held confidential. The identity of the sponsor of the research will also be held confidential unless it is to be disclosed as part of the research design.

## American Personnel and Guidance Association

In its "Ethical Standards," Section D: "Research and Publication," it states that the current American Psychological Association guidelines on research using human subjects shall be adhered to. It goes on to specify the following: members must be aware of and responsive to all pertinent ethical principles in planning and conducting research; ethical responsibility lies with the principal investigator but is shared by others working on the project; researchers must protect their subjects' welfare and must "take all reasonable precautions to avoid causing injurious psychological, physical or social effects"; subjects should be informed of the purpose of the research unless deception or withholding information is essential—in which case "corrective action" should follow; and participation is to be voluntary: "Involuntary participation is appropriate only when it can be demonstrated that participation will have no harmful effects." Finally, due care should be taken to disguise the identity of subjects in publication or data transmission.

## American Political Science Association

"Proposed Rules of Conduct" (1968). APSA's proposed rules are concerned not so much with subjects as with maintaining freedom and integrity of research, although "it is, of course, assumed that they [researchers] will conduct their research with due consideration for the rights of those whom it affects." In fact, none of the proposed rules is directly concerned with protecting the rights of subjects. In a discursive section entitled "The Clarification of Ethical Problems," however, reference is made to Shils's work on privacy, and to Ruebhausen and Brim, and the problems accompanying confidential data sources.

## American Psychological Association

A general code "Ethical Standards of Psychologists," in which work done by the Cook Committee "Ethical Principles in the Conduct of Research with Human Participants" is incorporated (adopted 1963), amended

1965 and 1972). The investigator is responsible for assessing the ethical acceptability of a proposed study and, once research is initiated, maintaining the study's ethical acceptability. To the extent that there is a deviation from any of the principles, the investigator is obliged to seek ethical advice and follow more stringent safeguards in protecting the rights and welfare of the research subjects. Full disclosure and openness and honesty are required; if undesirable because of methodological requirements, full debriefing is necessary. Participation is voluntary: Research should begin with an agreement between investigator and subject concerning the responsibilities of each, and the investigator is obligated to honor all commitments. The investigator protects the subjects from "physical and mental discomfort, harm, and danger"; if there is any risk, the subjects must be informed, must give their consent, and the risk, must be minimized as much as possible—including the correction of negative long-term aftereffects. Finally, information must be held confidential.

## American Sociological Association

"Code of Ethics" (1971). Like others in this section, the ASA's code lays down a number of general principles which indirectly serve to protect the rights and welfare of human subjects, broadly defined: For instance, maintaining scientific objectivity and integrity; presenting research findings without distortion, and so on. Three principles are directly concerned with the protection of research subjects: respecting the subject's right to privacy and dignity; protecting the subject from personal harm ("All research should avoid causing personal harm to subjects used in research"); and preserving the confidentiality of research data.

## Marketing Research Association

"Code of Ethics." Members pledge "to protect the anonymity of respondents and hold as privileged and confidential all facts or opinions of a specific nature concerning any individual respondent, within the limits of a particular study."

## Society for Applied Anthropology

"Revised Statement on Ethics" (1973). These principles are meant for practitioners working in the applied field, that is, any activity involving "manipulation" in the sense of social planning or intervention. They look toward the possible future development of professional board certification and licensing, as in medicine and law. The dignity, integrity, and internal variability of the community being served should be respected. The lives, well-being, dignity, and self-respect of any portion of the community should not be adversely affected unless minimally, and the net effect of the action in the long run is more beneficial than if no action were taken. Greatest care must be taken to protect respondents, especially with respect to confidentiality.

### Society for Research in Child Development

"Ethical Standards for Research with Children" (1973). Twenty-one principles are listed for consideration. The child's rights are more important than those of the investigator and each activity must be assessed in that light. Prior peer approval by means of institutional review committees is necessary; the final responsibility remains with the investigator. Any deviation from the following principles requires that the investigator seek consultation: The child must be free to participate or not (a freedom which is to be based on informed consent on the part of the child, its parents or guardians, and those persons whose interaction with the child is a focus of inquiry); there should be clear agreement between the investigator and the subject of the responsibilities of each; the investigator must honor all commitments and must not harm the child either physically or psychologically. Full disclosure is the ideal: When a particular methodology requires deception, a committee must give prior approval, and corrective action must be taken afterward. All information must be kept confidential. Special safeguards must be taken when consulting institutional records. If the investigator learns of circumstances which may seriously affect the child's well-being, he is obliged to discuss these with experts so "that the parents may arrange the necessary assistance for their child." The investigator should reflect on the repercussions of research. If possible, control groups should be given other beneficial treatment rather than no treatment at all. Instructors should communicate ethical concerns to their students, and journal editors should be on guard for ethical transgression.

## Associations Involved with and Related to Biomedical Research

### American Correctional Association

"Protocol for Medical Experimentation and Pharmaceutical Testing" (approved 1972). Briefly, this protocol requires usage of a review committee; informed consent; volunteer screening for physical and emotional preparedness; careful evaluation of the compensation provided, especially to check its compatibility with the general welfare of the institution; assurance that the research activity will not compromise ongoing programs or other correctional activities; and adherence to the Nuremberg principles and the Declaration of Helsinki. It warns the administration of correctional institutions not to be unduly influenced by arguments that prisoners constitute an ideal research population.

## American Dental Association

"Ethical Guidelines for Clinical Investigation: Ethical Policy of the American Dental Association Regarding the Use of Human Subjects in Clinical Research" (adopted 1972). This document lists six basic principles: research must conform to moral and scientific principles; can be conducted only by qualified personnel; its importance must be proportionate to the risk; a careful assessment of the risk-benefit balance must be made; special care is required if the subject's health or personality may be changed; and informed consent must be obtained. When research is combined with treatment it must be justifiable in terms of its therapeutic value for the patient. In the case of nontherapeutic research, the investigator is responsible for the subjects' welfare; the research, including its purpose and risk, must be explained; informed consent must be obtained; subjects' privacy and confidentiality must be protected and their integrity honored; participation must be voluntary and the subject must be able to withdraw at any time; the research must be stopped if it is too harmful.

## American Hospital Association.

"Statement on a Patient's Bill of Rights" (approved 1973). This statement, based on the legal precedent that institutions bear responsibilities toward patients, covers all aspects of in-patient care and treatment. Right No. 9 is directly pertinent: "The patient has the right to be advised if the hospital proposes to engage in or perform human experimentation affecting his care or treatment. The patient has the right to refuse to participate in such research projects." Other relevant rights, placed in the broader context of treatment, are those of informed consent, privacy, and confidentiality, as well as "the recognition of his dignity as an individual."

## American Medical Association

The AMA issues both a general statement, "Principles of Medical Ethics," and the more specific "Declaration of Helsinki and AMA Ethical Guidelines for Clinical Investigation." The Declaration of Helsinki was adopted by the World Medical Association in 1964, and the Ethical Guidelines for Clinical Investigation were adopted by the AMA in 1966. Both make a distinction between therapeutic and nontherapeutic clinical investigation. With respect to the latter, the Ethical Guidelines require adequate safeguards for the welfare, safety, and comfort of the subject; signed informed consent after disclosure of the investigative nature of the activity;

reasonable explanation of the procedure and its risks; and the offer to answer any inquiries. Minors and the mentally incompetent may be used only if the research is not suitable for mentally competent adults, an informed and prudent adult could be expected to volunteer himself or his child, and written consent is provided by the subject's legally authorized representative. Participation must be voluntary.

## American Nurses' Association

"Code for Nurses with Interpretive Statements" (adopted 1950; revised 1960 and 1968). Two of the code's ten principles are particularly relevant: the nurse's obligation to safeguard the individual's right to privacy by holding information confidential, and to participate in research activities only when assured that the rights of the subject are protected. The individual's rights are described as those of "privacy, self-determination, conservation of personal resources, freedom from arbitrary hurt and intrinsic risk of injury." The nurse is urged to communicate her concerns to appropriate persons if she believes the well-being and safety of the patient are adversely affected by the research activity. Another document, "The Nurse in Research: ANA Guidelines on Ethical Values," approved in 1968, consists essentially of an elaboration of the rights listed above.

## Association to Advance Ethical Hypnosis

"Code of Ethics and Standard." This code contains four general principles: the welfare of the subject is to be the prime consideration at all times; members are to use hypnosis only within the limits of their training and competence; rights and desires of subjects must always be respected; and hypnosis must be employed in accordance with the laws of the community. The code goes on to detail the do's and don't's of the practice of hypnosis: for instance, age recall or regression beyond five is unreliable and unwise.

## Society for Clinical and Experimental Hypnosis

"Code of Ethics." Four ethical principles are stated: members must also be members in good standing of the recognized professional association in their field, must not use hypnosis beyond their area of competence as defined by the professional standards of their field, must not use hypnosis as a source of entertainment, and must use hypnosis only if it contributes to the welfare of the patient or to the advancement of professional knowledge in their field. More specifically under this last principle, "research investigations utilizing hypnosis shall maintain the strongest safeguards for the well-being of the subject. Proper safeguards shall be maintained whenever a human subject is exposed to stress. The problem should be of sufficient importance to justify such a procedure, and adequate facilities during and after the procedure should be available to assure the well-being of the subject. When there is doubt as to appropriateness of the stress exposure, the member shall consult with one or more colleagues or specialists or with the Committee on Ethics before undertaking the procedure."

## Associations Supplying Documents Responsive to Current Federal Activities

### American Psychiatric Association

Its "Proposed Interim Statement on Human Experimentation" expresses support for the establishment of the National Commission but opposes the ban on fetal research and psychosurgery. "These measures would impose a moratorium on valid and vital research activities which could set the mental health field back for many years to come." The statement calls for new task forces within the association to study the matter further and then report back.

### American Public Health Association

A resolution adopted in 1972 evidences particular concern with research on "captive" populations, a concern reiterated in a letter to HEW. Here it is suggested that a distinction should be drawn between behavioral and biomedical research, and that separate guidelines should be developed for behavioral research. The comments and suggestions accordingly pertain only to biomedical research, particularly on children and captive groups.

### Child Welfare League of America

A document giving assurance of compliance with HEW policy lists five implementing guidelines to be used by the institutional review committee: risk benefit assessment; research designed so as to minimize possible risk; voluntary participation in research; informed consent "unless special circumstances make this unnecessary or undesirable in particular instances"; and protecting the confidentiality of data.

### National Association for Mental Health

"Resolution in Opposition to Unrestrained Experimentation Involving Children and Also Patients and Prisoners in Institutions" (adopted 1974). This document urges that research on these groups be conducted under conditions no less stringent than those stipulated by HEW, "with particular emphasis on the involvement of informed consumer representation in all review or protection bodies."

## Associations Subscribing to the Codes of Other Associations

Eight associations responded to our inquiry by stating they subscribe to or endorse the codes of ethics of other associations. Four of them use the American Psychological Association's code: Council for the Advancement of the Psychological Professions and Sciences, National Association for Applied Arts and Sciences, Psychologists Interested in Religious Issues, and the Society for Personality Assessment. Two use the American Medical Association's code: American Academy of Family Physicians, and the National Medical Association. The American Academy of Psychoanalysis uses the code of ethics of the American Psychiatric Association; and the National Council for the Social Studies is an affiliate of the National Education Association.

## Associations with Nonexplicit Codes

American Association of Criminology

American Society for Personnel Administration

American Association of Pastoral Counselors

National Association of Black Social Workers

American Association of School Administrators

National Association of Social Workers

American Bar Association

National Education Association

American Society for Information Science

Operations Research Society of America

Although these ten associations' codes of ethics do not contain material specifically addressing the issue of the protection of human subjects, all of them define and prescribe ethical and responsible conduct with respect to clients, the public, or professional colleagues. More specifically, the associations' principles all include a reference to the importance of contributing to the growth of knowledge. Each association's code contains references to appropriate professional conduct, for example, protecting the integrity and competence of the profession; resisting unethical practices and professional impropriety; accepting only appropriate remuneration, and so on. Nine of them also contain statements that deal with the need to protect the interest and welfare of the public. For instance, one finds statements about the need to respect the dignity of the individual and to treat all with justice and impartiality, the need to protect the welfare of the individual or the group, or to act responsibly when making public statements. Eight associations further invoke principles concerning the importance of preserving confidentiality with respect to the people or organizations they serve. Seven associations' codes contain formulations of principles regulating conduct with clients, sponsors, or employers; four specifically warn their members against the unethicality of misrepresenting their skills or competencies.

## ASSOCIATIONS WITH NO CODES OF ETHICS

Aside from the 39 associations whose codes of ethics were described above, there are another 21 professional associations among those we examined which do not have codes of ethics. They are as follows:

American Association for Social Psychiatry

American Association for the Advancement of Science

American Association of Dental Schools

American Economic Association

American Educational Research Association

American Educational Studies Association

American Geriatrics Society

American Institute of Hypnosis

American Psychoanalytic Association

American Society for Public Administration

American Society of Human Genetics

American Statistical Association

The Econometric Society

Human Factors Society

Industrial Relations Research Association

International Transactional Analysis Association

Linguistic Society of America

Psychonomic Society

Society for Pediatric Research

Four of these associations (American Institute of Hypnosis, American Psychoanalytic Association, American Society for Public Administration, and Human Factor Society) reported they are in the process of developing a code of ethics or statement of professional standards. Two others (American Association for Social Psychiatry and International Transactional Analysis Association) responded that they have standing Ethics Committees.

# APPENDIX B/ *Public interest groups and the protection of human subjects*

This appendix summarizes the results of an effort to discover the extent of interest in the protection of human participants in large-scale social research on the part of public interest groups sufficiently well-established to have an address and telephone numer and to be listed in a directory.* A list of 72 organizations that might conceivably have an interest in the topic was extracted, to which we added several others. Some of them proved to be defunct or at least could not be located. A total of 75 groups, representing a substantial segment of this admittedly ill-defined universe, was ultimately surveyed (see Table B.1).

A cautionary word is needed in interpreting the results of our informal telephone interviews with representatives from these public interest groups. Insofar as there was a general absence of position papers or other organizational documents relating to the protection of human subjects involved in large-scale social research, we have had to rely solely on the testimony of these individuals for our classifications. In the case of the smaller public interest groups, the person interviewed was probably fully aware of the group's major interests and activities; the opposite may well be true of some of the larger, less-cohesive ones.

A related problem pertains to the lack of understanding as to the scope and nature of social research, especially large-scale social research. Widely publicized scandals such as the Tuskegee Syphilis Project aroused public indignation and concern and are generally seen as abusive of the rights and welfare of those participating in "research." The overall findings of our

*C. C. Clark and M. K. Marcus, eds., *Information Resources for Public Interest,* Fifth draft ed. (Washington, D.C.: Commission for the Advancement of Public Interest Organizations, 1974).

## TABLE B.1 Public Interest Organizations

American Civil Liberties Union
American Friends Service Committee
American Institute for Public Policy Research
American Institute for Public Services
American Jewish Committee
American Public Welfare Association
Anti-Defamation League
Arkansas Communtiy Organization for Reform Now
Arkansas Institute for Social Justice
Business and Professional People in the Public Interest
Center for Community and Economic Development
Center for Community Change
Center for Law and Social Policy
Center for Science in the Public Interest
Center for Study of Responsive Law
Children's Defense Fund
Children's Foundation
Church of the Brethren
Church Women United
Citizen Action Group
Citizens Communication Center
Common Cause
Concern
Corporate Action Program
Council of Churches of D.C.
D.C. Public Interest Group
El Congresso
Friends of the Earth
Gray Panthers
Human Justice Commission—Indiana
Institute for Public Interest Representation—Georgetown Law Center
Jesuit Conference
Kennedy Institute for Bio-Ethics
La Raza
Law Student Legal Action Organizers
Lawyers Committee for Civil Rights Under Law

Leadership Conference on Civil Rights
League of Women Voters
Legal Aid Society of D.C.
Mexican-American Cultural Center
Mexican-American Legal Defense and Educational Fund
Migrant Legal Action Program
National Assocation for the Advancement of Colored People
National Center for Urban Ethnic Affairs
National Consumers Congress
National Consumers League
National Council of Churches
National Council of Negro Women
National Education Association
National Institute of Public Affairs
National League of Cities
National Organization of Women
National Sharecroppers Fund
National Urban Coalition
National Urban League
National Vista Alliance
Native American Rights Fund
Network
New American Movement
Office of Community Services—Alexandria, Va.
People United to Save Humanity
Professionals in the Public Interest
Public Advocates
Public Citizen
Public Citizen Litigation Group
Public Interest Campaign
Public Interest Research Group
Science for the People
Source Group
Southern Law and Poverty Center
Southern Regional Council/Government Monitoring Project
U.S. Catholic Conference
U.S. Commission on Civil Rights
Urban Information Interpreters
Youth Project

Source: Compiled by the authors.

survey indicate that concern with the protection of human subjects among public interest groups is primarily linked to biomedical research, especially research on "captive" or institutionalized subjects. It is not impossible, however, that if or when the important ethical principles underlying biomedical research come to be seen as germane to social research, this heightened concern may spread to include noninstitutionalized participants in social science research.

On the basis of their responses, the organizations surveyed were placed into three categories: active interest; latent interest or working on related issues; and no interest:

| | |
|---|---|
| Active interest | 11 |
| Latent interest or working on related issues | 35 |
| No interest | 29 |
| Total | 75 |

## ACTIVE INTEREST

As previously mentioned, the lack of documented response made it difficult to establish the precise degree of interest in the particular area of inquiry. Nonetheless, two organizations mentioned a specific concern with a sensitive point in social research, namely privacy. One organization is working on the issue, the second clearly recognizes its importance but because of limited funds has not yet begun any work on it. Strictly speaking, only these two groups can be said to be addressing some of the specific problems associated with social research. Nine other groups were also placed in this category, however, on the basis of the high degree of interest they expressed. Because of their general civil libertarian and human rights orientation, three organizations claimed to be very interested in our topic; another two described themselves as especially interested in inequitable social welfare and social program legislation and administration. One of these pointed out that it is not always easy to distinguish between social programs and social experimentation.

Finally, four organizations were included in this category because of their representatives' strong antipathy toward social research in general. One described himself as suspicious of social research because of its "unsubstantiated conclusions"; a second was against social research if the voluntarism of participants was in doubt because she is "against social control" and, furthermore, tends to think all social research a hoax because it is too commonsensical to require that much time, money, and effort. A third said flatly that all research involving human subjects "brings us back to the Nazi era"; and the fourth said that while opposing large-scale social experimentation, he is in favor of survey research provided it is done according to guidelines. He also stated the opinion that "everyone knows that data is abused," and referred to instances where interviewers were claiming to be conducting survey research when they were actually making welfare-related assessments.

## LATENT INTEREST OR WORKING ON RELATED ISSUES

The modal position of one subcategory of this diffuse category or class of organizations (containing 17 groups) can best be characterized by this quotation: "Confessing a lack of interest in the protection of human subjects would be tantamount to saying we are against motherhood and apple pie. Nonetheless, it is not one of the things we are working on at present."

One of these organizations, involved with work on minority groups in low-income areas, reported that it has not run into any protest but that it is unclear whether this is because research on minorities has diminished or whether it has become more accepted. Another group mentioned a crime survey being conducted at the time of our inquiry in which some resistance by men to being interviewed had been encountered. Evidently this was not because respondents object to being used but because of the attitude that nothing makes a difference—"You can't do anything anyhow." A third expressed wholehearted approval of research such as that underlying the 1954 Supreme Court shool desegregation decision, but disapproved (referring to the Moynihan Report) of improperly done research or "reresearch instead of action."

Eighteen other organizations expressed concern or claimed to be dealing with issues relating to the protection of human subjects primarily in connection with biomedical research or, to a lesser extent, with behavior modification. In addition, many of these groups showed some concern with specific types of people, such as children, prisoners, people in mental institutions, and women. But these concerns were linked principally to biomedical experimentation. Here are the issues of interest to these organizations:

| | |
|---|---|
| Biomedical research | 16 |
| Institutionalized populations | 8 |
| Behavior modification | 5 |
| Children | 3 |
| Mental health-therapy | 2 |
| Fetal research | 1 |

(Some of the 18 organizations expressed interest in more than one issue.)

It is noteworthy that several of these groups responded to HEW draft guidelines or took some other specific action. A number of them cosigned the response of the Leadership Conference on Civil Rights, prepared by its

Health and Welfare Task Force chaired by Marilyn G. Rose, to the proposed HEW regulations governing biomedical experimentation on human subjects.

For the interest groups in this broad category, it seems not unlikely that if their constituencies or the general public become more concerned about social research, they will follow suit by broadening their sphere of interest. At present, however, since resources are limited, they are focusing upon other issues.

## NO INTEREST

Of the 29 groups, 19 placed in this category reported interests and activities in well-defined areas unrelated to the protection of human subjects: for instance, consumer issues, agricultural and energy policy, nuclear issues, pollution and evironmental protection, and so on. Five other organizations described themselves as concerned mainly with fund-raising or organizing and coordinating activities. Four organizations, mainly legal-aid societies, do not take positions on issues. Finally, one organization's director, upon hearing that this study is sponsored by the National Institute of Mental Health, launched into an antigovernment and anti-HEW diatribe and refused to discuss the activities of his organization at all.

In conclusion, on the basis of our interviews, concern does not appear to be widespread among these public interest groups with protecting the rights and welfare of noninstitutionalized participants in large-scale social research. Some interest exists, notably in connection with the privacy and confidentiality issues, and there is some evidence of hostility toward social research. But on the whole, such troublesome issues as assessment of risk-benefit criteria and informed consent appear to be confined largely to the field of biomedical research.

# Bibliography

This compilation of works relating to the ethics of social research is intended as a guide to additional material as well as reference for works cited in the text. It is no exception to the general rule that bibliographies are selective. We focused particularly on works published between 1965 and 1976. Earlier work was not systematically reviewed, although a few particular relevant items are included. Entries are listed alphabetically by author. Each entry is followed by up to four keywords to act as cues for particular areas of reader interest.

Below is a list of the keywords with brief descriptions of their meanings:

Biomedical Research: refers to material dealing primarily with ethical issues in biomedical research.

Codes of Ethics: material covering the substantive nature of professional codes of ethics, the purpose and function of codes of ethics, professional response to codes of ethics, and so on.

Collective Concern: refers to the concerns, including risk, of identifiable social groups, such as the poor, and not to concerns of the wider collectivity or society in general.

Coercion: covers material dealing with coercive elements of research, including work by authors who see any research participation in the absence of informed consent as coercive; also, items addressing the problem of "manipulation."

Confidentiality: covers material dealing with the ethical and legal status of research data, the subpoena risk for data as well as researchers, ways and means of providing for de facto confidentiality, and proposed corrective action, including lobbying by professionals.

Data Banks: deals with the impact of computers on data processing, storage, and retrieval; surveillance activities; problems of unauthorized access and techniques of prevention; ways of conducting intra- and interfile analysis without violating confidentiality; and so on.

Deception: refers to the use of deception in behavioral research; critiques of deception including methodological ones; alternatives to deception.

Ethical-General: refers particularly to philosophical perspectives on ethics and to theoretical treatments of ethics as a focus of inquiry.

Field Investigation: refers to studies conducted in the field mainly in the anthropological mode; also, to a lesser extent, to "naturalistic experimentation."

Freedom of Inquiry: refers to material emphasizing "the right to know," the high value of scientific knowledge; and the deleterious consequences of placing restraints on free scientific or academic inquiry.

Informed Consent: covers material relating to this key ethical premise including empirical studies, discussions of the relationship between informed consent and aspects of research design, such as deception and participant or covert observation, and so on.

Institutional Review Boards: covers items dealing specifically with this mandatory review mechanism established by HEW, its efficacy in protecting the rights and welfare of research subjects, and reactions to it on the part of the research community.

Legal: material dealing with the legal status of or legal perspectives on such issues as privacy, informed consent, confidentiality of research data, and so on.

Legislation and Regulation: covers items relating to legislation and federal regulation of research activities.

Observation: pertains to discussions of the ethicality of "unobtrusive" methods of data collection such as participant, covert, overt, observation surveys, and so on.

Privacy: covers material pertaining to the legal development and status of privacy as well as discussion of the invasion or violation of privacy.

Professionalism: this refers to material concerned with the relationship between any aspect of professionalism (professionals, professional responsibility, professional associations, professional training, and so on) and protection of human subjects.

Psychological Experimentation: covers ethical concerns pertaining particularly to psychological research conducted in laboratories or other controlled settings.

Risk-Benefit: covers material referring to the balancing of risks (usually for the individual subject) versus benefits (usually for the wider collectivity).

Social Control: any discussion of control broadly defined; the control of social research, as well as perspective on social research emphasizing its societal control functions.

Social Experimentation: refers particularly to large-scale social science studies designed to draw comparisons and contrasts between two or more treatment conditions, and the ethical problems with which such research contends.

Social Policy: refers to material focusing on the relationship between social research and policy making.

Stress: items dealing with the potential or actual stress research causes in subjects such as lowered self-esteem, feelings of humiliation, anxiety, and so on.
Surveys: material dealing with the ethical problems in survey research.
Voluntarism: items discussing the voluntary status of research subjects, including the impact of using only volunteers on the validity of research findings.

Adams, M. 1973. "Science, Technology, and Some Dilemmas of Advocacy." *Science* 180:840–43.
This is a discussion of three crucial moral dilemmas facing the social worker required to strike a balance between the interests of the client and the interests of the public or society with respect to research: future gains versus immediate relief, prevention versus supportive help, and common good versus individual good. These issues are particularly pertinent to social workers since their training tends to focus on the individual and since they are frequently called upon to act as advocates for clients. ETHICAL-GENERAL

Afidi, J. 1971. "Informed Consent: A Study of Patient Reaction." *Journal of the American Medical Association* 216:1325–29.
This study tested 232 patients with respect to two letters giving extensive information about an experimental diagnostic procedure, angiograms. The findings indicate that most people wish to know as much as possible including the likelihood of possible complications. BIOMEDICAL RESEARCH, INFORMED CONSENT

Alpert, H. 1959. "The Growth of Social Science Research in the United States." In *The Human Meaning of the Social Sciences.* ed. D. Lerner. New York: Meridian Books.
Alpert sees decentralization as the most notable organizational aspect of social research in the United States since it leads to a division of labor where, for instance, private foundations can support research in areas too controversial for federal agencies. According to him, World War II was the mainspring for the government's induction into the field of social research. Research roots can be traced back to President Hoover's appointment of a committee to study recent social trends in the 1920s. SOCIAL EXPERIMENTATION, SOCIAL POLICY

Altman, 1975. *The Environment and Social Behavior: Privacy, Personal Space, Territory, Crowding.* Monterey, Calif.: Brooks/Cole.
An examination and theoretical interpretation of the research in the topical areas of the title. Alan S. Levy, in his review of the book

in *Contemporary Psychology* 21, no. 9, notes that privacy is defined as "the selective control of access to the self or to one's group." For Altman, privacy connotes an active process for which a person or group regulates interaction with others and thereby achieves self-definition. PRIVACY

American Statistical Association. 1977. "Report of the *Ad Hoc* Committee on Privacy and Confidentiality." *American Statistician* 31:59–78.

Concern that laws and regulations relating to information reporting, privacy, and confidentiality may have an adverse effect on the federal statistical information system prompted the appointment of this committee to "review and evaluate statistical implication of recent actions and reports, including the Privacy Act of 1974, the Buckley Amendment . . . and the recent HEW Report of the Secretary's Advisory Committee on Automated Personal Data Systems." Among the many issues facing them, the committee identified two areas of greatest concern and indicated a need for further inquiry in them: the need to balance an individual's right to privacy with society's "need to know," and the need to distinguish between data collected for administrative versus statistical and research purposes.

The report includes a review of the relevant legislation and its impact on the statistical system. In addition to the aforementioned acts, the Federal Reports Act, the Freedom of Information Act, and a few other statutes and proposed legislation were examined. The findings and recommendations center on the following areas: authority for and limitations on collection of data for statistical purposes; informing respondents; informing the general public; transfers of data with identifiers, file matching, release of statistical summaries and microdata without identifiers, and use of social security numbers; protection of confidentiality; and Freedom of Information Act exemptions. LEGISLATION, CONFIDENTIALITY

Angell, R. C. 1967. "The Ethical Problems of Applied Sociology." In *The Uses of Sociology*, ed. P. F. Lazarsfeld, H. L. Wilensky, and W. H. Sewell, pp. 725–40. New York: Basic Books.

Angell discusses the ethical problems facing the applied sociologist in the roles of consultant and practitioner, as well as when working in the field. He discusses ethical difficulties such as risk-benefit criteria development and assessment, deception (which he believes is unjustifiable in the applied research context, although it can be justified in the case of pure science), and the vital importance of protecting respondents' confidentiality. He goes on to warn against subpoena risk. He argues that deviants are entitled to the same protections as law-abiding citizens and that disclosure of deviant activity should be made only when there is "clear and present danger to individuals or collectivities." Again he argues that in the applied context organizational anonymity should be granted. CONFIDENTIALITY, DECEPTION, RISK-BENEFIT

Annual Chief Justice Earl Warren Conference. 1974. *Privacy in a Free Society —Final Report.* The Roscoe Pound American Trial Lawyers Foundation.

The conference examined questions on electronic surveillance, political informing, and data banks and dossiers for their effects and infringement on individual privacy. Informational privacy in the area of data banks and dossiers is of key concern. The dangers of loss of privacy and individual autonomy will increase as information systems are more integrated and centralized. The increased quantity of sorted data leads to increased power for data collecting agencies and creates a "dossier mentality." The conference recommended the establishment of principles of fair information practice; indicated the necessity for federal legislation embodying such principles to regulate information processors and the need for enforcement procedures; and suggested there be no coercion on individuals to reveal social security numbers unless required to do so by federal statute. DATA BANKS, LEGISLATION AND REGULATION, PRIVACY, SOCIAL CONTROL

Appell, G. N. 1974. "Basic Issues in the Dilemmas and Ethical Conflicts in Anthropological Inquiry." *Module* 19:1–28. New York: MSS Modular Publications, Inc.

Concerned less with what ought to be than with what is, and on the basis that presenting normative statements would assume resolution of the fundamental controversy in anthropology between cultural absolutism and cultural relativism, Appell discusses the major inherent dilemmas and ethical conflicts which occur in anthropological inquiry. Since anthropological research takes place on an interface with many conflicting ethical systems, anthropologists are frequently faced with situations of moral ambiguity. Conflicts can and do arise between the investigator's customs, rules, and principles, and those of the host community. For a variety of reasons, however, many anthropologists have not involved themselves with ethical questions. It is possible to become sensitized using the case discussion method endorsed by Appell which stimulates ethical discourse, provides exposure to a wide range of experiences, and helps develop judgment and skill in resolving situations of value conflict.

The issues Appell addresses include the misuse of knowledge, cultural and ideological contamination of anthropological inquiry, the problems of a nationally based anthropology with its parochial interests and pressures to conform to such interests, the paradox of incomplete cultural relativism, and the need to reorder the priorities of anthropological inquiry.

For Appell, it is necessary to develop organizational expression for concerns with the misuse of knowledge and a consensus on what constitutes the good society in order for anthropologists to control the use of their work. To achieve moral responsibility, it is necessary to strive for absolute truth in reporting research, not only because replication of the field experience (and hence verification) is impossible, but also because "the habit of truth creates trust, and trust is the mortar of all social relations, the mortar that holds society together, and the mortar on which a scientific profession must be based." FIELD INVESTIGATION, PROFESSIONALISM

————. 1971. "Three Cases Dealing with Dilemmas and Ethical Conflicts in Anthropological Inquiry." *Human Organization* 30:97–101.

Appell describes two approaches to ethical problems: the normative or legalistic one which establishes rules and principles to be applied in deciding on appropriate ethical action, and the case-method approach which empirically determines what the current ethical dilemmas are and what positions are taken. The following three cases illustrate the use of the latter method:

1. Problems in urban ethnic research: The researcher as participant-observer was privy to information which, if made public, could damage reputations and reveal illegal activities. The dilemma posed by the demand to publish versus the right of privacy was resolved when the diluted findings were recorded first in dissertation form, and later in a professional journal. The governing ethic was that recording ethnographic facts about a rapidly disappearing population is important.

2. A challenge to anthropological inquiry: Indian hospitality to a research project suffered because of suspicions about economic exploitation, personal gain, and indifference to Indian causes. At the time of writing the researcher had not yet been able to convince the council of the importance of the work and thus had not yet gained permission to do the research on the reservation.

3. An intelligence agent masquerading as an anthropologist can threaten the continued existence of bona fide anthropological work in foreign countries. Questions of relations with and obligations to the host country and fellow workers and appropriate action are raised in the case where a legitimate anthropologist accidentally uncovers a masquerader.

The three cases demonstrate the ethical quandries which can arise during the course of research as well as the difficulties of deciding where responsibility lies and to whom it is given. FIELD INVESTI-GATION, DECEPTION, OBSERVATION, PRIVACY

Askin, F. 1973. "Surveillance: The Social Science Perspective." In *Surveillance, Dataveillance and Personal Freedoms,* ed. Columbia Human Rights Law Review, pp. 69–98. New Jersey: Burdick.

Askin describes an American Civil Liberties Union sponsored suit, *Tatum v. Laird,* challenging the army's domestic intelligence-gathering system on the basis of the chilling (or inhibiting) effect it had on the plaintiffs. The plaintiffs' brief included an extended appendix prepared in consultation with social scientists, scientifically defining chill and offering detailed psychological and sociological evidence that chill can be caused by surveillance programs such as the army's. Askin details societal processes and situations which can result in chill. He also describes ways in which the public's awareness of surveillance is growing and the negative consequences of this awareness. He offers evidence that allegations of chill are not imaginary and speculative but empirically verifiable in the hope that it can help define the legal parameters of government surveillance. LEGAL, SOCIAL CONTROL

Baker, M. A. 1973. "Record Privacy as Marginal Problem: The Limits of Consciousness and Concern." In *Surveillance, Dataveillance, and Personal Freedoms,* ed. Columbia Human Rights Law Review, pp. 99–111. New Jersey: Burdick.

Baker discusses the problem of record privacy in the "context of organizational routines and everyday personal experiences." He points out that organizations tend to perceive maintaining record privacy as a nuisance; that privacy, confidentiality, and due process are given attention only under compulsion; and that they are severely limited by concerns with operating procedures and cost. As far as individual experiences are concerned, Baker outlines the ways in which record privacy problems tend to remain on the margin of our everyday existence. Records on individuals exist in such profusion that it is nearly impossible for a specific person to keep track of them all; nor are they usually of great importance in the conduct of an individual's everyday life. A further difficulty is ignorance about the potential use of much of recorded information which means that appropriate protests cannot be lodged. In short, individuals are not "document wise," and hence not in a favorable position to protect themselves. Record-keeping practices, nonetheless, have real rather than trivial consequences for dealing with confidentiality and due process problems involving personal records. As possible remedies, Baker suggests nearly unlimited access by individuals to records pertaining to themselves, proper procedures for challenges to and correction thereof (most important), automatic destruction of old records, and routine enforcement procedures to maintain record privacy. CONFIDENTIALITY, DATA BANKS, PRIVACY

Balter, M. B. 1974. "Coping with Illness: Choices, Alternatives, and Consequences." In *Drug Development and Marketing,* ed. R. B. Helms. A Conference Sponsored by the American Enterprise Institute for Health Research.

In discussing the inadequacy of current frameworks for examining the costs, benefits, and risks of drug development and treatment, Balter points out that we need to know more about attitudes toward drugs and illness. Such attitudes influence individuals' choices on how and where to seek treatment and thus affect the size and nature of those diagnosed and treated by our medical system. According to Balter, in order to prevent policy decisions being made without knowledge of public preferences, and to use instead the public as an active resource for developing standards and basic principles in the areas of cost, benefit, and risk of drug development and treatment, we need a major research effort to determine public attitudes. This raises the question whether the public can define a practical ethic or give principles to evaluate benefit and risk in matters concerning drugs. Balter feels the answer is yes if we are to operate on the principle of informed consent. The public should know of the probable long-term consequences of various proposed health policies and actions. The orientation should be toward consumers as the group best able to analyze the consequences of our national drug experience. BIOMEDICAL RESEARCH, INFORMED CONSENT, RISK-BENEFIT

Barber, B. 1975. "Some Perspectives on the Role of Assessment of Risk-Benefit Criteria in the Determination of the Appropriateness of Research Involving Human Subjects." Columbia University, New York.

This paper, prepared for the National Commission for the Protection of Human Subjects of Biomedical and Behavioral Research, discusses the issues involved in the assessment of the risk-benefit ratio in behavioral and biomedical research, the author's experiences as a member of a university peer review committee for nonmedical research, and the current and needed research on risk-benefit.

Barber argues for the "fundamental similarity, in principles and procedures, of risk-benefit assessment in biomedical and behavioral research." From this perspective, the following issues are examined: the differences and similarities in the ethical problems of behavioral and biomedical research; the need to distinguish between the amount and probability of inquiry; the similarity between the biological and social person; the ambiguities in risk-benefit assessments and recommendations of who should do such assessments; and the comparative risks of behavioral versus biomedical research.

The dearth of studies of risk-benefit assessment in behavioral research prompted his empirical examination of his experiences as a member of the Human Subjects Review Committee at Columbia University. Included are data from this study. Barber ends with a call for more and better research on the problem of risk-benefit assessment in behavioral research. RISK BENEFIT, BIOMEDICAL RESEARCH, INSTITUTIONAL REVIEW BOARDS

————. 1973a. "Experimentation on Human Beings: Another Problem of Civil Rights." *Minerva* 11:415–19.

This is a book review of P. A. Freund's *Experimenting with Human Subjects* (1972). Barber draws on his own work to support the contention that medical researchers and practitioners do not take ethical issues seriously. He discusses the whole issue within a framework which emphasizes extending civil rights to the human subjects of research. BIOMEDICAL RESEARCH, ETHICAL-GENERAL

————. 1973(b). "1973 Prepared Statement to the House Subcommittee on Health Hearings, *Protection of Human Subjects Act.*"

Barber is in favor of the act for three major reasons: (1) There is a need to control the use of human subjects in biomedical and behavioral science research because the present safeguards are either insufficient or insufficiently adhered to. (2) The biomedical professions have amply demonstrated that they cannot sufficiently control themselves in this respect. (3) The present bill will improve matters because it allows for government control in a sensitive area which is too important to be left to professional control only. LEGISLATION AND REGULATIONS

————. 1973(c). "Research on Research on Human Subjects: Problems of Access to a Powerful Profession." *Social Problems* 21:103–12.

Barber discusses problems of identity and legitimation in gaining access to a powerful professional group for the purpose of studying it. The research team feared that identifying themselves as sociologists of science would be insufficient to gain cooperation; therefore, they also made use of the roles, goals, and values they shared with the biomedical researchers they wished to interview. They also implied that they might have access to "countervailing" power. Finally, they used the potential conflict in their subjects between their roles as individual professionals and their roles as members of research teams. Barber states that as sociologists "we must not put our own needs and rights as scientists above the needs and rights of those we study, whether they are powerful or powerless. Like the biomedical research profession, for example, we must be respectful of the civil rights of those we study, who should be asked their informed consent to be so studied. An essential element of such consent is full information about the probable risk-benefit ratio for those being studied." INFORMED CONSENT, RISK-BENEFIT

————. 1967. "Experimenting with Humans." *The Public Interest* 6:91–102.

Since many scientific advances are possible only through experimentation, the role of experimentation should be publicly discussed and considered. Barber examines experimentation in four areas: drugs, medical research, social research, and biology. The modern world demonstrates a heightened concern for the individual, and from that perspective, social research runs the risk of invading the privacy of the individual or endangering his self-esteem. Voluntary informed consent is absolutely essential, although often difficult to obtain.

The main problem with existing codes lies in the translation of general principles to particular instances. Furthermore, while researchers have no right to make martyrs of their subjects, society has no right to make martyrs of researchers when, despite all precautions, something goes amiss. For these two reasons, Barber makes two main public policy suggestions: (1) Establish review and approval committees for all research involving human subjects, with both locals and outsiders as members, required to keep detailed written records of proceedings. It would also be desirable to include both a lawyer and a social scientist. (2) Develop a general viewpoint through a commission. CODES OF ETHICS, INFORMED CONSENT, INSTITUTIONAL REVIEW BOARDS, LEGISLATION AND REGULATION

————. 1963. "Tensions and Accommodations Between Science and Humanism." *American Behavioral Scientist* 7:3–8.

Conflict between science and humanism is inevitable because of different social and cultural characteristics. Humanism is characteristically pessimistic, concrete, and concerned with values; science is characteristically optimistic, abstract, and amoral. Both trends are necessary for societal functioning, but as a social movement science has been far more successful than humanism. ETHICAL-GENERAL

————, J. J. Lally, J. L. Makarushka, and D. Sullivan. 1973. *Research on Human Subjects.* New York: Russell Sage.

This is one of the few empirical studies measuring the extent of adherence to ethical principles among biomedical researchers and the efficacy of institutional review committees, especially focusing on the gap between professed ideology and the actual behavior of researchers. Two studies were conducted. The first, called the National Survey, elicited responses from 293 nationally representative biomedical institutions; the second, the Intensive Two-Institution Study, obtained responses from 387 biomedical researchers at two institutions considered to be representative of institutions in the national sample.

Data were collected on two key issues: voluntary informed consent, and the balance between risk and benefit in assessing the ethical propriety of proposed research. The data show two types of patterns: the majority of biomedical researchers using human subjects are aware of the importance of voluntary informed consent, are unwilling to take undue risk when confronted with hypothetical research proposals, and do not conduct studies in which the risk-benefit ratio is unfavorable for the patient; there exist a minority who are unaware or lack concern with the principle of informed consent, are willing to take undue risks, and to conduct studies with unfavorable risk-benefit ratios. These two patterns, the first labelled "strict" and the second "more permissive," are explained in terms of linkages to two independent variables, conflict among equal values and social control.

Other findings include a difference in treatment between ward or clinic patients and private patients, with the former more likely to be inducted in the research process; and the correlation, holding at both the wider scientific community and the local-institutional levels, between relative failure as a researcher and the tendency to be more permissive in judging ethical propriety of dubious research projects. Researchers who believe they have received just treatment are more likely to be "strict" than those who feel they have been unjustly treated. Socialization and work context are identified as other important explanatory variables. Overall, the findings indicate that there is considerable slippage between the Public Health Service regulations concerning the use of human subjects and the actual conduct of research. BIOMEDICAL RESEARCH, INFORMED CONSENT, INSTITUTIONAL REVIEW BOARDS, RISK-BENEFIT

Barnes, F. A. 1970. "Some Ethical Problems in Modern Field-Work." *British Journal of Sociology* 14:118–34. Also in *Qualitative Methodology*, ed. W. J. Filstead, pp. 235–51. Chicago: Markham.

Barnes contrasts ethnographic work done during the "colonial period" with that done subsequent to 1930 and notes that in the earlier period, less attention was paid to the ethical problems surrounding the relationship between the investigator and a study's sponsors, the general moral stance adopted by the sponsor, the difficulties of the investigator's role definition, and the problems surrounding the publication of results. "As professional sociologists and anthropologists we have an abiding interest in seeing that we are regarded as responsible profession- als by all those we work with, and the interests of the profession outlast those of the specific investigation or investigator. A professional code of ethics would not make any easier the solution of the many problems discussed here, but it might at least remind ethnographers that these problems do have to be solved and cannot be ignored." FIELD INVES- TIGATION, CODES OF ETHICS, PROFESSIONALISM

Barnsley, J. H. 1972. *The Social Reality of Ethics.* Boston: Routledge and Kegan Paul.

Operating essentially from a sociology-of-knowledge perspective (social existence determines consciousness), Barnsley, in this densely written monograph, makes a beginning attempt at laying the ground- work for a comprehensive sociology of ethics. The book is divided into three parts. In the first, he considers some of the conceptual problems facing a sociology of ethics, including problems of definition, and places the field within the broader domain of the sociology of culture. In the second part, he offers the reader an extensive critical review of the available research, especially emphasizing methodological issues. In the third part, he discusses types of ethical relativism and traces its implications for the field of sociology. This is a scholarly work (based on the author's dissertation) with its major contribution more concep- tual and theoretical than substantive. ETHICAL-GENERAL

Bauer, R. A. 1965. "Social Responsibility of Ego Enhancement?" *Journal of Social Issues* 21:47–53.

The author makes the point, with reference to "brainwashing," "hidden persuasion," and fears of "1984," that the power of psycholo- gists to control behavior is frequently exaggerated. Psychologists, in seeking to enhance their own status and self-image, often promulgate bad research and thus abdicate their social responsibility both to rein- force a positive public image of the psychologist and to conduct realis- tic research. PSYCHOLOGICAL EXPERIMENTATION

Baumrind, D. 1975. "Metaethical and Normative Considerations Covering the Treatment of Human Subjects in the Behavioral Sciences." In *Hu- man Rights and Psychological Research,* ed. E. C. Kennedy, pp. 37–68. New York: Thomas Y. Crowell, Inc.

In an effort to explicate the bases for ethical judgments, Baumrind first considers systems of moral judgments in which she contrasts Chris- tian and Buddhist views, theories of justification (obedience, deontolog- ical, teleological), the good life, and the function of morality. She then offers a detailed critique of the APA's current code of standards, its cost-benefit approach, its qualifications of the informed-consent principle, and its failure to deal adequately with the problem of experimental deception and manipulation. Finally, in discussing the value of behavioral science, she states that for her the activities of behavioral scientists and the values they promulgate are more important than the products of the behavioral science enterprise. CODES OF ETHICS, DECEPTION, INFORMED CONSENT, RISK-BENEFIT

————. 1972. "Reactions to the May 1972 Draft Report of the Ad Hoc Committee on Ethical Standards in Psychological Research." *American Psychologist* 27:1083–86.

Baumrind objects to the draft because it is not sufficiently explicit and unequivocal to provide for true guidance in cases where researchers are confronted with ethical quandaries. In addition it permits scientific considerations to outweigh ethical obligations to subjects when there is conflict between the two. While it requires that the research protocol be approved by both a committee of the investigator's peers and a committee of the prospective subjects' peers under such circumstances, it has no means of enforcing this requirement. Furthermore, it does not provide clear guidelines to help such committees decide whether the benefits of proposed research outweigh the risks.

The main thrust of her criticism is directed toward the use of deception in experimentation. She regards informed consent both as the most important ethical principle and the one most commonly violated in behavioral science research: "I am most outraged by human acts that deprive others of their freedom of choice and their reason." CODES OF ETHICS, DECEPTION, INFORMED CONSENT, PSYCHOLOGICAL EXPERIMENTATION

————. 1971. "Principles of Ethical Conduct in the Treatment of Subjects: Reaction to the Draft of the Committee on Ethical Standards in Psychological Research." *American Psychologist* 26:887–96.

Baumrind is particularly concerned with the abuse of subject trust and the use of deceptive practices in behavioral science research. She is critical of the committee's risk-benefits approach and its expressed willingness to strive for a compromise between scientific and humanistic values. She lists what she considers more preferable principles: the researcher should be responsible for the effect of experimental conditions on subjects; a given action under a given set of conditions can be assessed as good or evil—deceptive practices, perpetrated by psychologists in experimental settings, are considered highly reprehensible by her; scientific ends even if highly laudable do not justify unethical transactions; a full disclosure of the APA Code should be made to the public. CODES OF ETHICS, DECEPTION, PSYCHOLOGICAL EXPERIMENTATION, RISK-BENEFIT

————. 1964. "Some Thoughts on Ethics of Research: After Reading Milgram's 'Behavioral Study of Obedience.'" *American Psychologist* 19: 421–23.

Baumrind voices her objections to Milgram's study and similar research on a number of counts. Special precautions are needed for experiments which expose subjects to loss of dignity. Since subjects are more prone to behaving in an obedient fashion in the laboratory, it is not an appropriate place to study obedience and conformity. Finally, when subjects are not only asked to perform unworthy tasks but also, in a sense, made fools of since they accepted the experimental conditions as real, extensive postexperimental reassurance and correction are needed to repair losses of self-esteem. DECEPTION, PSYCHOLOGICAL EXPERIMENTATION, STRESS

Beals, R. L. 1969. *Politics of Social Research.* Chicago: Aldine.

Using data drawn mainly from anthropology, Beals attempts to explicate the thesis that all social research is located in a political setting. He points out that the federal government is extensively involved in social research and uses it for the formulation and implementation of policy. Social scientists who are increasingly surrounded by restrictions are evidence of the success of social science. In further articulating the political ramifications of social research, Beals argues that social scientists are creatures of their culture at two levels: in a particular set of institutional or structural arrangements, and in the sharing of national and subcultural sets of values. To illustrate these points, he refers to Ruebhausen and Brim, who indicated the relative recentness with which the moral claim of private personality became recognized; and to the viewpoint extant in mainland China which denies that science is above class and politics, believes that individualism and liberalism are vices, not virtues, and maintains that the scientist's first duty is to the class struggle. Modern complex societies are characterized by a variety of subcultures, the four major ones of which are the sciences, the humanities, the social sciences, and the governmental set of values and goals. While each subculture is likely to have its very own set of ethical principles, they share such major features as responsibility to the profession, responsibility to others—professionals, subjects, and humanity—and responsibility to self. In the case of the social sciences, Beals believes that the future of research depends on the extent to which the freedom, autonomy, and integrity of the discipline can be maintained in a developing welfare state which is increasingly the sponsor of such research, and the extent to which social science can contribute effectively to human welfare. FIELD INVESTIGATIONS, SOCIAL POLICY

Beaney, W. B. 1966. "The Right to Privacy and American Law." *Law and Contemporary Problems* 31:253–71.

As a legal concept the right to privacy can be defined "as the legally recognized freedom or power of an individual (group, association, class) to determine the extent to which another individual (group, association, class, or government) may (a) obtain or make use of his ideas, writings, name, or other indicant of identity, or (b) obtain or reveal information about him or those for whom he is personally responsible, or (c) intrude physically or in more subtle ways into his life space and his chosen activities." Tort is not a panacea for the protection of privacy, although it could be helpful if precedents involving substantial damage settlements were set. According to Beaney, the best solution, however, lies in the area of public law. From an examination of the record it is clear that the Supreme Court tends to uphold individual privacy against unreasonable governmental intrusion, increasing the likelihood that an expressed right to privacy with constitutional underpinnings will find support in the future. "What the Court has been doing in a somewhat tentative way is to insist that privacy-dignity claims deserve to be examined with care and to be denied only when an important countervailing interest is shown to be superior." In addition, there are several nonjudicial means of protecting privacy such as legislation at both state and federal levels, administrative choices, due process. In any case, "the values that find expression in legal decisions, statutes, or administrative rules and orders must reflect the consensus of the leaders of opinion and action in the wider society. While judges, lawmakers and administrators have a capacity for helping to teach us to select the more desirable of competing values, they in turn are instructed and informed by the acts and beliefs of those who shape the society of which they are a part. The protection of privacy-dignity values, then, is not solely a task for the law but part of a never-ending quest to increase the respect of all men for the essential values of human life." LEGAL, PRIVACY

Becker, H. S. 1964. "Against the Code of Ethics." *American Sociological Review* 29:409–10.

A letter to the editor in which Becker explains his position by pointing out that ethical codes are generally either equivocal or too vague, reflecting the lack of underlying consensus. He suggests that the American Sociological Association sponsor a symposium on the ethical problems characteristically facing sociologists. CODES OF ETHICS, PROFESSIONALISM

Beecher, H. K. 1970. *Research and the Individual.* Boston: Little, Brown.

This is a comprehensive treatment of experimentation on people primarily in the biomedical sphere. Beecher gives a good brief history of the growth of ethical concern in recent times. He identifies the fundamental issue as the relationship between the individual and society in terms of priority of claims. According to Beecher there can be no doubt that the individual comes first because a healthy society requires the moral treatment of its individual members; the individual should have priority over the state—there is the danger that an overemphasis on group rights will lead to totalitarianism; and finally, the individual is a concrete entity while society is an abstraction.

Beecher mentions the various value conflicts which bedevil the whole topic of human experimentation: the individual's right to be left alone versus the advancement of society through scientific research; the individual's desire for privacy versus the public's right to be informed and the principles of free speech and a free press; and he points out that compromises and adjustments need to be made.

Beecher describes the law as generally protective of the rights of the individual, but points out that since it rests on the moral consensus of society, it changes in accordance with changes in prevailing norms and moral standards.

Underlying the debate on experimentation with human subjects is concern with means-ends relationships. Some maintain that the end can never justify the means—a position to which Beecher subscribed in the past. Following G. E. Moore and Fletcher, he is now more in favor of situational ethics; that is, means ought to fit the end; both are relative; circumstances alter cases. BIOMEDICAL RESEARCH, LEGAL

————. 1969. "Scarce Resources and Medical Advancement." *Daedalus* 98:275–313.

Beecher states categorically that medical advances involve experimentation and that most problems arise because of scarce resources— suitable subjects are practically always in short supply. He points out that much research involves no discernible risk to the subjects. BIOMEDICAL RESEARCH, RISK-BENEFIT

————. 1966(a). "Consent in Clinical Experimentation: Myth and Reality." *Journal of the American Medical Association* 195:124–25.

Beecher argues it is a myth to believe that codes, all of which emphasize the notion of consent, offer some security. Codes can be dangerous because cases are always different, hence security can rest only with the responsible researchers who consult with their peers when faced with difficult decisions.

He points out that obtaining informed consent is frequently very difficult and represents an ideal toward which to strive and comments on the "particularly pernicious myth" that ends justify means. He maintains instead that a study is ethical or not from the beginning (a position, it might be noted, he later recanted). BIOMEDICAL RESEARCH, CODES OF ETHICS, INFORMED CONSENT

————. 1966(b). "Ethics and Clinical Research." *New England Journal of Medicine* 274:1354–60.

The discussion here is limited to experimentation conducted on patients not for their own benefit but for the benefit of patients in general. Beecher believes that ethical errors are increasing in both frequency and variety and accordingly discusses 22 unethical experiments. He holds as absolutely essential that researchers strive to obtain truly informed consent although, ultimately, the presence of a responsible investigator is an even better safeguard. Editors watchful for ethical transgression would be another means of ensuring greater ethical responsibility. BIOMEDICAL RESEARCH, INFORMED CONSENT, PROFESSIONALISM

Benne, K. D. 1965. "The Responsible Behavioral Scientist: An Introduction." *Journal of Social Issues* 21:1–8.

"Moral concern is both generated and quickened in the presence of unequally distributed power." Benne points out that when dealing with moral and ethical questions, one has to move beyond science into metascientific areas, and that this is critical especially now with the recognition that science is not and cannot be value-free. ETHICAL-GENERAL

Bennett, C. C. 1967. "What Price Privacy?" *American Psychologist* 22:371–76.

Bennett discusses privacy in the context of absolute privacy versus selective communication. He takes issue with those who claim an inalienable right to privacy. To make a public outcry over "rights" and "privacy" unnecessarily hinders an intelligent discussion of the real issue, the management of communication. Privacy can be incompatible with the peaceful coexistence of communities—our social systems depend on an exchange of information for cooperation. Therefore, our moral imperative is to encourage communication while respecting personal confidence, not to invoke blindly a right to privacy. Bennett suggests that when claims to privacy are expressed, we need to analyze the situation in terms of how damaging the revelation might be to the person involved, how many others may be harmed, and the importance of the revelation to the general welfare. The result of such an analysis will be a basis for "a rational assessment of the values at issue." PRIVACY, RISK-BENEFIT

Benson, J. K., and J. O. Smith. 1967. "The Harvard Drug Controversy: A Case Study of Subject Manipulation and Social Structure." In *Ethics, Politics, and Social Research*, ed. G. Sjoberg, pp. 115–40. Cambridge, Mass.: Schenkman.

Benson and Smith specifically address these questions: What are the practical limits to subject manipulation? Who establishes and upholds the limits in actuality? The answer to both is seen as lying within the professional mandate. As a case study they examine the Leary and Alpert investigation of psilocybin and the disputes surrounding it concerning the harmfulness of the research and control of drugs. They point out that the case involved a variety of complex normative issues such as the goals and methods of science, academic freedom, drug control, and the health of research subjects. "The interests of the research subject are, like those of society in general, defended only to the extent that they coincide with the mandates of powerful interest groups or organizations. As a research subject, as in other roles, the individual in mass society is at the mercy of powerful interest groups. He lacks the knowledge to decide intelligently whether or not to participate in a research project." INFORMED CONSENT, PSYCHOLOGICAL EXPERIMENTATION, PROFESSIONALISM

Berry, R. G., A. Castaneda, and J. D. Morton. 1970. "Psychology and the Law: A Symposium." *Canadian Psychologist* 11:2–29.

Berry states: "Each discipline must be given sufficient legal power to protect its clients or subjects through control of its documents and information and must be given sufficient control over its members to provide reasonable assurance to the community that a psychologist can be trusted with the privilege of establishing special social contacts with clients or subjects." Morton makes three suggestions: that certain experiments should not be conducted in a free society, that experiments should be conducted by properly qualified personnel, and that such personnel should be afforded legal protection. CONFIDENTIALITY, LEGAL, PSYCHOLOGICAL EXPERIMENTATION, PROFESSIONALISM

Berscheid, E., R. S. Baron, M. Dermer, and M. Libman. 1973. "Anticipating Informed Consent—An Empirical Approach." *American Psychologist* 28:913–25.

Although the codes of ethics of both the PHS and the APA require the use of informed consent as a general rule, in response to the claim that the use of deception can minimize the "demand characteristics" of experimental situations, both sets of standards do allow for some relaxation of this requirement if essential. The present study was designed to measure the extent to which informed consent "to a number of published social-psychological experiments could have been anticipated had a sampling procedure for determining likelihood of consent been used prior to experimentation." The results suggest that the procedure has both face and predictive validity and thus can be used as a means to determine whether consent can be expected in a given case. IN-FORMED CONSENT

Biderman, A. D. 1970. "Review of G. Sjoberg, ed., *Ethics, Politics, and Social Research." American Journal of Sociology* 76:1048–50.

While Biderman welcomes Sjoberg's edited volume for showing that social research ethics are closely linked to politics and for demonstrating how the sociological emphasis shifted from gaining acceptance and funding during the 1960s to attempting to reconcile intellectual, human, and ideological values, he deplores its individualistic bias. What is desperately needed is for social scientists themselves to become convinced of the importance and impact of their own work; so long as that is lacking "they have a weak foundation for a disciplined approach to the ethics and politics of research, either as objects of their sociological analysis or their social behavior." ETHICAL-GENERAL, PROFESSIONALISM

————. and E. T. Crawford. 1968. "The Political Economics of Social Research: The Case of Sociology," Bureau of Social Science Research Report (see especially pp.89-97).

The authors discuss a variety of "Diseconomies" associated with social research, focusing especially on the respondent's time and other "psychic or material" costs which research incurs on the subject. They touch on the neglected issue of protecting the rights and interests of collectivities, a particularly salient issue since they argue that the bulk of empirical work involves organized groups. Another point of concern arises as a result of "integrations of research conduct into structures in which responsibility toward sponsorship and toward the collective subject of research are elevated to a high level of governmental authority." While this perhaps is a way of effectively ensuring the well-being of the profession, the individual researcher cannot help but see it as a curtailment of autonomy. COLLECTIVE CONCERN, PROFESSIONALISM

Blanpied, W. A., comp. 1974. "Selected Bibliography of Recent Works." *The Ethical and Human Value Implications of Science and Technology: A Prelim-*

*inary Directory Reviewing Contemporary Activity*, Newsletter 8 of the Program on Public Conceptions of Science. Department of Physics, Harvard University.

A selective bibliography dealing with the areas of professional ethics, social responsibility of scientists, technology and social change, environmental ethics, limits on research, special problems in biology and medicine, special problems in practices of and limitations on social research, and the effects of science on the general culture. BIBLIOG-RAPHY

Blume, S. 1974. *Toward a Political Sociology of Science.* New York: The Free Press.

Blume argues in this book that science no longer can be seen fruitfully as an autonomous system; rather, it should be recognized as innately political. The book's first three chapters deal with the internal structure of the scientific community and various criticisms of the Mertonian paradigm. Blume sees scientific rationality as an ideology which is in competition with others, and the reward system of science as manipulable by nonscientific factors. In chapters four and five he discusses professional associations and various types of unions. In the remaining chapters he discusses science and the citizen, innovation and society, and finally offers a concluding chapter on the political sociology of science. PROFESSIONALISM

Blumgart, L. 1969. "The Medical Framework for Viewing the Problem of Human Experimentation." *Daedalus* 98:268–74.

Blumgart draws a contrast between the therapeutic and scientific alliance in medicine and points out that many important discoveries were made as a result of accumulated clinical experience. In his opinion, the ultimate guardian of subjects' welfare must be the wise, responsible, humane physician. BIOMEDICAL RESEARCH

Bok, S. 1974. "The Ethics of Giving Placebos." *Scientific American* 231:17–23.

This article deals mainly with the use of placebos in a prescriptive, therapeutic context, in which the ethical dilemma hinges on the fact that placebos can relieve suffering only if the patient does not know he is receiving a placebo. BIOMEDICAL RESEARCH, DECEPTION

Bonacich, P. 1970. "Deceiving Subjects: The Pollution of Our Environment." *American Sociologist* 5:45.

Bonacich has found himself confronted with subjects who do not believe what they are told under any circumstances because of past experiences with deceptive practices in behavioral science research.

This profound disbelief makes his own research very difficult and therefore he calls upon researchers to stop polluting our natural resources—subjects. DECEPTION

Boruch, R. F. 1974. "Costs, Benefits, and Legal Implications of Methods for Assuring Confidentiality in Social Research." Research Report NIE-020. Evanston, Ill.: Northwestern Evaluation Research Program.

   *Abstract:* "This report concerns methodological solutions to a particular class of ethical and sociolegal problems: assuring confidentiality of an individual's response to a social researcher's questions. The two types of solutions discussed here—procedural and statistical—are designed to minimize or eliminate the possibility that social research information on identifiable respondents can be or will be appropriated for nonresearch purposes, without severely undermining research goals. The techniques are cataloged and evaluated for cross-sectional, longitudinal, and experimental research, and they are illustrated with applications to research on social program evaluation. Special attention is focused on the costs of using these techniques, including reductions in the flexibility of research and the quality of research data. The implications for a statutory testimonial privilege for social researchers and for other legal issues are explored." CONFIDENTIALITY, LEGAL

———. 1972. "Strategies for Eliciting and Merging Confidential Social Research Data." *Policy Sciences* 3:275–97.

   *Abstract:* "This report presents, discusses and extends strategic models for representing the process of merging records from different sources when confidentiality of the records is required by law or custom. Examples and variations on the models cover simple situations, such as eliciting anonymous data from previously identified respondents, as well as more complex merge operations, such as merging files from different data archives and merging data under code linkage systems. The versatility and potential corruptibility of the models are also discussed." CONFIDENTIALITY

———. 1971. "Assuring Confidentiality of Responses in Social Research: A Note on Strategies." *American Sociologist* 6:308–11.

   Boruch describes two statistical procedures for protecting the confidentiality of a respondent. One, the randomized response technique, depends heavily on statistical machinations and involves responding randomly to one of two simultaneously presented questions—the question being investigated or an innocuous question. The second strategy, derived from "administrative models," requires consolidation of all background data on the identified respondent, presenting this and the question to the respondents, and having him answer and return all documents without identification. CONFIDENTIALITY

————. 1971. "Maintaining Confidentiality of Data in Educational Research: A Systemic Analysis." *American Psychologist* 26:413–30.

This is a work describing strategies available for maintaining data confidentiality, particularly with respect to longitudinal studies, primarily by reducing individual identifiability. Within survey administration Boruch discusses such techniques as manipulating identification (for example, through the use of aliases), manipulating question and response frequencies (for example, Warner's randomized response technique), manipulating survey logistics (for example, face-sheets detached by a third party). He also discusses confidentiality with respect to document processing and data maintenance. In the latter case, administrative safeguards, insulated data banks, and computerized security are discussed. CONFIDENTIALITY, DATA BANKS, SURVEYS

Boulding, K. E. 1967. "Dare We Take the Social Sciences Seriously?" *American Psychologist* 22:877–87.

Since all sciences are a part of the system they study, sociology is just another of many subcultures. Boulding laments the general lack of a social system approach, the failure to recognize and appreciate the interrelatedness of wholes, and calls for serious study of the "sociosphere" in part through the establishment of social data stations.

According to Boulding, the social sciences must establish their own value system and ethic for "evaluating and legitimating preference systems," and while he sees the roots of the scientific value system lying in Christianity, he comments on the deep conflict between the ethic of science and that of other institutions. ETHICAL-GENERAL

Bowers, R. V. 1974. "The Issue of the Use of Human Subjects in Relation to Social Science Progress." Paper presented at the American Sociological Association Annual Meeting, Montreal.

Bowers comments on the increasing restrictions placed on the conduct of social science and asks whether sociology will have to cease the move toward being an empirical discipline and instead become a more humanistically oriented discipline. He is afraid that the major impact of the new HEW regulations will be in the direction of evasions and "white-collar crime." He points out the danger of subject reactivity and the well-known Hawthorne effect, that is, the effect produced by undue attention to the subjects, in connection with obtaining informed consent, and the tension which restricting the fact-finding exercise of research places on sociology as the finder of solutions to pressing social problems. INFORMED CONSENT, LEGISLATION AND REGULATION, SOCIAL POLICY

Brandt, R. M. 1972. *Studying Behavior in Natural Settings*. New York: Holt, Rinehart & Winston.

The second chapter of this book is devoted to a discussion of the ethical problems connected with naturalistic studies of behavior. Following Kerlinger, Brandt distinguishes between the following types of research: laboratory experiments, field experiments, field investigations, and survey research. Field investigations are typically ex post facto and usually do not set out to manipulate independent variables; naturalistic observations fall under this type. Studying behavior in natural settings often necessitates the use of unorthodox methodology such as deception because of the need to see behavior free of conscious control.

A major difficulty facing social research is the conflict between the individual's right to privacy and self-determination and the public's right to know. The overprotection of an individual's privacy can be detrimental to society; on the other hand, it is essential that research participants be protected against unnecessary harm. The research community's status must be preserved—Brandt suggests that the concern with privacy might hide the fear that social science will undermine treasured ideas. Taking these points into account, it is clear that the main ethical issue with respect to the conduct of naturalistic research is invasion of privacy, especially with respect to what happens to the data after they are gathered, and what is done on the basis of the research findings. Thus it is vitally important that data are kept secure and depersonalized and collected according to a systems-analysis, task-centered approach, and not merely to gain power or influence particular people or groups.

Because naturalistic research frequently precludes gaining informed consent and yet is premised on the need to obtain information about regular patterns of behavior, the researcher is obligated to protect the research participants as best as possible. Subjects' anonymity and confidentiality of information must be scrupulously maintained. Whenever possible, provided the validity of the results is not impaired, informed consent should be obtained. When only unknown observations will do, permission to conduct the research should be sought from the greater community. In addition, a group of competent persons should decide and evaluate the likelihood of potential damage occurring, the value of the research, and the essentiality of the method chosen compared to alternative strategies. CONFIDENTIALITY, FIELD INVESTIGATION, INFORMED CONSENT, OBSERVATION

Brayfield, A. H. 1968. "Creating a Code for Social Scientists." *Research Symposium: Social Science and Individual Rights*. Washington, D.C.: American Society for Public Administration.

Our society witnesses two emerging rights: to develop as individuals and to create "human environments" optimal for such development. Knowledge and understanding which can be obtained through social research are needed to achieve these aims. To control the conduct of social research, researchers should establish a code containing the following elements: "a statement of the scientific canons of objectivity, consistency, and meaningfulness"; the role of pilot investigations; differentiation among types of measurement; and clarification of the problems of informed consent, confidentiality, peer-group evaluation of research, professional consultation and services, and utilization of research results. According to Brayfield, social scientists have an obligation to ensure that research is used. Unfortunately, the need for legislation to control these issues will probably arise. CODES OF ETHICS, LEGISLATION AND REGULATION, PROFESSIONALISM

————. 1967. "Inquiry on Federally Sponsored Research." *American Psychologist* 22:893–903.

A statement submitted to the Research and Technical Subcommittee of the House Committee on Government Operations emphasizing the design of human environments as a main function of the behavioral sciences. SOCIAL POLICY

Brock, T. C., and L. A. Becker. 1966. "Debriefing and Susceptibility to Subsequent Experimental Manipulations." *Journal of Experimental Social Psychology* 2:314–23.

*Abstract:* "This empirical study was designed to discover the usefulness of data collected from subjects having undergone previous debriefing. The question was whether previous experience in an experimental design using deception would contaminate subjects' trust or lead them to disbelieve a new experimental situation. The findings suggest 'that a sufficiently powerful independent variable can offset the desensitizing effects of debriefing, unless complete prior debriefing is coupled with explicit similarity between the debriefing situation and the test experiment.'" DECEPTION, PSYCHOLOGICAL EXPERIMENTATION

Brown, B. 1968. "The Ethics of Social Science Research." *Research Symposium: Social Science and Individual Rights*. Washington, D.C.: American Society for Public Administration.

A value-conflict exists between freedom of research and accountability, or between privacy and "the need to know." This conflict can potentially be resolved by weighing risks against benefits or by applying appropriate ethical considerations. Brown suspects that ethics is mainly a matter of a balance of power, easily resolved if one takes a fundamentalist approach but far more difficult from an applied ethics, "working balance of power," perspective. Then a balance must be sought "between the ends-to-means issue, new knowledge, and invasion of privacy." Brown refers to the current PHS policy on the protection of human subjects as a move in the right direction, but he warns that historically significant scientific advances have often been made by violating current ethical principles. FREEDOM OF INQUIRY, LEGISLATION AND REGULATION, PRIVACY, RISK-BENEFIT

Brush, S. G. 1974. "Should the History of Science Be Rated X?" *Science* 183:1164–72.

Brush argues that a consideration of the history of science gives lie to such notions as the sacredness of the scientific method, objectivity, and the hypothetico-deductive method. Instead, it should be stressed that so-called objective facts are useless in the absence of interpretation, and that interpretation is inevitably linked to theory and metaphysical preconceptions. ETHICAL-GENERAL

Bruyn, S. T. 1966. *The Human Perspective in Sociology—The Methodology of Participant Observation*. Englewood Cliffs, N.J.: Prentice-Hall.

Bruyn, using C. P. Snow's famous distinction between the "two cultures" of science and the humanities, argues that social science can act as a bridge between the two provided it emphasizes the "human perspective." According to him, the method of participant observation is ideal for this, and in the final chapter he spells out methodological procedures which can guide research adequate in terms of both objectivity and subjectivity. For our purposes, the book is deficient in not explicitly confronting some of the ethical difficulties associated with participant observation, although Bruyn does point out the close relationship between ethics and methodology. OBSERVATION

Bryant, E. C., and M. H. Hansen. 1976. "Invasion of Privacy and Surveys: A Growing of Dilemma." In *Perspectives on Attitudes Assessment: Surveys and Their Alternatives*, ed. H. W. Sinaiko and L. H. Broedling, pp. 68–77. Champaign, Ill.: Pendleton Publications.

The basic assumption underlying this work is that valid statistics are of great national utility. It is thus important that a distinction be drawn between administrative and statistical records. The authors fault recent legislative activity designed to protect privacy for not making this distinction. On the one hand, the Privacy Act of 1974 and the Buckley Amendment may severely hamper research; on the other, depending on interpretation, the Freedom of Information Act may permit widespread invasion of privacy. For adequate protection of privacy with respect to the production of statistical records, strong measures for protecting confidentiality are needed, for instance, following the Bureau of the Census model.

The authors offer a brief summary of the recent legislation mentioned above and then go on to trace the implications of these for statistics. They note that they are not aware of a single instance where the use of records for statistical purposes has been of detriment to an individual, and that in any case, provided there is strict maintenance of record confidentiality, such abuse is impossible. On the whole, the concept of invasion of privacy is irrelevant to statistical studies because data are not released in personally identifiable form. If, indeed, legislators are seriously concerned with this problem, it would be better to accord legal protection to the maintenance of confidentiality. Further statistical treatment of data already available (for example, administrative records) should be permitted so long as confidentiality can be assured, since this does not constitute invasion of privacy. No access should be allowed to data collected for statistical purposes unless required by law. CONFIDENTIALITY, LEGISLATION AND REGULATION, PRIVACY, SURVEYS

Calabresi, G. 1969. "Reflections on Medical Experimentation in Humans." *Daedalus* 98:387–405.

Calabresi comments on the paradox that we fuss about some human risks and deaths and yet are unconcerned about many others. To be more consistent, all nonessential driving should be banned and airports made much safer, for instance. The West is committed to humanism and values human lives, but accident law demonstrates that this commitment is not as great as is generally supposed. Frequently, the market-value structure determines at what pains lives will be safeguarded.

According to Calabresi, while obtaining informed consent is very important, it is not enough by itself; hence, he suggests the establishment of a compensation fund for those harmed by research and the setting up of institutional review boards to screen research proposals involving human subjects. BIOMEDICAL RESEARCH, INSTITUTIONAL REVIEW BOARDS, LEGAL

Campbell, D. T. 1976. "Protection of the Rights and Interests of Human Subjects in Program Evaluation, Social Indicators, Social Experimentation, and Statistical Analyses Based Upon Administrative Records." Background paper prepared for the National Commission for the Protection of Human Subjects of Biomedical and Behavioral Research. Northwestern University.

Campbell perceives the need to make major improvements in protecting the privacy and interests of individuals participating in social research. He offers a set of 25 specific suggested regulations designed to protect the privacy and interest of such individuals. These recommendations are made in the context of the following areas of concern: the use and function of institutional review boards; the borderline between administrative reports on social service delivery and program evaluation; rights and interests of respondents in informational surveys; subpoena and government audit; data processing and archiving practices; the rights and interests of participants in social experiments with regard to treatment variables; and the reanalysis of research data and statistical analysis of administrative records.

Also addressed are the interests of respondents ten or twenty years hence; what their interests and rights are in the topics on which data are collected, their rights to data produced, and the inadvisability of setting forth regulations governing the rights of class or category. Campbell includes definitions of selected terms as he uses them in the context of his paper. LEGISLATION, REGULATION, INSTITUTIONAL REVIEW BOARDS, PRIVACY

————, R. F. Boruch, R. D. Schwartz, and J. Steinberg. 1974. "Confidentiality-Preserving Modes of Access to Files and to Interfile Exchange for Useful Statistical Analysis." Paper prepared for the National Research Council's Committee on Federal Agency Evaluation Exchange.

A conflict exists between invasion of privacy, confidentiality, and the threats to individual freedom represented by the existence of data banks; and the demands for archival data use for program evaluation. The conflict can be resolved, however, on the grounds that "confidentiality-preserving modes of access to files and to interfile exchange for statistical analysis exist." This paper discusses procedures to safeguard confidentiality in two instances: intrafile analysis by outsiders, and interfile exchange of confidential data relating variables across files for statistical analysis. In order to protect confidentiality, the authors suggest that administrative and research records on individuals be kept separate and not merged into data banks, that data archives relevant to federal program evaluation conduct in-house statistical evaluation of data, and that common person identifiers be recorded in all files while limiting confidential material to the original file. The authors point out that single files cannot be released safely with only personal identifiers deleted since cross-comparison can invalidate this procedure, and that further precautions (such as restrictions on and refinement of public variables or error inoculation of public variables, and micro-aggregated release) are needed. When interfile exchange of confidential data is required, mutually insulated file linkage with random deletions of one person per list can be provided. CONFIDENTIALITY, DATA BANKS

Cannell, C. F., F. J. Fowler, Jr., and K. H. Marquis. *Interviewers and Respondent, Psychological and Behavioral Variables*. National Center for Health Statistics, HEW Series 2, no. 6.

This is a summary report of a methodological study by the Survey Research Center of the University of Michigan, carried out immediately following a Health Information Survey. Reinterviews with respondents showed a variety of positions and negative reactions to the experience and considerable vagueness about the information given in informal consent procedures. INFORMED CONSENT

Caplan, N. and S. D. Nelson. 1974. "Who's to Blame?" *Psychology Today* 8:99–104.

This is an examination of what the authors consider to be social science's oversimplification of the importance of powerful, systemwide forces and its attendant reinforcement of the negative labeling of groups already socially, politically, and economically vulnerable. The authors argue for the need to understand the relationship between knowledge and the social, political, and economic consequences of its use. Social science exhibits a reprehensible bias toward studying the powerless minorities at the same time that it ignores the powers responsible for many of the system's failures. The blame for political and technological failures erroneously falls not on those who have the power to prevent them, but on those who fall victim to them. "In fact, the social sciences are rapidly becoming the institution that 'certifies' these politically motivated transfers of blame." COLLECTION CONCERN

Carmody, J. 1973. *Ethical Issues in Health Services: A Report and Annotated Bibliography*. National Center for Health Services Research and Development, Department of Health, Education and Welfare.

A highly selective, annotated bibliography of articles published between January 1967 and December 1969 dealing with the ethical issues connected with health services. The five areas of literature covered are the right to health care, death and euthanasia, human experimentation, genetic engineering, and abortion. BIBLIOGRAPHY

Carroll, J. D., and C. R. Knerr. 1976. "Confidentiality of Social Science Research Sources and Data." A Project of the American Political Science Association, conducted by the Department of Public Administration, The Maxwell School, Syracuse University. Funded by the Russell Sage Foundation, New York City.

In an effort to investigate the issues of confidentiality in social science research, the Research Data Project was established under the auspices and guidance of the American Political Science Association. The two-year research effort resulted in part in the publication of this extensive monograph on the project's findings.

The question of confidentiality was examined on three levels: legal, ethical, and organizational. Does an investigator have a legal right to the confidentiality of the information he has obtained, and how can the right to confidentiality be established and maintained? What are the ethical obligations of a researcher to respondents and to other scholars? What should be the positions of various national scholarly associations on these legal and ethical questions, and what should they do to secure acceptance of their position by the courts, legislatures, administrative agencies, and the public?

Data-collection methods included acquisition of case histories, a national survey of the scholarly community, legal analysis of the status of scholarly research sources and data, a literature search, and contact with others conducting related studies.

The Research Data Project's summary conclusions are as follows:

The problems of confidentiality have been increasing in recent years.

Researchers sometimes promise confidentiality without always understanding the attendant legal and ethical implications.

A majority of the respondents in this study felt that enactment of researcher privilege statutes would improve the willingness of subjects to participate in research.

A First Amendment right not to reveal confidential data in civil proceedings is recognized by judicial authorities.

The courts will probably not uphold constitutional claims to confidentiality in criminal proceedings.

Existing testimonial privilege statutes for federal and state researchers are not always used by the scholarly community.

Scholars do not have an ethical obligation to promise confidentiality during research. However, once made, the obligation to keep the promise exists in the absence of overriding interests to the contrary.

The obligation exists to reveal sources and data developed in confidence when the subject of that information so requests.

A variety of research contract and grant provisions and research techniques exist to minimize problems of confidentiality.

A scholarly research regulatory "system" has evolved in recent years in the absence of input from the community itself.

A set of recommendations is offered regarding the appropriate role of the scholarly associations and community in dealing with the problems of confidentiality, including a code of ethics to be adopted by them. CONFIDENTIALITY, CODES OF ETHICS

Carter, R. K. 1971. "Clients' Resistance to Negative Findings and the Latent Conservative Functions of Evaluation Studies." *American Sociologist* 6:118–24.

This article consists of a number of case studies demonstrating the ineffectiveness of evaluation studies in bringing about changes which are incongruent with the initial positive expectations on the part of those who commissioned the evaluation. SOCIAL EXPERIMENTATION, SOCIAL POLICY

Cartwright, A., and P. Willmot. 1968. "Research Interviewing and Ethics." *Sociology* 2:91–93.

This article is a description of the procedures used by researchers in England to guide interviewers: The subject is to be told the kind of survey being conducted, the uses to which the gathered information will be put, and the assurance of confidentiality of responses. CONFIDENTIALITY, INFORMED CONSENT, SURVEYS

Chambliss, W. 1975. "On the Paucity of Original Research on Organized Crime." A footnote to Galliher and Cain. *American Sociologist*, 10:36–39.

Chambliss describes the methods he used in doing research on not easily accessible subjects. Using the method of participant observation and concealing his identity as a sociologist, he collected preliminary information on crime in the Seattle area. He collected "harder" data by divulging his professional identity to one of his contacts. He found that taping interviews with informants was essential, but that it caused considerable awkwardness if his intention to record was known beforehand. The technique he adopted was to tape the interview secretly and then to divulge this at the close of the interview allowing the informant to destroy the tape if so desired. DECEPTION, OBSERVATION

Chinoy, E. 1970. *Knowledge and Action: The Role of Sociology*. Northampton, Mass.: Smith College Press.

An original aim of sociology, according to the author, was to improve the social condition of men. A controversy concerning objective, disinterested inquiry versus wide-ranging, assumption-testing questions with a specific aim in mind has hallmarked the discipline since its earliest beginnings. Sociology has been used most often and most explicitly in organizational contexts. Its most important client has been and is the government.

One of the difficulties is sociology's lack of a well-established body of theory and lack of valid and reliable sets of measurements. Also, the use of sociological knowledge will inevitably be made by people at the top, the leaders, and may be used mainly to control the masses. It is for this reason that some argue that sociology's only role can be a critical one. Chinoy does not agree: ". . . for most people life consists of realities which they face day by day. It would be as immoral to insist that they await the sociological and political millenium that might come with the total transformation of society as it would be to manipulate their lives without their awareness." SOCIAL CONTROL, SOCIAL POLICY

Committee on Federal Evaluation Research. 1975. *Protecting Individual Privacy in Evaluation Research*. National Academy of Sciences.

The task of the committee, set up by NAS at the request of the Office of Economic Opportunity in 1971, was to examine the government's evaluation, research, and experimentation activities focusing specifically on the problem of confidentiality and the protection of individual respondents. Program evaluation satisfies the need for public accountability, but since it entails large-scale collection of information about individuals, often over long periods of time, it presents threats to individual privacy and may lead to misuse of data. The committee identified two particular risks: the unauthorized misuse of sensitive data, which raises the question of physical protection of data, and official misuse of data, which raises the question of legal protection of data. In view of the dangers inherent in collecting sensitive information, the recommendations are to minimize the risks of mishandling by collecting only information essential to the evaluation at hand (no loading) and not collecting personally identifiable information unless absolutely necessary. Identifiers, when used, should be separated from the record and stored so as to severely limit access.

In discussing the possibility of legal protection in the area of confidentiality, the committee felt that communications between researcher and respondent can be considered analogous to evidence (such as illegal wiretapping and privileged communications between lawyer and client) now regarded as inadmissable. In other words, protection should be extended to confidential information given for the purpose of bona fide evaluation research. There is discussion on how such privilege should be created, how broad it should be, whether it should be done by statute, and what kind of communication should be protected under what circumstances. CONFIDENTIALITY, LEGAL, PRIVACY

Confrey, E. A. 1968. "PHS Grant-Supported Research With Humans." *Public Health Reports* 83:127–33.

   This report is a detailed and authoritative review of PHS policy concerning research on human subjects and its underlying reasoning. A policy on grant-supported research using human subjects was announced on July 1, 1966 (first promulgated in February 1966 applicable to research grants and research training grants only). Confrey describes the various features of the policy: institutional responsibility, independent review, surveillance and advice, facilities, need to take community norms into account, possibility of designating separate review groups for particular areas, distinctions in research (the policy recognized that much behavioral research involves no personal risk but at the same time was based on the premise that important questions remain such as voluntary participation, maintenance of data confidentiality, and protection of subjects against misuse of findings). The policy was designed to reflect certain principles such as avoidance of extremes; complementary roles of the granting agency, the grantee institution, and the individual researcher; recognition of the diversity of institutional settings, types of research, subjects, and investigators; and the concept of a grant. In addition, Confrey describes the PHS's experience with the policy including a listing of some of the questions asked of the PHS in connection with the policy. Finally, he discusses the PHS's future plans "to serve as a catalyst in attaining better understanding of this problem." LEGISLATION AND REGULATION

Conrad, H. S. 1967. "Clearance of Questionnaires with Respect to 'Invasion of Privacy,' Public Sensitivities, Ethical Standards, etc." *American Psychologist* 22:356–59.
   The U.S. Office of Education is aware of the limitations of the questionnaire as an instrument of research and, therefore, is on the alert for inappropriate items which might appear in the questionnaires of extramural research projects supported by them. The office tallied the number of projects whose data-gathering instruments they reviewed in a five-week period. The 50 projects counted used a total of 109 instruments with more than 5,300 items, out of which only 10 items were found to be objectionable. Conrad points out that clearance criteria cannot be applied routinely but need to be sufficiently flexible to adapt to changing subject populations. Since social science cannot expect to operate free from societal restraints, he believes that the government should play the role of "honest broker" between the researchers' desire for scientific freedom on the one hand and the public's emphasis on personal privacy on the other. The ultimate responsibility lies with the people and the legislators and administrators who presumably respond to the people's will. FREEDOM OF INQUIRY, LEGISLATION AND REGULATION, PRIVACY, SURVEYS

Cook, S. W. 1976. "Ethical Issues in the Conduct of Research in Social Relations." In *Research Methods in Social Relations,* ed. C. Selltiz et al. New York: Holt, Rinehart and Winston, 3d ed., 2d rev.

Ethical questions often arise when social research is done on social relations. The research topic, setting, the type of participants, research procedures, data collection method and type, and the research report can all in some way evoke ethical questions. Cook enumerates ten questionable practices which can violate subjects' rights during the research process: involving people in research without their knowledge or consent, coercive participation, withholding the true nature of the research from the participant, deceiving the participant, leading the participant to commit acts which diminish self-respect, violating the right to self-determination (Cook specifically discusses research on behavior control and character change), exposing the participant to physical or mental stress, invading the privacy of the research participant, withholding benefits from controls, and failing to treat research participants fairly and showing them consideration and respect. Eliminating any of these practices may mean abandoning the research; therefore, researchers are often forced to balance benefits against risks. After reviewing and discussing these ethical dilemmas, Cook makes the following suggestions: the research problem should be important enough to outweigh the risks; in cases of uncertainty priority should be given to protecting the participants' dignity and welfare; whenever possible, harm to participants should be avoided and means for prompt alleviation should always be available; if questionable practices are used, subjects should deem them reasonable and not come to distrust the investigator; participants should benefit from the research; upon completion, the participant should, if asked, be willing to submit again to a similar procedure; the researcher should be willing to submit his own family to the procedure; and plans should be made to deal with the long-term aftereffects, if any, of the research. Responsibilities to participants remain beyond the completion of the project and include clarifying the nature of the research when methodological considerations demanded deception, honoring any commitments made when obtaining the participants' cooperation, providing such information about the research and its results as the participants desire, alleviating any discomfort or stress incurred during the research process, and maintaining promised confidentiality and anonymity. INFORMED CONSENT, RISK-BENEFIT, STRESS, VOLUNTARISM

Cooke, R. A., and A. S. Tannenbaum. 1977. *A Survey of Institutional Review Boards and Research Involving Human Subjects.* Washington, D.C.: U.S. Department of Commerce, National Technical Information Service, PB-270 60.

A report on a study carried out by the Survey Research Center (SRC), University of Michigan, for the National Commission for the Protection of Human Subjects of Biomedical and Behavioral Research under the monitorship of Bradford Gray; the only comprehensive study on the topic. SRC interviewed a total of 3,900 respondents including members of 80 IRBs, investigators, and subjects. The report of 90 pages of text and 167 pages of tables provides data on the composition of the IRBs, the procedures they use in reviewing and monitoring projects, the nature of the research they review, and the time and effort they devote to the process.

The study covers boards that deal with both biomedical and behavioral research and contains comparative procedural and attitudinal information on the treatment of the two areas of interest to the social scientist, particularly in respect to its tabulated data related to informed consent and risk-benefit assessment. INSTITUTIONAL REVIEW BOARDS, RISK-BENEFIT, INFORMED CONSENT

Corwin, R. G., and S. Z. Nagi. 1972. "The Case of Educational Research." In *The Social Contexts of Research*, ed. S. Z. Nagi, and R. G. Corwin. New York: John Wiley.

Educational research is taken as a case study to demonstrate some of the concerns arising from the relationship between researchers and subjects from a moral viewpoint. The two main areas of concern are experimentation and confidentiality. Experimentation involves a major strain between the viewpoints that it is a way of testing knowledge before too many people are exposed and harmed by the innovation, and that humans cannot be harmed or put to risk and, in the case that the innovation is positive, that the control groups are deprived of possible benefits. The primary means of accommodating these concerns is the principle of obtaining informed consent, but this raises the difficulty that such foreknowledge can interfere with the results obtained. As possible solutions, the authors suggest that professional journals publish a variety of views on controversial research topics and that community members be actively involved in research by acting not only as consultants but also by being placed on steering committees.

Confidentiality is linked to invasion of privacy. The norm of scientific research is to guard response anonymity but this is not always possible in the case of, for instance, longitudinal studies. Secondary analysis may also lead to problems since permission given freely for one kind of study may be denied if the subjects know of other uses to which the data may be put. In addition, there is the difficulty of self-fulfilling prophecy. "Knowledge about the personal characteristics of an individual often becomes the basis for grouping or stereotyping him into categories which in turn can influence his behavior in a direction that conforms to the stereotypes. In fact, the situations themselves are often structured by others in a way that would produce the stereotyped characteristics." CONFIDENTIALITY, INFORMED CONSENT, PROFESSIONALISM, SOCIAL EXPERIMENTATION

Cox, D. E., and C. N. Sipprelle. 1971. "Coercion in Participation as a Research Subject." *American Psychologist* 26:726–28.

"Volunteer status of research subjects may or may not be an ethical issue depending on a multitude of factors that are not within the scope of this report. However, volunteer status does appear to be a technical issue relating to this experiment (operant verbal conditioning of heart rate) and may be related to other experiments. It would appear that the practice of using coercion, however mild and disguised, to secure research subjects should come under scrutiny as a possible error in the design, conduct, and generality of research." COERCION, PSYCHOLOGICAL EXPERIMENTATION, VOLUNTARISM

Cranberg, L. 1965. "Ethical Problems of Scientists." *American Scientist* 53:303A–04B.

Cranberg identifies ten dichotomous ethical problems dealing mainly with conflicts of interests and the management of science. He states that the ethical problems of scientists are similar to those facing other professions, that public scrutiny is helpful in setting up moral consensus, and that what is most needed is systematic study of operating systems of ethical self-regulation. ETHICAL-GENERAL, PROFESSIONALISM

Culliton, B. J. 1976. "Confidentiality: Court Declares Researcher Can Protect Sources." *Science* 193:465–67.

This article discusses the proceedings and court decisions of a case involving the attempt by a private industry to subpoena the interview records of a researcher. In refusing to force a Harvard professor to turn over his confidential notes, a California court has in effect ruled "that an academic research has the same right to protect confidential sources of information as does a journalist.... compelled disclosure of confidential information would without question severely stifle research into questions of public policy, the very subjects in which the public interest is greatest," wrote San Francisco judge Charles B. Renfrew of the U.S. District Court. CONFIDENTIALITY, LEGAL

———. 1975. "Fetal Research II: The Nature of a Massachusetts Law." *Science* 187:411–13.

This is an example of *Science*'s current coverage of the ethical and public problems in connection with biomedical research. BIOMEDICAL RESEARCH

————. 1974(a). "Grave-Robbing: The Charge Against Four From Boston City Hospital." *Science* 186:420–23.

Culliton comments that the "rights" movement has caught the public imagination. The defendants in this case have been charged with grave-robbing because of their failure to ask permission from the mothers to perform autopsies on dead aborted fetuses. It must be noted that the women involved gave written consent to experimental participation. BIOMEDICAL RESEARCH

————. 1974(b). "Manslaughter: The Charge Against Edelin of Boston City Hospital." *Science* 186:327–30.

Dr. Edelin's case is cited as an example of some of the broad moral and legal questions to which biomedical research is presently being subjected. At issue in this case is whether a fetus is a person, and when a fetus can be considered viable. BIOMEDICAL RESEARCH, LEGAL

Curran, W. J. 1969. "Government Regulations of the Use of Human Subjects in Medical Research: The Approach of Two Federal Agencies." *Daedalus* 98:542–94.

An excellent historical treatment of developments in the Food and Drug Administration and the Public Health Service, especially in the case of the National Institutes of Health, in relation to problems concerning experimentation on humans.

Curran points out that prior to the 1960s there were no federal or state regulations governing the use of human subjects; the general legal position was that researchers experimented at their own risk. In order to help the courts decide on reasonable practices, discussion on these issues started in the late 1950s and early 1960s and generally focused on the development of a code or set of guidelines or principles and a study of the existing research practices in reputable organizations. The FDA program started two years before that of the PHS, mainly because of Senator Kefauver's subcommittee and the thalidomide tragedy. A "Statement of Policy Concerning Consent for Use of Investigation of New Drugs on Humans" was published in August 1966.

Unlike the FDA's regulatory program, NIH's main task is to support a national program of health science research. Its own clinical research center has operated under a set of guidelines since its beginning in 1953. There was sporadic discussion whether the guidelines should also be applied to extramural projects. In late 1963 the problem was discussed in earnest, and an ad hoc committee was formed in 1964. In December 1965 a policy was instituted which provided institutional review, the appropriateness of obtaining informed consent, and a risks-benefits assessment for proposed studies. In July 1966 these requirements, instead of being confined to research and research training grants, were extended to all PHS grants. In December 1966 statements relating mainly to behavioral and social science were issued, giving the grantee institution the responsibility to ensure that the research was conducted in accordance with community norms and with due regard to ethical issues. BIOMEDICAL RESEARCH, LEGAL, LEGISLATION AND REGULATION, RISK-BENEFIT

————, E. M. Laska, H. Kaplan, and R. Bank. 1973. "Protection of Privacy and Confidentiality." *Science* 182:797–802.

A Multi-State Information System (MSIS) for Psychiatric Patient Records seeks to comprehensively protect the confidentiality and privacy of patient records by implementation of administrative, technical, and legal safeguards. An electronic data system, in which only a few authorized personnel have access to a computer terminal, helps ensure confidentiality of patient material. An analysis of the laws in seven MSIS-participating jurisdictions was undertaken, and questions such as the general law of personal privacy, confidentiality, privileged communications in the general medical area, and testimonial privilege were examined. CONFIDENTIALITY, DATA BANKS, LEGAL, PRIVACY

Dalenius, T. 1974. "The Invasion of Privacy Problem and Statistics Production—An Overview." *Sartryck ur Statistic Tidskrift* 3:213–25.

After emphasizing that the aim of data production is the dissemination of information, Dalenius lists three major techniques to cope with the invasion of privacy problem: by restricting data collection, for instance, through the use of anonymous schedules; through sampling (he draws a distinction between "object" and variate sampling); or through the collection of nonrevealing data, for instance, by using "interval observations," randomized response technique, or collecting "combined" data. A second major technique is data contamination, and a third is restricted publication, for instance, by providing only tabulations.

In conclusion, Dalenius indicates the need for better public relations in the whole area of statistics production, especially by emphasizing the benefits instead of possible dangers of statistics, and he calls for the development of new techniques and the further elaboration of existing ones (for example, randomized response technique). PRIVACY, SURVEYS

Dalglish, T. K. 1976. *Protecting Human Subjects in Social and Behavioral Research: Ethics, Law and the DHEW Rules: A Critique.* Center for Research in Management Science. University of California, Berkeley.

*Abstract:* This is a critical study in four parts of the development of legal controls on university research involving human subjects. It focuses on the social and behavioral sciences, rather than medical.

Part I describes the problems of research using human subjects, its scope and extent, and its larger context. The HEW Rules are portrayed as part of a trend in legal development toward increasingly formal, detailed prescriptions on conduct.

Part II reviews the ethical and legal framework for the HEW Rules. Ethical codes of the major professional social and behavioral science associations are analyzed for their potential for protecting research subjects. The doctrines of privacy, confidentiality, anonymity, and privilege are discussed as centrally relevant to human research, and their legal status and treatment in the ethical codes are examined.

Part III analyzes the HEW Rules and their implementation and interpretation at Berkeley. The rationale for peer review boards is described, and various issues relating to such boards (especially Berkeley's) are examined. The Berkeley search for alternative procedures is discussed. Future trends in human subjects' protection are noted. Also discussed are the concepts of "risk," "benefit," and "informed consent" in detail, focusing on their treatment in the HEW Rules and by the Berkeley review board. Numerous case decisions by the Berkeley board are cited.

Part IV discusses the implications of the HEW Rules (for academic freedom, for the governance of universities and research, and for the protection of human subjects). It closes with a variety of recommendations for national policy and further research. INSTITUTIONAL REVIEW BOARDS, LEGISLATION AND REGULATION, SOCIAL CONTROL

Davidson, H. A. 1969. "Legal and Ethical Aspects of Psychiatric Research." *American Journal of Psychiatry* 126:237–40.

Davidson raises questions about current standards concerning confidentiality and the use of experimental medication. In connection with confidentiality he is critical of the American Medical Association's "protection of the community" clause on the grounds that this is too vaguely stated a principle to be of much use when having to make concrete decisions. In connection with experimental medication, he draws a distinction between innovation and experimentation, with preference for the latter, on the grounds that it is conducted in a more systematic and rigorous fashion. Finally, he states that "there is still no substitute for personal judgment, the facing of responsibility, and the guidance of the human conscience." BIOMEDICAL RESEARCH, CONFIDENTIALITY

Davis, C. R. 1975. "The Buckley Regulations: Rights and Restraints." *Educational Researcher* 4:11–13.

The General Education Provisions Act, or the Buckley Amendment, allows students' parents or the students themselves (if 18 or older or if attending an institution of postsecondary education) access to information directly related to the student and forbids the transferral of such data to third parties without written consent. Failure to comply can lead to withdrawal of Office of Education funds. The regulations do not apply to the National Institute of Education. Parents or students are permitted to challenge any inaccuracies or errors. Some exceptions in connection with the requirement of obtaining informed consent for transferral of data to third parties are permitted—mainly other educational institutions and state or federal agencies. Organizations concerned with predictive tests and improving instruction are included, provided the data are not personally identifiable, the purpose of their use is known, and the data are destroyed after completion of the study. Davis speculates about the meaning of "improving instructions," the effects of the new bill on longitudinal studies and other kinds of research, and wonders whether the time has not come to protect the rights of researchers. "Researchers have long maintained and honored their own codes of ethics, and the ethical obligation to provide informed consent in pertinent types of research has been a tradition in the field, as evidenced by codes such as that of the American Psychological Association." CONFIDENTIALITY, INFORMED CONSENT, LEGISLATION AND REGULATION

Denzin, N. K., and K. T. Erikson. 1968. "On the Ethics of Disguised Observation." *Social Problems* 15:502–06.

Denzin disagrees with the viewpoint that observation in the absence of consent is unethical, and he proposes that anything which advances science is acceptable, provided it does no harm. In addition, he points out that it is difficult to distinguish between public and private behavior; that, according to the theoretical perspective propounded by Goffman, we all wear masks; and that all research potentially limits the ability of future investigators to conduct studies. In rebuttal, Erikson states that we never really know when we harm subjects, that disguised observation can never fulfill the requirements of obtaining informed consent, and finally, that other professions, notably law, religion, and medicine, have free license only when they are serving the needs of their clients, not when they are conducting research.

INFORMED CONSENT, OBSERVATION, PROFESSIONAL-
ISM, RISK-BENEFIT

Deutscher, I. 1972. "Public and Private Opinions: Social Situations and
Multiple Realities." In *The Social Contexts of Research*, ed. S. Z. Nagi and
R. G. Corwin. New York: John Wiley.

Deutscher points out that there are two aspects to the issue of
confidentiality in social research: the ethical, which has received most
of the attention, and the methodological. His main point is that behavior is situationally variable, that people hold many honest opinions
which vary with the context in which they are elicited, a situation
which gives rise to the paradox that "one of the few instances in which
an attitude is unlikely to be translated into an opinion or an act in any
social context is when it is elicited in a rigorously controlled interview
situation by highly trained interviewers employing a technically high
quality instrument." He goes on to add: "The interview is structured
in such a way as to maximize the opportunity to elicit a private opinion.
The facts of social life are that real utterances of opinion always are
public in the sense that they occur in the presence of others. . . . In real
life there is neither anonymity nor guarantee against possible sanctions. . . ." CONFIDENTIALITY, SURVEYS

————. 1966. "Words and Deeds: Social Science and Social Policy." *Social
Problems* 13:235–54.

In survey research, states Deutscher, the assumption is made that
verbal responses reflect behavioral tendencies. In view of LaPiere's
work, however, such an assumption is badly in error. The question then
becomes, Why is survey research still popular? According to LaPiere,
because questionnaires are cheap, easy, mechanical, and give quantitative results; according to C. Wright Mills, because questionnaires are
easy to administer, made safe because of their triviality, and because big
money tends to encourage large-scale, bureaucratic-type research of
small-scale problems. Deutscher uses a sociology of knowledge paradigm for explanation. Because of sociology's low status, those dominat-
ing the field during the 1930s were determined to prove that sociology
was a science and that sociologists were not moralizers. There was thus
an overemphasis on reliability. Now that sociology is somewhat more
secure, Deutscher suggests that more attention can be paid to problems
of validity and to following Mills's dictum that the discrepancy between talk and action is the central methodological problem of the
social sciences. To this end, he recommends refining LaPiere's model
and obtaining verbal and interaction behavior from the same population under natural social conditions. OBSERVATION, SOCIAL POL-
ICY, SURVEYS

Dohrenwend, B. S., J. Williams, Jr., and C. H. Weiss. 1969. "Interviewer Biasing Effects: Toward a Reconciliation of Findings." *Public Opinion Quarterly* 33:121–29.

This is a discussion of three papers with divergent findings with respect to the relationship between an interviewer's role performance and consequent biasing effects. Because of the inconclusive nature of the three papers when taken together, it is suggested that better measures of friendliness and sociability are needed and that the topic of the interview must also be taken into account when attempting to map the relationship between social distance and bias. Energy should be directed to establishing what combination of social distance, interviewer behavior, and topic maximizes and minimizes bias. SURVEYS

Dumont, M. 1974. "The Arrogance of the Professionals: Viewpoint." *Behavior Today* 5:150.

The author bewails self-righteous professionalized social control and describes it as a process "which confounds the political process with liberal rhetoric of compassion and nationality." While none of the rhetoric is malicious—"in fact, its most characteristic feature is the absence of ideology and moral judgment"—he warns against science being used to further governmental ends. PROFESSIONALISM, SOCIAL CONTROL

Duncan, S., Jr., M. J. Rosenberg, and J. Finkelstein. 1969. "The Paralanguage Experimenter Bias." *Sociometry* 32:207–19.

This study demonstrates the interaction between a subject's set or perception of the situation and the message received. In other words, subjects respond unconsciously to paralinguistic cues such as intonation, especially under conditions of high evaluation anxiety. PSYCHOLOGICAL EXPERIMENTATION, STRESS

Durkheim, E. 1958. *Professional Ethics and Civic Morals*. New York: The Free Press.

The first three chapters of the book deal with professional ethics. Durkheim distinguishes between two kinds of moral rules: universal or general, and more specific kinds. Professional rules of conduct are strikingly diverse because they depend on different professional duties. Frequently real opposition occurs between different moral sets. Another set of conflicts arises as a result of individual interests being contrary to the group's interests, and vice versa; a bridge between the two is afforded by professional ethics in many cases.

For Durkheim, the professions are important because of their identity and solidarity-providing functions. He also believes that organization and the raising of moral standards are concomitant processes. A system of morals is always the affair of the group and can operate only if the group protects it by its authority. There is no form of social activity which can do without moral discipline and there is only one moral power—collective power—which stands above the individual. In general, all other things being equal, the greater the strength of the group structure, the more numerous the moral rules and the greater their authority over the members. ETHICAL-GENERAL , PROFESSIONALISM

Edsall, G. 1969. "A Positive Approach to the Problem of Human Experimentation." *Daedalus* 98:463–79.

Edsall makes a variety of points concerning the problem of human experimentation. He states that it is difficult to draw a clear-cut distinction in medicine between treatment and experimentation; usually the distinction is made on the basis of the purpose of the activity. The accepted legal position sees the individual as physically inviolable and stresses that violation can occur only for the patient's direct benefit. Experimentation, however, can indicate the errors in accepted or traditional methods of treatment.

The main principle underlying the emphasis on informed consent is that the individual should be able to exercise free judgment, but there are difficulties in establishing criteria for what constitutes "informed" and "consent." It must be remembered that there is an inseparable relationship between risk and progress. Finally, community welfare must be seriously considered, and the rights of volunteers to volunteer must be taken into account, too. BIOMEDICAL RESEARCH, INFORMED CONSENT, RISK-BENEFIT, VOLUNTARISM

Edsall, J. T. 1975. "Scientific Freedom and Responsibility." *Science* 188:687–93.

This is a report on the American Association for the Advancement of Sciences' (AAAS) committee on scientific freedom and responsibility. One of the committee's major conclusions is that the issues of scientific freedom and responsibility are inseparable. It must be recognized that freedom is gained; it is not an inalienable right. Moratoria like that established at the Asilomar Conference should be placed on certain kinds of research depending on risk-benefit assessment. In some cases restriction may be necessary. On the whole, data should not be kept secret except perhaps in the case of compelling reasons of national security, and even then for a limited time only. With respect to applied science and technology the risk-benefit assessment of innovations or the use of new knowledge is even more crucial because of the likelihood of unanticipated consequences.

Edsall indicates the need for arbitration mechanisms when violations of professional standards and ethics are at issue, and he suggests that the various professional societies work actively toward developing policies promoting the general public interest. He discusses the AAAS's role and suggests that another committee reexamine these issues in about five years. In the meantime, *Science* should continue covering issues relating scientific freedom and responsibility. FREEDOM OF INQUIRY, LEGISLATION AND REGULATION, PROFESSIONALISM, RISK-BENEFIT

Eetgerink, H. 1975. "Uitwerking Volkstelling Heeft Jaren Vertraging." *De Telegraaf*, March 3, 1975.

A newspaper report on the reaction to the Netherlands Census of 1971. Some 300,000 people refused to cooperate. This, in addition to some technical difficulties, has meant delays in data analysis and the production of results which in turn has had negative implications for the policy process. SOCIAL POLICY, SURVEYS

Ellis, N. R. 1974. "More Legal Restraints on Research: Will Protection of Subjects Defeat Its Own Ends?" Paper presented at the American Psychological Association Annual Meeting, New Orleans.

Research has a negative public image. It is often viewed only as resulting from an individual's need to collect data for degree purposes or merely as an ivory-tower venture. The public tends to be especially suspicious of behavioral science research because it does not produce a tangible product. The new HEW regulations are unduly restrictive and will prove to be very lucrative for the legal profession. Ellis objects to the criterion that the proposed research must be of direct benefit for the subject participating in it and suggests instead that everyone who is suitable should be obliged to participate since, ultimately, research will benefit all. In addition, the present regulations have the undesirable effect of reinforcing the public's negative attitude toward research and putting researchers on the defensive. They also provide a basis for seriously hindering research with red tape. Finally, while human rights deserve protection, the right of mankind to acquire knowledge should not be overlooked. FREEDOM OF INQUIRY, LEGISLATION AND REGULATION, RISK-BENEFIT

Epstein, L. C., and L. Lasagna. 1969. "Obtaining Informed Consent: Form or Substance." *Archives of Internal Medicine* 123:682–88.

This study found an inverse relationship between the length of a form giving information about a mock experimental drug and comprehension. The authors conclude that information given to subjects should be concise and pertinent in order to facilitate understanding and rational decision making. BIOMEDICAL, INFORMED CONSENT

Epstein, Y. M., P. Suedfeld, and S. J. Silverstein. 1973. "The Experimental Contract: Subjects' Expectations of and Reactions to Some Behaviors of Experimenters." *American Psychologist* 28:212–21.

This study addresses the general topic of the social psychology of experimentation, specifically "the set of attitudes and expectations which the subject himself brings into the laboratory." The results indicate that subjects do indeed have opinions about the experimenter's obligations toward subjects and vice-versa, expect to be given certain information about the experiment, and believe that subjects are justified in withdrawing from experiments under certain conditions. The authors measured the expectation, desirability, and appropriateness ratings of 14 possible experimental occurrences. They found that while being deceived, being asked personal questions, and not being told the purpose of the experiment, for instance, are not considered particularly desirable, they are considered somewhat appropriate by subjects. There is some suggestion that an undesirable feature such as experimenter unpunctuality inhibits test performance for those subjects who were aware of it and to whom it was not justified. DECEPTION, INFORMED CONSENT, PSYCHOLOGICAL EXPERIMENTATION, VOLUNTARISM

Erikson, K. T. 1967. "A Comment on Disguised Observation in Sociology." *Social Problems* 14:366–73.

Participant observation is unethical when the identity of the observer is obscured because it is a blatant invasion of privacy which may cause great harm. It damages the general reputation of sociology and may cause future scholars to be denied access to population groups they wish to study. It leads to bad science because the impossibility of a perfect masquerade means the group's interaction is distorted and hence such subterfuge casts doubts on the validity of the results. As a general principle, it is unethical to deliberately misrepresent the purposes of one's research. DECEPTION, OBSERVATION, PRIVACY

Etzioni, A. 1973. "Regulation of Human Experimentation." *Science* 182: 1203.

Etzioni warns against government regulations restricting freedom of inquiry and is in favor of the scientific community establishing its own set of ethics because subjects need protection; and if the scientific community takes the responsibility upon itself, science will be least hampered. Furthermore, subjects falling outside federally funded research also need protection and "concern with the humanitarian aspects of scientific work should not have to be imposed on researchers." He suggests the setting up of a three-tiered system: human-subject review committees composed of scientists, nonscience academicians, and representatives of subjects at the local level; appeal boards at the regional level; and a nationwide board to evolve review standards and clarify generic questions. FREEDOM OF INQUIRY, LEGISLATION AND REGULATION, PROFESSIONALISM

Farley, R. 1971. "Social Science and Social Policy—A Review of Some Recent Books." *American Sociologist* 6 (Supp. June):75–76.

There is an intricate relationship between social science and social policy according to the books reviewed. It would appear that Farley's view is closest to the position presented by Moynihan: social science is most useful when it measures the results of social policies and helps identify trends, but it is of little value in the formulation of public policy. SOCIAL POLICY

Farr, J. L., and W. B. Seaver. 1975. "Stress and Discomfort in Psychological Research." *American Psychologist* 30:770–73.

Subjects' opinions of procedures which potentially cause discomfort or stress and subjects' definitions of what constitutes invasion of privacy were the object of an inquiry which used 86 introductory psychology students at Pennsylvania State University as subjects. Hypothetical experimental procedures describing threats of varying severity to physical and psychological comfort and possible invasions of privacy were presented for rating on a scale of 1 to 5. The procedures were designed to represent many different areas of psychological research and a wide range of stress arousal, and the scale values derived can be used as a comparison for considering the magnitude of stress and discomfort in other experimental procedures. Although the values arrived at reflect hypothetical situations and the subjects did not experience the situational and social pressures which accompany the normal consent-giving state, the authors note that gaining informed consent often involves little more than the type of brief description of procedures outlined in this case. Invasion of privacy was rated generally low for the procedures described. This unexpected finding suggests that revelation of personal data may be considered legitimate in psychological experimentation and that invasion of privacy in psychological research is not as critical an issue as thought. The authors suggest that procedures which were rated greater than 3 (moderate amount of tension and stress) should be used with caution and impose serious responsibilities on researchers to protect the welfare of their subjects. INFORMED CONSENT, PRIVACY, PSYCHOLOGICAL EXPERIMENTATION, STRESS

Fellner, C. H., and J. R. Marshall. 1970. "Kidney Donors: The Myth of Informed Consent." *American Journal of Psychiatry* 126:1245–51.

This study found that three systems operate in the selection of a genetically related kidney donor: volunteer self-selection, the medical team's best selection choice, and the family. Of the three, only the medical team takes the American Medical Association's ethical guidelines into account. Twenty donors were interviewed; of these, six were interviewed before as well as after surgery. Another ten prospective donors, awaiting surgery, were also interviewed. The decision to volunteer was immediate in most cases. The family serves to exclude certain members, a process which is most efficient very early in the selection process. Little evidence of postoperative depression was detected; instead many donors felt they had done one of the most meaningful things in their life.

Citing Schwartz, the authors mention three variables which come into play when making moral decisions, namely awareness of the consequences, ascription of responsibility, and moral norms. All three are present at the time of first contact with the potential donor. The donors thus, on the whole, make immediate decisions well prior to the gaining of information necessary for "informed consent." This is understandable since all information necessary for moral decisions, as opposed to other kinds of decision-making, was available. Donorship tends to lead to increased self-esteem and a better self-concept. INFORMED CONSENT, VOLUNTARISM

Feuillan, J. 1974. "Everyman's Evidence: Should There be a Testimonial Privilege for Survey Researchers?" Paper presented at the Joint Meeting of the American and World Associations for Public Opinion Research.

This paper explores the problems concerning the subpoena risk for confidential information gathered in the course of research. The author suggests that the professional social science associations work at producing model legislation so as to secure testimonial privilege for researchers at both federal and state levels. CONFIDENTIALITY, LEGAL, LEGISLATION AND REGULATION, PROFESSIONALISM

Fichter, J. H., and W. L. Kolb. 1970. "Ethical Limitations on Sociological Reporting." In *Qualitative Methodology*, ed. W. J. Filstead, pp. 261–270. Chicago: Markham.

Fichter and Kolb identify four variables which an investigator should take into account when attempting to solve the difficult decision of what ought, and what ought not, to be reported: the sociologist's definition of the nature of science; determination of the extent to which a person or a group will be injured by the publication of data concerning their behavior; the degree to which individuals or groups are members of the same moral community as the sociologist; the degree to which the larger society, the local community, or the group, needs the data of the research. COLLECTIVE CONCERN, CONFIDENTIALITY, RISK-BENEFIT

Fillenbaum, S. 1966. "Prior Deception and Subsequent Experimental Performance: The 'Faithful' Subject." *Journal of Personality and Social Psychology* 4:532–37.

The overall results of this study indicate that deception, if mild, is seen as legitimate by subjects, and that despite awareness of deception, subjects will follow instructions and perform well for the sake of experimental validity and, possibly, to create a good impression. In addition it was found that while between one-third and one-half of the subjects were suspicious to begin with, it was difficult to increase this proportion through experimental manipulation, or to induce subjects to act on the basis of their suspicions. The author remarks on the "docile role" of subjects in the laboratory situation and calls for a "theory of behavior settings." DECEPTION, PSYCHOLOGICAL EXPERIMENTATION

Fiske, D. W. 1975. "A Problem of Bias in Behavioral Research." *Science* 189:373–74. Book review of *The Volunteer Subject,* by R. Rosenthal and R. L. Rosnow. New York: Wiley-Interscience, 1975.

The book reviewed systematically investigates research on the specific characteristics of volunteer subjects and the effects of volunteer status on empirical findings. "The topic is important only insofar as volunteers are not representative of the population of interest with respect to whatever behavior is being studied. While the authors have amassed hundreds of studies on the characteristics of the volunteer subject, they found relatively few on the differences between volunteers and nonvolunteers in their behavior in experiments, presumably for the obvious reason that it is difficult to study the behavior of nonvolunteers. The few results they do present are quite striking and indicate that the use of volunteer subjects can affect the researcher's findings and conclusions, at least in some areas of investigation."

The reviewer faults the work for not paying sufficient attention to the particular areas of research in which volunteer status makes a difference, and for not giving the reader sufficient background information on how they located the studies they reviewed. VOLUNTARISM

Fletcher, J. 1967. "Human Experimentation: Ethics in the Constant Situation." *Law and Contemporary Problems* 32:620–49.

This is an investigation of the position informed consent—the indispensable *sine qua non* ethical principle for Fletcher—plays in medical experimentation. The author calls for studies investigating some of the restrictions which various factors impose on free choice. BIOMEDICAL RESEARCH, INFORMED CONSENT

*Footnotes.* 1975. "Debate Rages Over Rules for Research." *Footnotes* 3:1 and 16.

This article, in the official American Sociological Association newsletter, comments on the clear distinction between biomedical and social science research and the far more obscure distinction between behavioral and social science. It reports that there is a "general fear" among social scientists that restrictive regulations will be applied unfairly to social research, too; unfair because social science research activities are mainly harmless and innocuous. LEGISLATION AND REGULATION, PROFESSIONALISM

Fox, G. L. 1974. "Problems of Ethics and Family Research: Some Observations." American Sociological Association Annual Meeting, Montreal.

Fox identifies three basic concerns: subjects' right to privacy, the protection of subjects' welfare, and researchers' vulnerability. She notes that the new HEW guidelines tend to make explicit the "noncontractual elements of contract" and is afraid of the unanticipated and unintended consequences of well-meant legislation, for instance, the weakening of self-regulation among professional sociologists. LEGISLATION AND REGULATION, PROFESSIONALISM

Fox, R. C. "Ethical and Existential Developments in Contemporaneous American Medicine: Their Implications for Culture and Society." *Milbank Memorial Fund Quarterly, Health and Society* 54:445–83.

As the title suggests, this paper deals with some current developments in the medical field which are interesting from a sociological point of view since they indicate that a "serious reexamination of certain basic cultural assumptions on which modern medicine is premised may be taking place." These current developments are reflected in the establishment of new organizations (for instance, the Institute of Society, Ethics and the Life Sciences), new intellectual disciplines (bioethics), and new perspectives (ethics is increasingly important in medical decision making), and are accompanied by three other institutionalized responses: new guidelines or codes, moratoria on various kinds of research, and legal decisions and statutes such as the Supreme Court's ruling on abortion.

On the whole, Fox suggests, medicine is moving away from an ethic based on the sanctity of life to one based on the quality of life.

In addition, there is growing skepticism that medical innovations invariably improve mankind's lot. BIOMEDICAL RESEARCH, ETHICAL-GENERAL

Fox, R. G. 1968. "Legal Aspects of Confidentiality." *Australian Psychologist* 3:53–75.

   According to Fox, a psychologist in Australia is legally obliged to divulge confidential information only when called as a witness in court. Outside the court, professional ethics prohibit disclosure unless special consent thereto has been granted by the client or subject. In another case, if the psychologist knows that a serious offense has been committed and fails to inform the proper authority, he is himself guilty of the offense of misprision of felony. In reality, however, the psychologist has a number of defenses against this. Fox discusses the lack of testimonial privilege for psychologists and believes that the best to be hoped for in this regard is application of the exercise of judicial discretion, depending on the particular circumstances in each case. CONFIDENTIALITY, LEGAL

Frankel, L. R. 1976. "Restrictions to Survey Sampling—Legal, Practical, and Ethical." In *Perspectives on Attitude Assessment: Surveys and Their Alternatives,* H. W. Sinaiko and L. H. Broedling, ed. pp. 54–67. Champaign, Ill.: Pendleton Publications.

   Frankel, following Kish, makes a distinction in nonsampling errors and biases in survey research between those resulting from nonobservation (usually because of nonresponse) and those resulting from observation (for instance, interviewer error, faulty communication, and errors in response, coding, and tabulation), and goes on to discuss legal restrictions, ethical considerations, and some practical difficulties.

   In Frankel's estimation, sample survey techniques started being abused about 15 years ago when everyone began conducting surveys, including sales personnel who saw survey research as a useful means to gain access to potential buyers. At a 1973 American Statistical Association conference, there was a general feeling that declining response rates were the result not so much of people refusing to be interviewed as of interviewers being unable to contact respondents. Because of changes in life style the probability of finding a person older than 14 years home in the afternoon, estimated in 1960 to be .692, had dropped to .620 in 1971.

   Under legal restrictions, Frankel discusses the Census Bureau's legal protection to maintain data confidentiality through statutes, protection which has also been accorded to data collected under such acts as the Crime Control Act of 1973, but points out that confidentiality cannot be assured for many data-gathering activities. He also states that in order to protect the right of privacy many local authorities either restrict or prohibit interviewing.

Following Tybout and Zaltman, Frankel identifies three basic rights of respondents: the right to participate or not, the right to safety, and the right to be informed about the survey's findings and results. Each of these is at risk of being violated during the survey research process. At the point of initial contact, an interviewee's "peace" may be disturbed. Deception often occurs with respect to the length of time an interview takes. Failure to inform respondents of the purpose of the research may lead to ethical difficulties not because of the risk to the individual respondent but to the class of which he or she is a member. Promises of confidentiality frequently have no legal basis. Promises of anonymity are occasionally falsely given, and the assurance that the gathered information will be used only for "statistical purposes" can be misleading because of the ambiguity of the term.

Frankel mentions alternatives to survey research techniques: observation following von Frisch's work on bees; randomized response; split sample and projective techniques; and greater use of technology such as Larzarsfeld's and Stanton's "program analyzer." ETHICAL-GENERAL, LEGAL, SURVEYS

Frankel, M. S. 1972. *The Public Health Service Guidelines Governing Research Involving Human Subjects: An Analysis of the Policy Making Process.* Program of Policy Studies in Science and Technology, George Washington University, Washington, D.C.

The first part of this paper traces the historical development of the PHS guidelines up to May 1969, concerning research using people as subjects, with an afterword devoted to the April 1971 guidelines. The second part consists of an analysis of the policy-making process in order to discover the reasons for its formulation. Frankel identifies five basic values governing the PHS policy makers: to do no harm to subjects, and certainly not to expose subjects to risk without consent; to keep government interference to a minimum; to maintain cooperation between the PHS, research-conducting institutions, and the individual investigator; to retain the diversity of scientific research; and to allow the search for knowledge as much freedom as possible. In order to satisfy these values, the policy makers, according to Frankel, adopted a "mixed-scanning strategy" (a term taken from Etzioni), a strategy in which "policy makers make fundamental decisions regarding the basic direction of policy and subsequent decisions are made incrementally and within the contexts set by the original fundamental decisions." LEGISLATION AND REGULATION

Freidson, E. 1974. "Problem of Defining and Protecting Social Research." Paper presented at the International Conference on Research in Conflict with Law and Ethics, University of Blalefeld, West Germany.

Freidson draws a distinction between institutional research, usually located within and at the service of the establishment, and independent research, analogous to an independent, free, and critical press. The question is: How can the independent researcher be protected against institutional encroachment? It is first necessary to differentiate between kinds of social research along the dimension of data needs, extent of intrusion into people's privacy, and extent to which investigators can protect subjects' privacy without legal privilege, in order to arrive at a definition of "social researcher" useful for preparing protective legislation.

Some research uses data already available, for instance historical and economic research. Within the social sciences there is also a well-established tradition of doing documentary research, although this sometimes poses problems of access. It is only empirical research which relies on verbal information and observation of persons that is faced with the two main issues of informed consent and protecting the well-being, including privacy, of subjects.

The survey method does not usually entail problems of protecting confidentiality while the panel study method does. Survey research is not appropriate, however, for studying either deviance or the established institutions. In-depth interviewing and participant-observation methods are better suited for this, but in neither case is it possible for the researcher to remain unaware of his informant's identity. The above methods rely on the researcher's "concrete social role" as a researcher —an open strategy which can be compared with deceptive techniques violating both privacy and trust.

According to Freidson, the field method is the most capable of gaining independent information about matters important to an informed public, but it is least able to protect itself against legal encroachment. This limitation will inevitably make open research more difficult. For Freidson, one of the most important functions of social research is the collecting, analyzing, and publishing of information independent of the established institutions.

For the purposes of gaining testimonial privilege, Freidson offers a definition of a social researcher. CONFIDENTIALITY, LEGAL, LEGISLATION AND REGULATION, PRIVACY

———. 1964. "Against the Code of Ethics." *American Sociological Review* 29:410.

In this letter to the editor, Freidson urges his colleagues to vote against adoption of any code of ethics by the ASA on grounds that debate is preferable to an artificial delineation of issues. Underlying his concern is the question whether sociologists are primarily practitioners, in which case a code of ethics, state licensing, and enforcement systems are needed, or whether sociologists are primarily scientists and scholars, in which case no ethical code is needed. CODES OF ETHICS, PRO-FESSIONALISM

Freund, P. A. 1969. "Legal Frameworks for Human Experimentation." *Daedalus* 98:314–24.

Freund characterizes the law as dialectic (deeply concerned with the physical integrity of individuals), as a system which mediates between conflicting rights, and as adaptable to changing values. LEGAL

————. 1967. "Is the Law Ready for Human Experimentation?" *American Psychologist* 22:394–99.

The law cannot yet offer precise answers to ethical questions and problems. Closer interplay between law and medicine is necessary. To that end it must be remembered that the law is conservative, "deeply protective of human integrity and life," dialectic in method—that is, based on reciprocity of roles, safeguards and so on—but also creative and innovative.

The topic of human experimentation is surrounded by moral dilemmas. The Nuremberg defense took the position that the community ought to have precedence over the individual—"the welfare of the species overrides the welfare of the particular man"—but this position was not found acceptable. In the end perhaps we have to learn to accept limits to the search for knowledge. BIOMEDICAL RESEARCH, LEGAL, RISK-BENEFIT

Friedrichs, R. W. 1970. "Epistemological Foundations for a Sociological Ethic." *American Sociologist* 5:138–40.

The code of ethics passed by the ASA in 1968 will bring about further divisiveness in a discipline already caught between adopting "system" or "conflict" as its basic frame of reference and marked by critical reexamination of its previously presumed value-freeness. Friedrichs comments on the paradox of a professedly value-free discipline attempting to codify ethics on an empirical basis. He is critical of Bidney's and Northrop's attempts to arrive at a derivative ethic on rational grounds since both these efforts approach persons as means and not ends. In his opinion, sociology's main emphasis should be on rationalizing and humanizing our common social existence. CODES OF ETHICS

Gallagher, C. E. 1968. "The Role of Legislation in Protecting Privacy." *Research Symposium: Social Science and Individual Rights.* Washington, D. C.: American Society for Public Administration.

    Legislation would be premature on public questions not yet fully understood. Our technology enables us to gather unlimited amounts of information, but should we? The consequences of surveillance must be fully understood before we create such institutions as the national data bank. "We must weigh ethics as well as technology." The evolution to an elitist society where individual choice is gone must be avoided. COLLECTIVE CONCERN, DATA BANKS, LEGISLATION AND REGULATION, PRIVACY

Galliher, J. F. 1973. "The Protection of Human Subjects." *American Sociologist* 8:93–100.

    The ASA's code of ethics has three rules dealing specifically with subjects' right to privacy. On the whole they probably reflect the values held by most sociologists. Nonetheless, there is a good deal of controversy surrounding the adoption of a code of ethics. There is general agreement that certain classes of subjects (for instance, the poor) need protection but that others (well-entrenched, powerful groups) do not, and that protecting the one category against unwelcome research also means protecting the other. Although the code demonstrates an individualistic bias, it protects not only individuals but also powerful groups. Furthermore, the postulate that all subjects need protection and that the ASA guidelines offer sufficient protection where needed is doubtful.

    Galliher suggests that the code be modified to allow for free research on all publicly accountable behavior, and that harm to subjects and the violation of data confidentiality be calculated on an individual cost versus societal-benefit ratio, the assessment to be performed by professionals. He warns that "subterranean" research will not be able to receive federal funding because it explicitly violates the HEW guidelines. CODE OF ETHICS, PRIVACY, PROFESSIONALISM, RISK-BENEFIT

Gaylin, W., and S. Gorovitz. 1975. "Academy Forum: Science and Its Critics." *Science* 188:315.

    This is a comment on the "adversarial" tone of the National Academy of Science's forum on "Experiments and Research with Humans: Values in Conflict." The authors point out that both abuses and triumphs have occurred in experimentation involving humans, and that public understanding and debate would have been better served if, at the forum, lawyers had discussed the danger of overregulation and

scientists had focused on abuses instead of vice-versa. BIOMEDICAL
RESEARCH, LEGISLATION AND REGULATION

Gergen, K. J. 1973. "The Codification of Research Ethics: Views of a
Doubting Thomas." *American Psychologist* 10:907–12.

Gergen raises a number of points expressing his qualms about
premature and overly absolutist codification of ethics. In the first place,
more research is needed to establish whether subjects are concerned
with ethics. In the second place, such things as "harm" are relative—
some ethical systems, for instance, maintain that self-doubt is a virtue.
Furthermore, deception is a pejorative term and can be called diplomacy or propriety in other contexts. He suggests using "advisory statements" rather than ethical principles. CODES OF ETHICS,
DECEPTION, STRESS

Gibbons, D. C. 1975. "Unidentified Research Sites and Fictitious Names."
*American Sociologist* 10:32–36.

Gibbons argues that place names should be disguised or left un-
specified only when individuals have been promised anonymity and
when divulging the true name of the research site would break that
promise. Similarly, when organizations request and are promised confidentiality, such promises should be honored, and care should be taken
that no direct data are supplied which identify the organization. CON-
FIDENTIALITY

Gibbons, J. D. 1973. "A Question of Ethics." *American Statistician* 27:72–76.

Gibbons is in favor of codes of ethics for two main reasons. Codes
of ethics are necessary to resolve conflicts of interests and would be
especially helpful as a defense in those cases where the statistician,
because of his obligation to remain neutral, has to resist advocacy
pressures. Second, with reference to the public's needs, there is a great
need for professionalism. CODES OF ETHICS, PROFESSIONAL-
ISM

Glass, B. 1965. "The Ethical Basis of Science." *Science* 150:1254–61.

Glass points out that values evolve. He sees ethics as a "philosophy
of morals, a moral system that defines duty and labels conduct as right
or wrong, better or worse." He emphasizes that scientific activity is
human activity and remains thus unavoidably subjective; it attains relative objectivity depending on the degree of intersubjective agreement.
From this perspective, scientific and humanistic studies are not radically
different.

Glass believes that an ethical basis for science can be derived from
two notions: science is an evolutionary product and it is ineluctably
subjective. Since knowledge production is a social activity, its key

feature is social. Science cannot operate in a vacuum—it has an obligation to help develop and regulate social life. It must also be truthful and,
hence, cannot be bridled; rather, "science cannot prosper where there
is constraint upon daring thinking, where society dictates what experiments may be conducted, or where the statement of one's conclusions
may lead to loss of livelihood, imprisonment, or even death." ETHI-
CAL-GENERAL, FREEDOM OF INQUIRY

Glazer, N. 1959. "The Rise of Social Research in Europe." In *The Human
Meaning of the Social Sciences,* ed. D. Lerner. New York: Meridian
Books.

    Glazer argues that social science's most distinctive feature relates
to its methods, not its subject matter or conclusions. He points out that
social science started to develop in the first half of the nineteenth
century, stimulated, he believes, by the vast upheavals following the
Industrial Revolution. Reality changed drastically because of huge mi-
grations to the cities and the resulting states of upheaval, chaos, and
social disorganization. It was the need to collect information which
gave the initial impetus to the growth of social science. SOCIAL POL-
ICY

Golann, S. E. 1969. "Emerging Areas of Ethical Concern." *American Psychologist* 24:454–59.

    This is a report of a 1969 questionnaire survey of the APA mem-
bers. In addition, it gives a history of the APA's concern with and
approach to the problem of ethical guidelines and describes the Cook
Committee's empirical, case-study-based approach focusing on seven
main areas: stress, consent, unnecessary impositions, confidentiality, privacy, and deception. Golann points out that ethics education in graduate departments leaves a lot to be desired. ETHICAL-GENERAL,
PROFESSIONALISM, PSYCHOLOGICAL EXPERIMENTA-
TION

Goldberg, E. M. 1970. "Urban Information Systems and Invasion of Privacy." *Urban Affairs Quarterly* 5:249–64.

    This is a general discussion of information gathered by computer
systems and the danger of violating individual privacy. DATA
BANKS, PRIVACY

Gothie, D. L. 1973: *A Selected Bibliography of Applied Ethics in the Professions:
1950–1970.* Charlottesville: University Press of Virginia.

    This is meant as a selective reference guide and source book of
information on applied ethics ("ethical or moralistic behavior as observed in actual practice by institutions, groups, and individuals under
societal conditions rather than in unilateral, individualist situations") in

a variety of professions: business and management, engineering, general ethical philosophy, government and politics, health sciences, law, science, and the social sciences. Very brief annotations accompany some of the entries. BIBLIOGRAPHY

Gray, B. H. 1975(a). "An Assessment of Institutional Review Committees in Human Experimentation." *Medical Care* 13:318–28.

    *Abstract:* "A study of the functioning of an institutional review committee, when combined with the Barber et al. survey data on 300 institutions, allows for a useful provisional assessment of the strengths and weaknesses of existing procedures for protecting human research subjects. The evidence shows that there is an important role for such committees; however, most committees are relatively permissive. While one committee's performance showed that such committees can have an impact on proposed research, the absence of effective monitoring procedures and lack of feedback from research subjects limits the impact of the review procedure on the actual conduct of research. The question is also raised whether the review procedure, because of its legitimizing functions, may have some regressive consequences for the protection of human subjects." (It must be noted that the works by Gray and Barber *et al.* were confined to examination of the review procedures for biomedical research only.) BIOMEDICAL RE-SEARCH, INSTITUTIONAL REVIEW BOARDS

————. 1975(b). *Human Subjects in Medical Experimentation.* New York: John Wiley.

    Gray points out that in the discussion and debate surrounding the ethics of experimenting on humans relatively little is known about subjects' perspectives. This work marks a step in redressing that unbalance. Gray chose subjects who had participated in studies which had the advancement of knowledge as their primary goal, and he found that not altruism but ignorance and perceived constraints often accounted for subject participation. Through interviews he was able to recount the manner in which subjects became involved in the research activity. He offers detailed analysis of the subjects' decisions to participate, an analysis which highlights the fact that in many instances, despite the existence of signed consent forms, the requirements of *informed* consent were not met. On the basis of his interviews, he draws up a typology of subject-types: unaware, unwilling, benefitting, indifferent, and committed.

    In order to more closely approximate the ethical idea that subjects volunteer for experimentation with full knowledge of what they are to undertake, Gray suggests the establishment of an institutionalized mechanism to detect ethical evasions or laxity which would supplement the activities of the institutional review committee. BIOMEDICAL RESEARCH, COERCION, INFORMED CONSENT, LEGISLA-TION AND REGULATION

————. 1974. "Social Control by Peer Review: The Case of Human Experimentation." Paper presented at the American Sociological Association Annual Meeting, Montreal. (Not to be quoted or cited without permission.)

This is a preliminary report on Gray's detailed study of a single review committee on clinical investigation in medicine, a work complementing Barber's (1973) more survey-research-oriented study. Gray focuses on two key ethical issues in particular: on the research benefits which should outweigh the costs, and on obtaining informed consent. In connection with the first point he found that the committee he studied was unwilling to judge the research design of proposals in terms of competence. In connection with the second point, he found that despite the existence of signed consent forms, 39 percent of the subjects he interviewed became aware only by talking to him that they were participating in a research project, while a majority of the others did not understand certain vital aspects of the research. Four subjects were unwilling participants. He also found that some investigators completely bypass the review process or fail to follow the committee's recommendations. BIOMEDICAL RESEARCH, INFORMED CONSENT, INSTITUTIONAL REVIEW BOARDS, RISK-BENEFIT

Green, P. 1971. "The Obligations of American Social Scientists." *The Annals* 394:13–27.

Green warns against loss of independence on the part of the social sciences because of their increased reliance on government funding. He makes a variety of suggestions to counteract this tendency, for instance, diversifying funding sources as much as possible; taking care that the research products do not strengthen "the Presidency or other institutions of centralization" or are not merely used to manipulate public opinion; seeking closer association with "political outsiders" (persons and institutions outside the establishment); and adopting and enforcing codes of ethics which are clearly against manipulative social science. "From their first introduction to our techniques, future social scientists ought to be instructed that, for example, every behavioral investigation or attitude survey potentially affects the interest of its subjects; and that no people, except on their own terms, ought to be made an object of the kind of study that could lead to further rationalization of social controls over them." COERCION, CODES OF ETHICS, INFORMED CONSENT, SOCIAL CONTROL

Halleck, L. 1969. "The Psychiatrist and the Legal Process." *Psychology Today* 2:25–28.

"It is ironic that practitioners of medicine, a profession dominated by respect for individual values, should have become so deeply involved in problems of social control." Halleck believes the law is overconcerned with punishment and not enough with community protection and rehabilitation. "To be useful to the courts in an insanity trial the psychiatrist must make a judgment as to the responsibility of an offender for a particular act. Yet there is no body of act or theory in the behavioral sciences which offers the psychiatrist any guidance in this task." LEGAL, PROFESSIONALISM, SOCIAL CONTROL

Hamscher, J., and M. Reznikoff. 1967. "Ethical Standards in Psychological Research and Graduate Training: A Study of Attitudes Within the Profession." *Proceedings of the 75th Annual American Psychological Association Convention* 2:203–04.

On the basis of a factor analysis of the 251 (50.3 percent) returned questionnaires mailed to all Connecticut psychologists, the authors conclude there is an inverse relationship between research involvement and ethical concern. The implications of this fact for the profession and the need for continued research in the area are discussed. PROFESSIONALISM, PSYCHOLOGICAL EXPERIMENTATION

Hanson, J. 1969. "Values and Social Science." *Social Science* 44:81–87.

Hanson argues that social science cannot be value-free because of the constellation of social and psychological factors influencing social scientists, constellations which in turn influence social science itself. By social factors he means such things as climate of opinion, socialization, and professional ideology, while the psychological factors he refers to can be illustrated by a concept such as mental rigidity.

According to Hanson, the influence of values can be traced in the scope of the discipline, the research problem selected, and the acceptance or rejection of hypotheses, principles, and theories when faced with counterevidence. ETHICAL-GENERAL

Haug, R. 1974. "The Erosion of Professional Autonomy: A Cross-Cultural Inquiry on the Case of Medicine." Paper presented at the American Sociological Association Annual Meeting, Montreal. (Not for quotation or citation without the author's permission.)

This paper offers qualitative and impressionistic data from the USSR and the United Kingdom to support the position that professional autonomy is eroding and that the medical profession in the United States has lost some of its high status. PROFESSIONALISM

Heuser, W. L. 1959. "Some Present Opinions on Social Ethics and Economic Science." *Southwestern Social Science Quarterly* 40:255–58.

Is economics a pure science or is it connected to social values and ethics? Heuser measured then current opinion on the relationship between economics and ethics by soliciting responses from 49 economists and 20 philosophers whose names were randomly selected from the *Handbook of the American Economic Association* and the *Journal of the American Philosophical Association.* Questions asked included whether economists as such should make public policy recommendations and whether economists in teaching situations should make normative statements. The data suggest that only a minority believe economists should not proffer advice on matters of public policy. PROFESSIONALISM, SOCIAL POLICY

Hobbs, N. 1968. "Ethical Issues in the Social Sciences." In *International Encyclopaedia of the Social Sciences,* Vol. 5, ed. D. L. Sills, pp. 160–67. New York: Macmillan and The Free Press.

"Ethics is concerned with standards of conduct among people in social groups," and thus, social science research is closely linked to ethical problems. In connection with his discussion of the use of deception in research, Hobbs points out that in studying the effects of group pressure on judgment, Russian psychologists used only naive subjects, as opposed to "stooges," analyzing naturally occurring trends and accepting the loss of experimental efficiency. Aside from deception, Hobbs discusses stress in social science research especially in connection with the Milgram experiments, protection of research data—the scientific investigator is not legally protected to keep his data strictly confidential—invasion of privacy, and the issue of informed consent. He also discusses the relationship between social science and social issues, and he touches on the social control of scientific inquiry by professional associations. He closes on the note that it is important to keep ethical matters under debate and discussion "in order to provide increasingly instructive principles for clarifying ethical issues in social science research." DECEPTION, INFORMED CONSENT, PRIVACY, SOCIAL CONTROL

Hofmann, G. 1972. "The Quest for Relevance: Some Implications for Social Research." *et al.* 3:50–57.

Hofmann discusses ethical problems and the ASA's formation of a professional ethics committee. Sociologists can no longer follow the pure scientific ethos; most agree that maintaining subjects' trust is important and that sociologists should hold themselves accountable for their activities. Ultimate ends can sometimes justify ethically questionable methods. The legitimacy of research thus has to be decided on a case-by-case basis. We must discard the notion that science's ultimate goal is to know and must rather concentrate on creating a good society where the well-being of persons will be the most important aim. ETHI-CAL-GENERAL, RISK-BENEFIT

Holden, C. 1975. "Privacy: Congressional Efforts are Coming to Fruition." *Science* 188:713–15.

The Buckley Amendment and the Privacy Act of 1974 indicate patterns of the future with respect to protection of privacy. In general the Privacy Act stipulates that data be used only for the purpose for which they are collected and that individuals be aware of those purposes, and for clarifying the position of contractors or extramural researchers. CONFIDENTIALITY, LEGISLATION AND REGU-LATION, RISK-BENEFIT, SOCIAL POLICY

*Human Organization.* 1972. "Learning at Rough Rock." 31:447–53.
John, V. P. "Learning at Rough Rock." pp. 447–49.

John considers questions on the purpose of cross-cultural research, the validity of research in general, the interpretation of cross-cultural observations, and the living up to responsibilities entailed by researchers in minority settings. One possible solution is for the researcher to be employed by the minority group so that the usual power relations are reversed, giving the researcher an entirely new perspective on his or her work. To illustrate her points, John draws on her own experiences of working with the Navaho and shows how their cultural interpretations of reality are different from the dominant cultural one, and how researchers can be limited by the preconceptions stemming from their own cultural matrix. COLLECTIVE CONCERN, FIELD INVESTIGATION

Hessler, R. M., and P. K. New. "Toward a Research Commune?" pp. 449–50.

Hessler and New present two dilemmas: should research on the poor be done, and are the right questions being asked. At issue is the trust of subjects. As solutions, they suggest that since nonwhite communities want immediate answers to their problems, the researcher should work with the local residents as partners, allowing them to share in the design and execution of the study, and that the researcher should adopt the basic values of the community. An experiment involving Tufts Medical School and Chinatown residents tested these theories. Since the community wanted to implement a community action program while the researchers, as is traditional, wanted to publish their findings, the problem of relevance was also raised. The

authors suggest that "community members should act as peer reviewers and pass judgment on the value and relevance of the study." They
point out that researchers are no longer omnipotent and should accordingly adjust their research strategies and methodologies. COL-
LECTIVE CONCERN, FIELD INVESTIGATION

Walsh, J. L. "Comment on 'Learning at Rough Rock' and 'Toward a
Research Commune?,'" pp. 451–52.
   The problem of the "adequacy of established procedures for the
conduct of social research" has been brought up by many researchers. The solutions presented by John and by Hessler and New are
biased because of their partisanship. The traditional sociological approach calls for theories to be generated and tested in strictly controlled situations. Insights arrived at in this fashion, however, may
also be invalid because of imposed conceptual schemes. Problems
thus exist with both approaches. The main difficulty with the John-
Hessler-New approach is its theoretical posture. Walsh opts for a
merger of the insights of the "research commune" suggestion with
the traditional perspectives. FIELD INVESTIGATION

Cohen, L. M. "Comment on 'Learning at Rough Rock' and 'Toward a
Research Commune?'" pp. 454–55.
   How can an outsider relate to minority-group subjects? Cohen
expresses agreement with John's call for reassessing the interplay of
investigator and subject but hopes this will not limit research and that
social scientists themselves will decide on the feasibility and desirability of proposed studies. Cohen points out that the researcher's presence in a given situation is influenced by different types of "outsiders"
who want information on a community. She also states that the
university as well as the researcher has a commitment to the community being studied since community belief in and cooperation with
the research depends in part on the total visible commitment of those
for whom the researcher works. COLLECTIVE CONCERN,
FIELD INVESTIGATION

Gearing, F. "Comment on 'Learning at Rough Rock' and 'Toward a
Research Commune?'" pp. 455–56.
   Anthropological inquiry is subversive: embattled communities
need cohesion to improve their lot, and knowledge generated by
studies subverts this cause because the knowledge is appreciated by
potential allies or enemies. Therefore, the two solutions of John and
Hessler and New are short-term. Gearing feels that to turn from
cross-cultural studies altogether would be wrong, but that to educate
the embattled is excellent in that it will facilitate cross-cultural ex-

change. In the long run, though, he hopes that it will be possible for "subversive anthropology" to work because of potentially reciprocal benefits. COLLECTIVE CONCERN, FIELD INVESTIGATION

Gladwin, T. "Comment on 'Learning at Rough Rock' and 'Toward a Research Commune?'" pp. 452–53.

John and Hessler and New emphasize the importance of local inputs but fail in their attempt to decolonize applied social science. Social scientists are not really the servants of the people they study, since they bring personal goals to the situation. One solution might be to employ a commercial model, in which an investigator works for a company and produces results which are then company property which it uses as it desires. FIELD INVESTIGATION

*Human Organization,* 1958–60. "Freedom and Responsibility in Research: The 'Springdale Case.'" Vols. 17–19.

Editorial. "Freedom and Responsibility in Research: The 'Springdale Case.'" 17, no. 2:1–2.

The appearance of *Small Town in Mass Society,* published as a result of a two-and-one-half-year research project investigating small-town dynamics, provoked controversy on two counts: the responsibility of an author of a community study to his subjects (individual identity and protection thereof), and the responsibility of the author to the project director ("ownership" of project data). Anonymity for the community members was pledged, but the small size of the town made it impossible to conceal individual identities. The author of the book (Vidich) contends that what he writes is "public knowledge," but others maintain that what is printed is quite different in import from what is spoken. Questions are discussed about how to allow for individual responsibility and creativity on a team research project where the findings cannot be published individually. CONFIDENTIALITY, ETHICAL-GENERAL, FREEDOM OF INQUIRY

Vidich, A. J., and J. Bensman. "Comment on 'Freedom and Responsibility in Research.'" 17, no. 4:2–5.

The editorial criticism of Vidich's position is too narrow. The real issues are the purposes of inquiry and the problems it purports to solve. The paper discusses the rationale for the use of some project material and the deletion of other material for their book. Scientific investigations of primitive populations have not encountered resistance because of the unsophisticated nature of the subjects, but an articulate group will resist the attention research brings. The researcher can ignore such groups, deal with them inoffensively, or do interesting and significant research. In considering the ethics of responsibility, the researcher can either obey the philosophy of the controlling interests of businesses, governments, foundations, research centers, and colleges, or he can deal with fundamental issues related to the basic problems of social science. The choice seemingly evolves to one of doing research for a sponsor and accepting the sponsor's social constraints or working independently and conscientiously alone. COLLECTIVE CONCERN, FREEDOM OF INQUIRY, SOCIAL CONTROL

Risley, R. "Comment on 'Freedom and Responsibility in Research.' " 17, no. 4:5.

If social research is to be conducted realistically, the researcher must accept two principles: before the project starts it is essential to arrive at a clear understanding with the subjects about the events being studied, the degree of anonymity to be offered, and the nature of publications; each member of a research team is to be bound by the terms of such an understanding as is the project director. Individuals on the project are not free to use data for their own purposes. There can be no responsible mode of operation without such standards. Violations arouse distrust to the extent that the conduct of social research will be endangered. ETHICAL-GENERAL, FREEDOM OF INQUIRY

Ries, R. E. "Comment on 'Freedom and Responsibility in Research.' " 17, no. 4:6.

The pursuit of objectivity in scientific research can exclude value judgments, often with morally reprehensible results. Vidich's claim that he was acting in the name of science when he published his report exposing the privacy of persons and using data cooperatively gathered is not justifiable since questions of moral responsibility should not be subordinated in scientific inquiry. There are no ethics of absolute ends. "A meaningful social science is one in which we recognize the value implications of our own behavior." ETHICAL-GENERAL, FREEDOM OF INQUIRY

Becker, H. S. "Comment on 'Freedom and Responsibility in Research.' " 17, no. 4:6–7.

Questions of project director-staff relations and the rights and obligations of each should be resolved at the time of hiring. The problems of Vidich versus Bronfenbrenner would never have arisen had positions been clearly stated early in the game on data availability and the researcher's obligations to those studied. Appeals to objectivity cannot release a researcher from commitments made to those studied. FREEDOM OF INQUIRY

Bronfenbrenner, U. "Comment on Freedom and Responsibility in Research." 18, no. 2:49.

The "Springdale" project developed an explicit code of professional ethics before field operations began. Vidich became thoroughly acquainted with the principles upon joining the project, and the community residents were told that no material would be published that would reveal individual or group identities. The "Principles of Professional Ethics" developed by the Cornell Studies in Social Growth is presented in its entirety. CONFIDENTIALITY, ETHICAL-GENERAL

Bell, E. H. "Comment on Freedom and Responsibility in Research." 18, no. 2:49.

Responsibility to the community does not conflict with responsibility to science. The author's experience in going over his manuscript with a community gave him a broader understanding of the issues and substantiated his contention that the fulfillment of responsibility to the community can strengthen scientific integrity. COLLECTIVE CONCERN, FREEDOM OF INQUIRY

Cornell Program in Social Psychiatry. "Memorandum of Understanding Concerning Basic Principles for Publication of Program Research." 18, no. 4:147–48.

A statement of six principles governing research and multiplication of goals, methods, or results is offered: professional recognition must be given to junior staff members for their contribution to the project; equity of past and present staff; quality of published work; privacy and self-respect of the individuals and community studies; protection of the long-range investment of time, work and money; recourse to higher university authority for staff members who disagree with the project director about publication of material. ETHICAL-GENERAL

Vidich, A. J. "Freedom and Responsibility in Research. A Rejoinder." 19, no. 1:3–4.

The role of the code of ethics in the "Springdale" controversy is discussed. The author accepted it as a principle but not as a legal directive, since it had been constructed on the basis of three to four years of previous experience. It could not cover all future contingencies, nor did it expressly cover the role of a "participant observer." The community was never fully informed of Vidich's role, and the code never accounted for it. Nor was it ever revised for this or other new issues which demanded, therefore, an allegiance to situational ethics. Vidich objects to the evolution of the project into an "entirely statistical report." Anonymity does not need to be equated with a

statistical report. To please all objects of research is a social obligation, and to do scientific justice to one's findings can, in some cases,
conflict with this need. CODES OF ETHICS, ETHICAL-GEN-
ERAL

Evans, W. M. "Conflict and the Emergence of Norms: The 'Springdale
Case.' " 19, no. 4:172–73.
 Conflict can create norms. Codes of ethics adjudicate controversy
via codes, and not by power or personal influence. In the "Springdale
case," norms regulating interstaff relations were missing as was the
mechanism for handling conflicts which arose because of different
interpretations of the code of ethics. Should the "Springdale" study
continue, it is probable that "the code of ethics would be modified
to prevent the recurrence of such conflict." A procedure to adjust
disputes might be established. The Cornell University Social Psychiatry Project illustrates the norm-generating power of conflict.
CODES OF ETHICS

Humphreys, G. 1975. "1984 at HEW?" Letter to the Editor. *APA Monitor*
6:3.
 Humphreys comments on the case of a researcher applying for a
small grant to do secondary analysis on data gathered in another part
of the country in 1969. The application was denied on grounds of
failure to obtain parental consent, and because of the potential risks to
the subjects both as individuals and as class representatives. A letter to
the Human Rights Review Committee at the researcher's institution
mentioned the investigator's "apparent failure to consider the probable
school consequences of the study." Humphreys points out that the data
were not in personally identifiable form and were to be analyzed only
in terms of group statistics. COLLECTIVE CONCERN, IN-
FORMED CONSENT, LEGISLATION AND REGULATION

Hyman, H. 1972. *Secondary Analysis of Sample Surveys:* New York: John
Wiley.
 This monograph does not focus on ethical problems. It does note
the usefulness of secondary analysis as nonintrusive when, for some
reason, community tensions are high, and also as a countermeasure
against a too-rapid depletion of social science's natural resource, subjects. Hyman contends that secondary analysis, "the extraction of
knowledge on topics other than those which were the focus of the
original surveys," can solve some of the problems besetting surveys:
cost, limited generalizability, and inability to deal with social change
because of the overemphasis on social statistics and relative neglect of
social dynamics. COLLECTIVE CONCERN, SURVEYS

Jacobs, H. 1970. "The Journalistic and Sociological Enterprise." *American Sociologist* 5:348–50.

This is a discussion of the ethical responsibilities of journalists and sociologists. An ethical or veracious dilemma for journalists is often a scientific and methodological problem for social scientists. Both are similar, frequently dealing with publicly accountable behavior. In publishing, both have the power of influence but the social scientist must be more cautious because of the possibility of subtle bias. Since the author noticed that respondents are frequently unclear about the sociologist's job and often confuse it with that of therapeutic personnel, she points out that the sociologist has ethical responsibility for establishing the understanding of roles. ETHICAL-GENERAL

Jaffe, L. 1969. "Law as a System of Control." *Daedalus* 98:406–26.

The conduct of research involves a variety of different interests: the individual's to protect his or her well-being; the researcher's, to protect his or her vocation; the collectivity's, to further the acquisition of knowledge. Jaffe notes that although the state is not considered to be more important than the individual, the individual is often compelled to sacrifice his immediate interests for the community's benefit. LEGAL, RISK-BENEFIT

Jonas, H. 1969. "Philosophical Reflections on Human Experimentation." *Daedalus* 98:219–47.

One of the difficulties with human experimentation is that frequently no nonhuman substitutions are possible. It is a topic marked by genuine conflict of higher-order values. Jonas discusses a number of issues such as the dubious distinction between individual and society when phrased in terms of "rights"; the sacrificial theme present in experimentation; the rationale to limit the individual's freedom in favor of the body politic which exists for the good of all; the fact that progress is an acknowledged social goal, making human experimentation of great societal interest. He closes on the note that society will not be threatened by a slow conquering of exotic diseases but by an erosion of moral values. BIOMEDICAL RESEARCH, RISK-BENEFIT, COLLECTIVE CONCERN

Jonsen, A. R. 1975. "The Ethics of Experimentation." Letter to the Editor. *Science* 188:98–100.

Jonsen comments on the neglect of value conflict in the forum conducted by the National Academy of Sciences in February 1975 which failed to discuss this very issue with respect to biomedical experimentation and research: ". . . the panelists almost to a man seemed to miss the public perception of the problem: research appears to involve a threat to the integrity and dignity of significant populations." Jonsen indicates three important factors necessary to determine the ethical principles which should underline research: While biomedical research is necessary and useful, the occurrence of abuses should be acknowledged, as should the problems in subject selection, risk-benefit criteria, and informed consent. Ethicists, people trained in dispassionate analysis of moral arguments, should be more fully utilized. Both the professions and the public need considerably more education with respect to these issues. In closing Jonsen refers to Handler's concluding comments at the forum: "It is never trivial to determine what is human and appropriate to human dignity." BIOMEDICAL RESEARCH, ETHICAL-GENERAL

Jorgensen, Joseph G. 1971. "On Ethics and Anthropology." *Current Anthropology,* June, pp. 321–34.

*Abstract:* "I address myself to the question of a need for an ethical code, even a decision-making ethics committee, for professional ethnologists, and social anthropologists. The focus here is on only one of the relationships ethnologists have in their professional lives: their relationship with the people they study. The first concern is with a distinction between normative ethics and metaethics. The assertion that a normative ethic for ethnologists should or can be based on scientific method or principles (metaethic) is analyzed and rejected. I maintain that such a code can only be based on our understanding of human behavior in many situations and can only be evaluated by observing the conduct of the ethnologists who adhere to it (metaethic). The second concern is with the contexts in which people live. I suggest that a normative ethic for anthropologists should be assessed in light of the present social environments in which we work as well as our expectations for future environments. The third [concern is] for consent and confidentiality, the conditions under which confidentiality may not be desired, the dangers of truth, validity of research reports as an ethical consideration, and the effects of the researcher on the host community. The fourth and final concern is with the establishment and the enforcement of an ethical code in such a way as to prevent the conducting of clandestine research under the cover of the title 'anthropologist.' The question of how an ethics committee might be selected is not taken up here, but is opened for discussion." CODES OF ETHICS, CONFIDENTIALITY, INFORMED CONSENT

Josephson, E. 1970. "Resistance to Community Surveys." *Social Problems* 18:117–29.

A Columbia University School of Public Health Study of adolescents' health in a well-known slum encountered local community resistance. (Three graduate-student interviewers mobilized public sentiment against the project; Josephson suspects something similar has happened in a number of other cases.) He analyzes this resistance in terms of its sources, forms, and implications for research. Since research can, in fact, be manipulative, it is often feared as an invasion of privacy. Potential subjects must be involved in the planning of research projects that will be done in their communities. It is also suggested that much improved ethical codes be established, and that the utility of research be demonstrated in such a way that the communities clearly perceive its value. CODES OF ETHICS, COLLECTIVE CONCERN, PRIVACY, SOCIAL CONTROL

Jung, J. 1971. *The Experimenter's Dilemma.* New York: Harper & Row.

The advantage of experimentation lies in its ability to eliminate alternative explanations of findings by controlling for as many extraneous variables as possible. Problems arise, however, because of the reactive nature of human subjects, because of sample bias, and because of experimenter bias.

This monograph examines each of the problem areas in turn and includes 12 selected readings dealing specifically with such topics as the demand characteristics of experimental settings, the relationship between experimenter attributes and subject responses, and so on.

Jung points out that the awareness of being in an experiment can affect subjects' behavior in a variety of ways: effects of the placebo or power of suggestion, the Hawthorne effect, or being the center of attention; demand characteristics of the situation; socially desirable responses; evaluation of informed consent; and the notion that while subjects should be permitted to withdraw at any time, this can create serious methodological difficulties. Subjects should be protected from harm. Data should be kept strictly confidential.

In discussing future developments Jung mentions the particularly troublesome nature of deception. He points out that role-playing has often been suggested as an alternative but it suffers from tapping what people imagine they would do in a particular situation, not what they would actually do. Greater focus on indirect, nonreactive measures would be a possible solution to some of these problems. Some way should be found to lessen the discrepancies between field and laboratory findings. Perhaps we need more naturalistic observations, although ethical problems also arise in that context. DECEPTION, FIELD INVESTIGATION, INFORMED CONSENT, PSYCHOLOGICAL EXPERIMENTATION

Kalven, H. J. 1966. "Privacy in Tort Law—Were Warren and Brandeis Wrong?" *Law and Contemporary Problems* 3:326–41.

Kalven's basic premise is that privacy is intimately linked to human dignity and the needs of human existence. The protection of privacy is a very important matter and Kalven worries that it cannot be accomplished by means of tort law. Privacy as such does not exist in common law and he is concerned that the common-law approach would mean that people most harmed by invasions of privacy would be those least likely to bring suit. He is cognizant of the tendency for privacy actions to move into the area of defamation suits. LEGAL, PRIVACY

Karst, K. L. 1966. "The Files: Legal Controls Over the Accuracy and Accessibility of Stored Personal Data." *Law and Contemporary Problems* 31:342–76.

Karst focuses on selective disclosure. On the whole he believes that the public's right to know will supersede individual efforts to restriction, but with respect to accuracy of data, the matter is somewhat different. He indicates the difficulty in separating fact from opinion and that problems often arise not from error but from half-truths—information which does not tell enough. Evaluative statements are difficult, especially when the language used by the original rater is different from that of subsequent perusers. There is also the risk of leakage, either deliberate or accidental, in computer time-shared systems. Because it is not possible to separate between the various restrictive mechanisms which could be employed to make the use of such data ethical and the utility of such data, he believes our main concern should be with data accuracy, not accessibility. DATA BANKS, RISK-BENEFIT

Kash, D. E. 1972. "Politics and Research." In *The Social Contexts of Research*, ed. S. Z. Nagi and R. G. Corwin, pp. 97–128. New York: John Wiley.

This is a general discussion of the relationship between politics and research especially since World War II, which includes a description of likely future linkages between the two systems. Kash attempts to establish the thesis that the old federal research policy, which tended to assume that research objectives and federal policy objectives were the same, is being changed. He attributes this change to such factors as the suspicion that much of research is irrelevant to the solution of important and pressing problems, the rise of antiscientism, and the increasing doubts about the worth of technological advances. These factors result in the paradoxical perception of research as both the source and solution of many problems. Kash sees political solution to this state of affairs to be greater emphasis on programmatic research directed to solving concrete national problems, which means researchers will have far less freedom in defining their own problems. The main characteristics of linkages in the future between politics and research are the following: Less money will be available for research, with applied research first priority; research funds will go directly to university administrators who hence will gain greater control; social science research funding will grow and will be directed particularly at policy-relevant and interdisciplinary research. SOCIAL POLICY

Katz, J. 1972. *Experimentation with Human Beings.* New York: Russell Sage.

It is impossible in a brief annotation to do justice to this exhaustive volume, organized more or less as a law-school casebook. Katz offers us case studies from medicine, psychology, and sociology to illustrate some of the issues surrounding the use of humans as research subjects and excerpts drawn from the writings of persons working in a broad variety of disciplines relevant to the area.

Katz contends that the tension between freedom and scientific inquiry and protection of human inviolability raises the question of when societal benefit should outweigh individual cost. To answer that, we need to know whether there should be limits to free inquiry and what the consequences of such limits would be, who can legitimately place such limits, and how they should be enforced. The Jewish Chronic Disease Hospital and the Wichita jury recording cases raised the following "contrapuntal" issues: need of individuals and society to continually expand the boundaries of knowledge versus men's fear of the unknown and desire to perpetuate the status quo; the belief that injury to life and limb is inevitable at some point in all human endeavors versus the belief in the paramount value of human life; and the need and wish to rely on professional expertise versus the individual's desire to have control over those decisions affecting him or her.

The following material attempts to demonstrate the inclusiveness of Katz's work:

Bertrand Russell distinguished between two motivations in the love of knowledge: love of an object and the desire to have power over it. According to Russell, the development of science has marked a change from contemplation to manipulation.

Everett Hughes pointed out that professions tend to protect their own and there is therefore no guarantee they will always act in the public's best interest.

There is ample evidence that medicine has a long history of experimentation on humans in most cases without their consent. Interference with self-determination and privacy, interference with psychological integrity, and interference with physical integrity are factors which can constitute harm for the individual.

The book also covers social science research. For instance, Laud Humphreys investigated "impersonal sex in public places," based on the ethical principles that social science should not ignore an area of research because of its difficulty or social sensitivity, that the methodology used should distort the subject matter as little as possible, and that respondents should be protected from harm at all costs. These views were attacked by columnist von Hoffman: "No information is valuable enough to obtain by nipping away at personal liberty, and that is true no matter who is doing the gnawing, John Mitchell and the conservatives over at the Justice Department or Laud Humphreys and the liberals over at the Sociology Department." Horowitz and Rainwater, in a rebuttal, pointed out that Humphreys had investigated public acts (conducted in public restrooms) and that social scientists should have the right to study behavior—in particular, publicly accountable behavior.

Another example of the kind of material to be found in the book is drawn from Hoagland: "Fear that the behavioral and social sciences may be used for evil purposes has slowed their development and blocked their use for constructive purposes. We need a larger investment of talent in this field, commensurate with their importance. As someone has said, understanding the atom is child's play compared to understanding child's play."

The book also has both a condensed table of contents and a very extensive analytical table of contents; a table of cases, authors, books, articles, and other sources; and a subject index. BIOMEDICAL EXPERIMENTATION, ETHICAL-GENERAL, PSYCHOLOGICAL EXPERIMENTATION, SOCIAL EXPERIMENTATION

Katz, M., ed. 1969. *Sciences of Man and Social Ethics: Variations on the Theme of Human Dignity.* Boston: Branden.

This volume attempts to introduce ethics, which Katz defines as the discipline which measures the extent to which aspects of self-images correspond to objective reality, as a research discipline. Hartman, one of the contributors, offers four axiological proofs (epistemological, logical, ontological, and teleological) of the infinite value of man and goes on to argue that the value of society can never be greater than the value of a single individual. ETHICAL-GENERAL

Keeney, B. C. 1970. "The Bridge of Values." *Science* 169:26–28.

Keeney discusses some of the problems surrounding building a bridge beween the humanities and the sciences, but he sees a reconciliation possible through the increasing recognition by both scientists and humanists that we cannot dispense with values since they and our basic assumptions are one and the same thing. He cites Seaborg to the effect that the modern era has brought fact and value, science and morality, into direct confrontation with each other—a confrontation which it is hoped will be resolved so as to lead to new levels of rationality and humanity. ETHICAL-GENERAL

Kelley, V. R., and H. B. Weston. 1975. "Computers, Costs and Civil Liberties." *Social Work* 20:15–19.

> *Abstract*: "The need to control costs has led many state mental health systems to set up automated data banks in which a patient's name is directly linked with his record. Many consider this a primary threat to confidentiality and civil liberties. In contrast, Iowa's community mental health centers are developing a system that avoids releasing identifiable personal information." CONFIDENTIALITY, DATA BANKS

Kelman, H. C. 1972. "The Rights of the Subject in Social Research: An Analysis in Terms of Relative Power and Legitimacy." *American Psychologist* 27:989–1015.

> Kelman discusses the ethical problems surrounding both the processes and products of social research and identifies as matters of central concern the invasion of privacy and the manipulation and control of subjects that arise from certain research practices. He points out that subjects tend to be recruited from the relatively powerless segments of society and organizations, and that this disadvantaged position is exacerbated by subjects' limited power within the research situation. Researchers focus on disadvantaged groups for several reasons: social deviance control is sought by the establishment; there is the tradition of helping those with social problems; and these groups are more readily available because of their power deficiency. For Kelman, the problem of abuse in research stems in part from this uneven distribution of resources. The research situation itself, wherein investigators are assumed to have legitimacy and subjects perceive themselves as lacking the capacity and right to question research procedures, contributes to an unequal distribution of power. Kelman discusses a number of different ethical problems such as violating subjects' right to privacy, deceiving them about the nature of the research, violating their psychological well-being, or using data to subjects' disadvantage. In line with his earlier writings on the subject, he focuses particularly on the noxious consequences of deception.
>
> Corrective approaches to the above problems can be found by adhering to the principle of voluntary informed consent. However, since the subject's position in society or in a given organization often makes "voluntarism" difficult, and because of the unequal distribution

of power in the research situation which throws doubts on the extent to which subjects can be fully informed, institutional mechanisms clearly defining, for instance, the rights and obligations of both investigator and subject are also needed. Kelman emphasizes the proper ethical training of researchers—"norms for the treatment of subjects must become a central part of the operational code of social scientists, alongside norms for proper methodology or honest reporting." Review committees should present a balanced viewpoint so that all biases and perspectives are considered. Codes of ethics could be supplemented by a subject's bill of rights detailing such items as the appropriate way of obtaining consent, the right to refuse participation, and the right to withdraw from the research. Ombudsmen might provide valuable additions to ethics committees.

With respect to misuse of the research products, Kelman notes that social scientists have made important contributions to social change and thus cannot be faulted wholly for serving only the elite; nonetheless, structural inequalities again create situations in which data misuse can occur. To correct this, he suggests that all population segments should be able to effect the formulation of problems and should be able to safeguard their interests in the interpretation and use of results. COERCION, COLLECTIVE CONCERN, PRIVACY, SOCIAL CONTROL

———. 1968. *A Time to Speak*. San Francisco: Jossey-Bass.

This is primarily a collection of Kelman's previously published papers relating to the ethical problems of social and behavioral research. In connection with deception, a major ethical problem in social-psychological research, Kelman suggests that we foster awareness of the ethical and methodological dilemmas surrounding the use of deception; that we counteract and minimize the negative effects of choosing subjects carefully, by not only debriefing subjects but also by giving them the opportunity to work through their negative feelings, and by developing new experimental techniques such as role-playing. DECEPTION, ETHICAL-GENERAL, PSYCHOLOGICAL EXPERIMENTATION, SOCIAL EXPERIMENTATION

———. 1966. "Deception in Social Research." *Transaction* 3:20–24.

Kelman points out that deception is generally done for the good reason that people tend to modify their behavior if they know what is being measured. He is thus concerned not so much about deception per se but that it is done without sufficient weighing of pros and cons. The issue of deception must be examined with respect to its ethical implications, actual effectiveness, and implications for future behavioral research. Alternatives to deceptive practices should be sought such as telling subjects they will not be given complete information at the beginning of the experiment. It is crucial that the participation and motivation of subjects be actively sought rather than passively bypassed. DECEPTION

————. 1965. "Manipulation of Human Behavior: An Ethical Dilemma for the Social Scientist." *Journal of Social Issues* 21:31-46.

Kelman comments on the basic dilemma facing those who value freedom that any kind of behavior change involves some form of manipulation. For Kelman himself, being human is predicated on the ability to choose. He does not believe there is an ultimate solution to the problem, but sees increasing awareness and encouraging reflexiveness, deliberately establishing safeguards against manipulation, and consciously espousing freedom of choice as the goal for research and practice as ways to mitigate the undesirable effects of new developments. COERCION

Kershaw, D. N. 1975. *The Experience with Ethical Issues in the Conduct of Social Experiments.* New Jersey: Mathematica.

On the basis of his experience in a variety of social experiments, including the New Jersey Negative Income Tax Experiment, Kershaw notes that the development and application of ethical principles for social experimentation differ from those for medical experimentation because of the less controlled and more public nature of the former contrasted to the scientifically controlled laboratory setting of the latter. He uses 10 of 12 points set forth by Veatch (*Ethical and Legal Issues in Social Experimentation,* ed. A. M. Rivlin and P. M. Timpane, Brookings, 1975) as groundwork for his own discussion of the ethical conduct of social experiments.

Benefit/harm ratio: Since the long-term effects of experiments cannot be effectively determined, they cannot be considered. The researcher's objective for short-term effects should be a restoration of what Kershaw calls the status quo ante for the subject.

Voluntary informed consent: Not all risks can be anticipated. (Kershaw gives the example of a Negative Income Tax experiment subject who consented to appear on television, but as a result was ridiculed by colleagues, and then was fired after a fight with his foreman. He could not find another job, was left by his wife because he could not support the children, and was threatened with imprisonment because he could not meet child-support payments.) Subjects do not need to be informed of all the technical aspects of a study but should be informed of possible harm. Kershaw points out that excessive inducements can create "involuntary" consent. Communitywide studies can be ethical if the duly elected officials give their approval.

Confidentiality: No legal basis exists for protecting the confidentiality of research data. This is a critical issue. Kershaw suggests that principles already existing for confidential communications be applied to social experiments or that such research be covered by statute.

Right to withdraw from research: This should be guaranteed and special care should be taken that such subjects are left in the status quo ante.

Adequacy of research design: No unnecessary experiments should be undertaken. Necessity should be established on the grounds of the data's relevance to policy decision, exhaustion of all nonexperimental avenues, existence of theory sufficient to specify a set of carefully designed testable hypotheses, and ability of the experiment to yield the needed data.

Outside review: One possible solution to the problem of adequate review would be to establish a professional society of social experimenters, members of which could act as peer reviewers.

Purpose of research: It is not necessary to tell subjects which forms of behavior the experiment is designed to measure so long as they know what use will be made of the information they provide and what policy outcomes might result from the findings.

The presence of a control group or placebo: No need exists to inform subjects of the existence of experimental conditions other than their own, provided they are allocated to treatment condition before contact.

Review and subject protection agents: The right to appeal disputed decisions and the existence of panels established for that purpose should be well publicized.

Statement of basic rights of the subject: The subject's rights and responsibilities and the experiment's "regulations" are to be made very clear before the decision to enroll in the experiment is made. INFORMED CONSENT, CONFIDENTIALITY, RISK-BENEFIT SOCIAL EXPERIMENTATION

———, and J. C. Small. 1972. "Data confidentiality and Privacy: Lessons from the New Jersey Negative Income Tax Experiment." *Public Policy* 20:257–80.

Kershaw and Small present a strong argument in favor of legal protection for the confidentiality of information revealed to an experimenter by a respondent-subject. The New Jersey Negative Income Tax Experiment is described, including the steps taken at the outset to guarantee confidentiality to participating families, such as a clause to that effect in the contract with the Office of Economic Opportunity and the requirements that all staff members had to sign a "confidentiality agreement." Despite this, local welfare officials and the local county prosecutor's office subpoenaed records of families suspected of having received overlapping welfare and experimentally linked payments. Pressure to reveal records also came from the General Accounting Office and the U.S. Senate, which desired information for family-assistance policy formulations.

The authors discuss the current powers of the state in matters of subpoena, the relevance of the notion of executive privilege, and the model provided by the Census Bureau of protecting the confidentiality of data. They conclude that the passage of a statute dealing specifically with social experiments is necessary to encourage full and open disclosure by subjects by legally protecting the confidentiality of their responses. CONFIDENTIALITY, LEGAL, SOCIAL EXPERIMENTATION

Kharchev, A. 1965. "Ethics as Object of Sociological Research." *Social Sciences Information* 4:170–78.

Kharchev points out that there has always been a conflict between the interests of the group and those of the individual, and that ethics traditionally is the method of "coordinating personal and social interests." ETHICAL-GENERAL

Knerr, C. R., and J. D. Carroll. 1977. "Researchers and the Courts: Development of a Testimonial Privilege." Paper presented before Annual Meeting of the American Association for Public Opinion Research.

The practice of researchers entering into confidential relationships with subjects is likely to continue. Researchers recognize that a conflict exists between the scientific norms of openness and replication and the granting of confidentiality. However, they have no need of individual identities in general, being primarily interested in aggregate responses. Also, they realize that anonymity improves participation and veracity. The article discusses the legal flaw in assuring confidentiality: subpoenas of records can breach confidences established. An ethical dilemma arises: one must choose between breaching confidences or refusing to obey subpoenas. Examples are given of subpoenaing of researchers and their varying reactions and degrees of cooperation; and of the various actions taken by prosecutors and the courts, ranging from dropping of all charges to imprisonment of the researcher.

In discussing the constitutional protections available in criminal and civil proceedings, the authors note that whereas the first amendment has been used in a few instances to defend the right to confidentiality of researchers, in general it does not afford a good protection. Various laws at both the state and federal level designed to protect researcher-subject communications are reviewed with an eye to the following: what the limits are on the protections they offer, whether they have been held to be constitutional, where they apply, and which provisions protect whom and what. CONFIDENTIALITY, LEGIS-LATION AND REGULATION

Kolb, W. L. n.d. "Statement on the Ethics of the Profession of Sociology." Mimeograph.

Sociology has prospered in the free democratic societies of the West which value the existential freedom of individuals—the individual is "free to will as he wills." Paradoxically, already at the theoretical level, sociology is not premised on such a conception of human nature —a matter which gives rise to considerable ethical tension. According to Kolb, the thrust of the sociological enterprise ought to be directed to "the task of creating and maintaining human freedom." ETHICAL-GENERAL

Konvitz, M. R. 1966. "Privacy and the Law: A Philosophical Prelude." *Law and Contemporary Problems* 31:272–80.

Konvitz conceptualizes privacy as the right to be left alone and thus wishes to stress the notion that the individual can publicly perform acts which still require recognition of privacy: Privacy applies not only to the bedroom but also to the streets. OBSERVATION, PRIVACY

Krasner, L. 1965. "The Behavioral Scientist and Social Responsibility: No Place to Hide." *Journal of Social Issues* 21:9–30.

Recent developments, such as techniques of behavior modification and control, societal demands for social science knowledge, increasing professional preoccupation with ethics, and the continuing existence of some old myths such as that of "mental illness," have made it imperative that behavioral scientists carefully examine their social responsibilities. Krasner recommends the careful mapping and presentation of the anticipated consequences of social scientific endeavors in the hope such awareness will lead to wise choices. ETHICAL-GENERAL, PROFES-SIONALISM

Kraut, R. E., and J. B. McConahay. 1973. "How Being Interviewed Affects Voting: An Experiment." *Public Opinion Quarterly* 37:398–406.

This is a report on a study conducted in one low-income ward in Boston. The investigation interviewed one sample of citizens, as though they were conducting a typical preelection survey on vote intentions, and compared their voting records with those of a control group. It was found that the interviewed group participated in the election to a significantly greater extent than those who were not interviewed. SURVEYS

Lakoff, S. A. 1971. "Knowledge, Power and Democratic Theory." *The Annals* 394:5–12.

Lakoff remarks on the growing tendency at all levels of government to make use of social scientific analyses to formulate policy. He specifically discusses the implications of this for democratic government. "The essence of the democratic idea is the belief that, to the extent possible, each individual and the society collectively must be free to make well-informed choices. Insofar as scientific norms prescribe openness and the freedom to challenge given truths, they are eminently compatible with the essential norm of democracy. Because science, in the Baconian sense of the term, does not claim access to wisdom, there can be no disputing the need for ultimate power of decision to rest with those affected by the use of knowledge rather than with specialists who make it available. SOCIAL POLICY

Lang, G. E. 1971. "Professionalism Under Attack: The Case of the Anthropologists." *Social Science Information* 10:117–32.

This article reports on the results of a pilot study designed to investigate some attitudinal and other changes by members of the American Anthropological Association. The data consist of systematic observations made by eight highly trained observers during sessions at the 1969 annual American Anthropological Association meeting and follow-up mail questionnaires sent to 1,909 registrants and another 571 nonregistrants drawn at random from the membership directory. Lang suggests that the concept of "academic professionalism" is changing as result of attacks from both without and within the profession. While not denying the value and worth of science, many anthropologists are concerned about the morality of the profession, especially in reference to the "political uses" of anthropological research findings. They are generally insistent that the wishes of the community being studied be taken into consideration. COLLECTIVE CONCERN, FIELD INVESTIGATION, PROFESSIONALISM

Lansing, J. B., G. P. Ginsburg, and K. Braaten. 1961. *An Investigation of Response Error.* Bureau of Economic and Business Research. University of Illinois, Urbana.

This monograph, a technical report based on a series of studies undertaken by the Survey Research Center of the University of Michigan, presents findings of the Consumer Savings Project of the Inter-University Committee for Research on Consumer Behavior.

One of the studies showed that most of the respondents to an interview study on savings accounts, when recontacted by mail afterward, said they found the study interesting, were favorably disposed toward being interviewed again, and liked the interviewer as a person. SURVEYS

Laswell, H. D. 1959. "Strategies of Inquiry: The Rational Use of Observation." In *The Human Meaning of the Social Sciences*, ed. D. Lerner. New
York: Meridian Books.

Laswell is critical of traditional patterns of problem-solving because of their insufficient contextuality, lack of transition, failure to
foster vivid perceptions, and disproportionate treatment of alternatives.
Policy-thinking could be improved by a clarification of values, the
consideration of historical sequences, and a careful examination of the
available theoretical and descriptive models of social processes. In addition, since policy-thinking is always future-oriented, projective hypotheses about the sequence of significant future occurrences and the
policy alternatives to be invented, evaluated, selected, and possibly
applied should be presented. SOCIAL POLICY

Le Compte, M. D. 1970. "The Uneasy Alliance of Community Action and
Research." *School Review* 79:125–32.

In order to answer the question of whether research and action
programs are basically incompatible, it is necessary to look at the relationship between funding and the application of social science knowledge to action programs and the nature of the research design with
respect to particular programs or institutions. Success of research in
community action programs (CAP) depends on the involvement of the
community in the research process. Researchers often lack rapport
with the "insiders" of community action programs, are accused of being
spies and critics of CAP agencies, and elicit skepticism about the benefits of the research to the program. A place can be made for research
in community action programs provided such research can do without
as much rigor as is customary, is willing to place more emphasis on
participant-observation, and can demonstrate concern with the ongoing process of "institution building." COLLECTIVE CONCERN, SO-
CIAL EXPERIMENTATION

Lengyel, P. 1972. "Introduction: Ethics, Institutionalization and Policies."
*International Social Science Journal* 24:635–47.

Lengyel points out that concern with ethical issues waxes and
wanes. He identifies two major approaches to the current discontent:
that which acting on the assumption that social science has already
proved its worth demands policies favorable for its continuing development, and that which, more conscious of the discipline's internal divisiveness, argues for greater consensus on issues including ethics. In
connection with the controversy surrounding value-freeness, he indicates the importance of distinguishing between critiques of the institutionalization of social science and critiques of basic scientific principles.
ETHICAL-GENERAL

Lerner, D., ed. 1959. *The Human Meaning of the Social Sciences*. New York: Meridian Books.

Lerner sees social science as the characteristic mode of self-study of modern societies and its development mainly as an empirical, quantitative, policy-related method of inquiry, not as a system of benefits. It arose during an age of great upheavals as an important activity valued for its ability to throw light on cloudy issues. Social research is possible only in societies which highly value self-improvement through self-study, and it is now an indispensable part of social policy.

According to Lerner, social research is the direct enemy of ideology because ideology prescribes a preferred future while social research describes the actual present. Democracies need the cooperation of the governed; one way of achieving this is through attitude research. Lerner points out that a deep fear of being manipulated and having one's privacy invaded has developed in the West, but for him there is nothing in the social sciences which permits the manipulation of persons against their will; the better viewpoint is that the social sciences have given us increased control over our social environments. COERCION, SOCIAL EXPERIMENTATION, SOCIAL POLICY, SURVEYS

Light, D. Jr. 1974. "Professional Superiority." Paper presented at the American Sociological Association Annual Meeting, Montreal. (Not to be quoted without permission.)

According to Light, the professions which he places in a structurally superior position have an implicit social contract with society. Professional authority is offensive in some forms because of its precariousness and claim to autonomy which undermines the original contract. There is a strong tendency to place professional authority in a firm bureaucratic-legal framework, thereby legitimating it; charisma, a characteristic of groups as well as of individuals, and traditional authority based on experience, are other legitimating factors.

Violations of the social contract occur because of the individual's tendency to claim professional autonomy as his own, although this is not a necessary element of professional work. Light says that such excesses can be controlled by legal and organizational counterforces. PROFESSIONALISM

Markovic, M. 1972. "Ethics of a Critical Social Science." *International Social Science Journal* 24:672–85.

Markovic describes two humanistic attacks on positive science: those which stress idiographic science over nomothetic, qualitative inquiry over quantitative, understanding over the "covering law" approach; and those from the left, for instance the Frankfurt School, which claim that all positive science has a system-supporting function, and that dialectic social theory thus can be nothing else than a critique of existing social reality and extant scientific theories. Existentialists likewise assert that science has a conservative function.

Markovic argues that such viewpoints confuse practice and theory. According to him, science can establish the parameters of an existing entity and delineate the sets of conditions under which qualitative change can occur. "Humanism needs science in order to transcend its utopian and arbitrary character, that is, to translate its theoretical aspirations into a practice." ETHICAL-GENERAL

Martin, D. C., J. D. Arnold, T. F. Zimmerman, and R. H. Richard. 1968. "Human Subjects in Clinical Research—A Report on Three Studies." *New England Journal of Medicine* 279:1426–31.

This is a report on three studies: prisoners volunteering for a malaria experiment were asked their reasons for volunteering; noninstitutionalized groups (divided into low-income, fire and police personnel, professional) were compared to prisoners for willingness to volunteer and opinions about volunteering; and a community sample of 105 persons were asked about their attitudes in connection with the selection of donors and recipients for heart transplants. Results of the first study, comparing volunteering with nonvolunteering prisoners, indicate that volunteering is not a strictly logical process based on information about the research activity, but more a mix of altruism, money, and a way of enhancing prestige or status. The second study found that all the groups tended to be less likely to volunteer for experiments involving greater risk or inconvenience, but that, on the whole, lower rather than higher socioeconomic groups were more willing to volunteer. It was also found that more women than men tend to be willing to volunteer and that the degree of obligation to others, especially to family, reduces willingness to volunteer. In the discussion, the authors emphasize the fact that voluntary consent is not necessarily related to extent of understanding; that it is perhaps better understood in terms of an individual's reference groups. They comment on the reluctance of the professionals, especially men, to volunteer, and strongly recommend that the public's opinions and attitudes be solicited concerning biomedical experimentation on humans. BIOMEDICAL RESEARCH, VOLUNTARISM

McEwan, P. J. M. 1971. "Some Problems of Medical Ethics." *Social Science and Medicine* 5:583–93.

In medicine as well as in other professions, the term "ethics" refers to professional canons of conduct. McEwan identifies three different areas of morality: individual, professional canons of conduct, and social morality—that is, any regulating relationship attempting to embody basic morality. Of these, individual morality is the most important. Medicine is faced with four kinds of applied problems: those of judgment (who should get what, when, and why), those of definition (for instance, what is death?), those of personal practice and belief (for both doctor and patient), and the establishment of priorities, a process dependent on public opinion. The main problem to be solved is how society can more effectively relate the technically possible to the socially desirable. BIOMEDICAL RESEARCH

McNeil, J. N., C. E. Llewellyn, Jr., and T. E. McCollough. 1970. "Community Psychiatry and Ethics." *American Journal of Orthopsychiatry* 40:22–29.

This is a review of some of the ethical foundations for community psychiatry. Following Polanyi who says that all science is personal knowledge, the authors state that community psychiatry cannot be seen as a value-free enterprise, and they go on to add "a code of professional ethics does not provide the common ground between the profession and the community which is necessary for concerted action. We must turn to the larger context of the civic community psychiatry." The ethical issues in community psychiatry include the following: the individual versus social needs—balance between the two required; threats to individual freedom involved—is the doctor on the patient's side or with those trying to exert social control; the idea of informed consent as basic to individual freedom; priorities and rejections—community psychiatry must not reject those most in need of care; research and evaluation as necessary; overthrust and overcontrol—the independence and freedom of community members must be respected at all times. Finally, with respect to public policy, the basic ethical principle of informed consent applies to society as such and is thus of crucial significance. INFORMED CONSENT, RISK-BENEFIT, SOCIAL CONTROL, SOCIAL POLICY

Mead, M. 1969. "Research with Human Beings: A Model Derived from Anthropological Field Practice." *Daedalus* 98:361–86.

Mead points out that it is possible to substitute voluntary participation for informed consent in line with her contention that subject participation in a collective enterprise should be emphasized. The usual model of research in anthropology uses informants and pays them for their time. The only viable approach is to be completely truthful about the research purpose, taking into account that full justice must be done to presenting facts within their correct cultural framework.

For Mead, trust is the most crucial element in discussions about ethics: the more powerless the subjects, the more important the matter of ethics; the higher the status, on the assumption that trust follows status, the greater the accountability.

She sees rules governing experimentation as a means of controlling experts and, thus, in some respects, as a denial of trust. The solution does not lie in a cost-benefit assessment; rather, the research model which stresses the subject's collaborator role should be adopted. In this respect, participation in experiments can be seen as a form of responsible citizenship activity. This is especially true when government funds are involved, since their use implies public support. In connection with the issue of informed consent, she points out that assent to experimental conditions (for example, the subject knows he may or may not take placebos), is sufficient. Four appendixes accompany this article, the first of which specifically discusses the problems of falsification. Deception denigrates the subject, has deleterious effects on the investigator, and invalidates the experiment itself because of the human ability t͡  ͡ ick up multiple subtle cues. The alternative to using humans for giving false cues is to rely on technology. Debriefing is not necessary then because trust in humans has not been violated. DECEPTION, FIELD INVESTIGATION, INFORMED CONSENT, VOLUNTARISM

————. 1961. "The Human Study of Human Beings." *Science:* 133:163–65.
Studying human beings raises a number of ethical problems: both researcher and subject must consent to the research, the researcher must guard against individual and cultural bias, must systematically take into account the effect of the method employed on the behavior observed, must protect subjects from damage during and after investigation, must protect his discipline and science in general from a loss of confidence, and must take great care to protect others from the potential ill-effects of research, too.

For Mead, the major ethical question is whether it is scientifically or morally desirable to deceive subjects. According to her, participant observers operating under subterfuge give false nonverbal cues and thus are liable to distort results. Concealed observation damages the fiduciary relationship of both actual and potential researchers and subjects. COLLECTIVE CONCERN, DECEPTION, OBSERVATION, VOLUNTARISM

Melmon, K. L., M. Grossman, and R. C. Morris, Jr. "Emerging Assets and Liabilities of a Committee on Human Welfare and Experimentation." *New England Journal of Medicine* 282:427–31.
From the abstract: "The University of California San Francisco Medical Center Committee on Human Welfare and Experimentation has reviewed 340 applications for research involving human beings

during its first two years of operations. The committee delegated review to three-man ad hoc groups selected on the basis of expertise and objectivity. Seventeen protocols were rejected by at least two ad hoc committees because risk-benefit ratio could not be assessed (seven), because of inadequate precautions (eight) and because of unacceptable risk (two). The decisions of the Committee were on the whole well accepted, ad hoc groups have increasingly adopted the standards defined by the parent committee, and wide involvement of the faculty in the reviewing process has led to greater recognition of the legal and moral obligations incurred by those who study man." INSTITUTIONAL REVIEW BOARDS

Menges, R. J. 1973. "Openness and Honesty Versus Coercion and Deception in Psychological Research." *American Psychologist* 28:1030–34.
    Menges lists the dilemmas of ethical researchers:

How can informed consent be obtained if the proposed investigation is too complex for easy comprehension? through its use there is an interactive effect with the treatment condition? previously collected data is exposed to secondary analysis?
How can subjects be allowed to withdraw at any time if there exists a previous relationship between the subjects and the investigator, such as teacher or therapist, or if withdrawal spoils random assignment conditions?
What happens when debriefing procedures contaminate future subjects or lead to lowered self-esteem?

    Menges investigated all the articles published in five psychology journals during 1971 and identified a total of 993 studies, of which 185 (18.6 percent) used some kind of deception. He comments on the difficulty of obtaining informed consent if subjects participate as part of a course requirement, or if the respondents are not aware that research is being conducted. He also remarks that the "openness and honesty" the APA statement on ethics calls for may not mean what these terms usually mean, and that while a case can be made for using deception as a means for finding answers to certain important questions, the methodological artifacts deception creates are little understood. He suspects that subjects and researchers will continue being suspicious of each other. COERCION, DECEPTION, INFORMED CONSENT, PSYCHOLOGICAL EXPERIMENTATION

Milgram, S. 1964. "Issues in the Study of Obedience: A Reply to Baumrind." *American Psychologist* 19:848–52.

Milgram responds to Baumrind's (1964) criticisms of his obedience study by asserting that the study was of scientific and general importance and by explaining that the stress caused in the subjects was an unexpected outcome since it had been expected that subjects would not comply. He also explains the various debriefing conditions the subjects received; for instance, obedient subjects were reassured about their obedience, disobedient subjects were reassured about their disobedience. All received a written report about the study and a follow-up questionnaire which indicated that 84 percent were glad to have participated, 15 percent were neutral, 1.3 percent were sorry. Many subjects expressed the feeling that the experiment had been worthwhile and important. A further follow-up conducted a year later found no sign of long-term injury. Thus, in Milgram's judgment, the subjects were not exposed to harm, and, contrary to Baumrind, he maintains that the laboratory is an ideal setting for studying obedience precisely because of its demand characteristics. PSYCHOLOGICAL EXPERIMENTA-TION, STRESS

Miller, A. G. 1972. "Role-playing: An Alternative to Deception? A Review of the Evidence." *American Psychologist* 27:623–36.

Miller sums up the advantages of role-playing as twofold: It is more ethical than deceiving and treats subjects with humanity and dignity; it avoids response styles of subjects which render research less valid. Nonetheless, after reviewing the negative commentary on role-playing and presenting a detailed discussion of four empirical studies contrasting role-playing with deception, he concludes that because of empirical and epistemological problems, role-playing provides a poor alternative to deception if the emphasis is on providing generalizable predictions about behavior. DECEPTION

Miller, A. R. 1974. "The Right to Privacy: Data Banks and Dossiers." In *Privacy in a Free Society.* Final Report, Annual Chief Justice Earl Warren Conference on Advocacy in the United States, sponsored by the Roscoe Pound-American Trial Lawyers Foundation.

According to Miller, data-gathering activities can be well-intended efforts to achieve socially desirable objectives, but frequently they are not. There is a need to strike a balance between data collection and individual rights. Miller calls for a framework to protect the public that would prohibit the recording of certain types of information, would limit general access to data while permitting individuals access to data in their own files enabling them to challenge data accuracy, and would prevent the storage of useless or irrelevant data. Enforcement of these principles should be by legislation, administrative regulation, and judicial process. Miller discusses the right to information-privacy in a constitutional context and notes that the courts are a long way from defining it as a constitutional right. DATA BANKS, LEGISLATION AND REGULATION, PRIVACY

————. 1971. *The Assault on Privacy.* Ann Arbor: University of Michigan Press.

This work carefully examines "personal privacy in the computer age." It traces out the effects of the cybernetic revolution and the threat it poses to personal privacy and the changes in information processing, focusing especially on the practices of federal agencies. The book is particularly useful in its treatment of existing legal theory and practices concerning the protection of privacy. It criticizes suggestions for needed legal innovations, for instance, or attempts to subsume privacy rights under common-law property-right tort, and argues that the best approach is legislation at the federal level. Finally, Miller lists a number of techniques available for safeguarding the privacy of computer-stored and processed information, such as technical and procedural methods, controls on input/output and storage, and managing the information managers. DATA BANKS, LEGAL, PRIVACY

Millikan, M. F. 1959. "Inquiry and Policy: The Relation of Knowledge to Action." In *The Human Meaning of the Social Sciences,* ed. D. Lerner. New York: Meridian Books.

Millikan sees the frequently unsatisfactory relationship between those who commission social science research (policy makers) and those who perform it (social scientists) as the result of misunderstandings on both sides. The policy makers are guilty of inductive fallacy, that is, that social problems can be solved by the collection of more facts. Against his better knowledge, the social scientist panders to his misconception, but more facts are no help if the relationship between them and the problem is unclear. Some people believe that social science research is useful only if it can predict complex social behavior in some detail, yet it is not clear whether human behavior will ever follow a purely deterministic pattern (or whether it should). Furthermore, the discipline has not yet reached the stage of developing models that are sufficiently complex to provide such predictive accuracy. For these reasons, Millikan sees social science's prime contribution to policy making as a process of making explicit previously implicit concepts and assumptions, testing their generality, and delineating their scope conditions. It can expose judgments, and the basis on which these judgments are made, to careful and systematic scrutiny. "The purpose of social science research should be to deepen, broaden, and extend the policy maker's capacity for judgment—not to provide him with answers. Thus, the test of effectiveness will lie not in whether the research leads to a new and unfamiliar conclusion but in whether it clarifies and makes explicit the logical basis for a conclusion already perceived or suspected." SOCIAL EXPERIMENTATION, SOCIAL POLICY

Moore, J. W. 1973. "Social Constraints on Sociological Knowledge: Academics and Research Concerning Minorities." *Social Problems* 21:65–77.

Moore says that sociology is epistemologically burdened with feelings of omniscience and neutrality. She is highly critical of much of the research done on minorities because of this stance, which she says should be replaced by true minority participation. COLLECTIVE CONCERN

Motulsky, A. G. 1974. "Brave New World." *Science* 185:653–63.

Most ethical systems are not phrased in absolutes; most of us are philosophic utilitarians. Motulsky points out that the greatest good for the greatest number is achieved by consensus, not edict, and thus calls for open discussion of ethical dilemmas and controversies as the preferable procedure. ETHICAL-GENERAL

National Academy of Sciences. 1975. *Experiments and Research with Humans: Values in Conflict.* Academy Forum, Third of a Series.

This National Academy of Sciences Forum was convened to discuss some of the problems associated with biomedical and behavioral research. The general theme of "risk-benefit" guided the specific discussions of the two-day meeting. Implicit throughout the forum's discussions was the recognition of an increasing demand for the right to know why, where, and how participation in research will be determined.

Some of the particularly complex and controversial problems associated with fetal and child research were discussed in depth. Participants recognized the need to devise intelligent controls for such research and establish procedures for its use. They also discussed the problems associated with research on special groups (such as prisoners, military personnel, and the poor) who, because of their unique situations, cannot usually give independent informed consent. BIOMEDICAL RESEARCH, INFORMED CONSENT, RISK-BENEFIT

National Urban Coalition. 1976. "Final Summary Report and Recommendations of The National Minority Conference on Human Experimentation," and Conference Papers on Selected Topics.

The National Urban Coalition was awarded a federal contract to conduct a conference on minority-group attitudes, perception, and views on human experimentation. In addition to identifying the special concerns of minorities in this area, it was to submit the results to the National Commission for the Protection of Human Subjects of Biomedical and Behavioral Research, in order to enable the commission to make recommendations on the problems and concerns of minorities. This report includes the conference summary report on the issues and concerns of the meetings, as well as the recommendations from the workshops, which discussed those areas of concern to the participants: psychosurgery, children, prisons, and health care.

Conference participants presented a series of papers on the ethical issues involved in social and behavioral research. The variety of topics addressed include the following papers: James S. Jackson, "Ethical and Human Use of Human Subjects: Issues in the Psychological Testing of Minorities"; Mary S. Harper, "Ethical Issues on Mental Health Research from a Minority Perspective"; John J. Cardwell, "Social Conscience and Social Experimentation: From a Minority Perspective"; and William A. Darity, "Ethics in Human Experimentation in Health Care Delivery." BIOMEDICAL RESEARCH, ETHICAL-GENERAL, INFORMED CONSENT, PSYCHOLOGICAL EXPERIMENTATION

Nedzi, L. 1971. "Public Opinion Polls: Will Legislation Help?" *Public Opinion Quarterly* 35:336–41.

Because of his concern about the possible negative effects of polls, hoping at the same time to enhance, not decrease, the reputation of pollsters, Congressman Nedzi calls for serious congressional investigation of polls. He maintains that certain minimal disclosure is vital of such background information as the size of the sample and locations drawn, methods used to contact respondents, and name of analyst. In addition, he would like Congress to address itself to the following questions: are public opinion polls trustworthy, do they guide opinion as well as measure it, is disclosure of results desirable, can "leaked" polls be regulated, do adverse polls lead to "bandwagon" effects, is legislation desirable, is policy made on the basis of polls? LEGISLATION AND REGULATION, SURVEYS

Nejelski, P., and K. Finsterbusch. 1973. "The Prosecutor and the Researcher: Present and Prospective Variations on the Supreme Court's *Branzburg* Decision." *Social Problems* 21:3–21.

The continuing development of the social sciences must be predicated on assured confidentiality of data. However, in the Branzburg case and others, the Supreme Court majority opinion ruled that newsmen must answer "relevant and material" questions asked in "good faith." One minority opinion (Stewart et al.) wished to emphasize that the material sought is crucial and that there is no other way of obtaining it, while another (Douglas) wished to grant absolute immunity to journalists.

Nejelski and Finsterbusch detect two current legal trends: preventing "inflexible determination," and a great reluctance to create testimonial privilege, because of the Court's attempts to balance conflicting interests and to make it easier for the legal process to arrive at the truth. After pointing out that the majority opinion is in favor of legislation and prosecutorial guidelines, the authors call for social science lobbying to establish privileges for researchers and propose the following action agenda: Research administrators should develop defensive record-keeping techniques; ethical codes should be established; documentation should be prepared proving the value of research and the importance and nature of confidentiality; a clearinghouse should be set up in which some professional organization assumes leadership with respect to the confidentiality issue; the social science community should provide models for prosecutorial guidelines, statutes, and research agreements; and direct action should be taken by means of publicity, lobbying, litigation, and boycott. CONFIDENTIALITY, LEGAL, LEGISLATION AND REGULATION, PROFESSIONALISM

————, and L. M. Lerman. 1971. "A Researcher-Subject Testimonial Privilege: What to do Before the Subpoena Arrives." *Wisconsin Law Review*, pp. 1085–1148.

Focusing particularly on the criminal-justice researcher, the authors explore the question of when a researcher should be required to divulge confidential information about a research subject or respondent. They point out that a subpoena can be issued for either a civil or criminal case, can require testimony by the individual or the production of records, and can be issued at any stage of the litigation process. Legislative and administrative agencies possess subpoena powers similar to the courts.' Subpoena risk is a focal issue because social research would be severely hampered if respondents could not be reasonably secure that the information they transmit is to be kept confidential.

Three main forms of maintaining data confidentiality by researchers are identified: professional codes of ethics, project guidelines, and protective administrative techniques.

The authors believe that prosecutorial activities would be little hindered if researchers could not be used as information sources. Indeed, many prosecutors recognize the importance of the knowledge gained if respondents can be assured of the confidentiality of their responses and have deliberately refrained from seeking information from researchers. The interests of a variety of parties bear on the testimonial privilege: subject, researcher, sponsor, facilitator, state, and society. Society's interest is the most important but it is also the most difficult to identify and assess.

The authors emphasize the need for the researcher-subject relationship to be protected by recognition—not creation, since a constitutional base exists—of testimonial privilege. "The researcher-subject relationship finds a second basis for overlap." This means that if socially justifiable, traditional forms of privileged communication can be extended through the doctrine of functional overlap.

The authors acknowledge that privileges are increasingly avoided, but they argue that if the constitutional underpinnings of researcher-subject are recognized with reference to freedom of expression, right of privacy, and rights of criminal defendants, the claim that privilege interferes with the judicial process loses much of its force. CONFIDENTIALITY, LEGAL

Nelson, S. H., and H. Grunebaum. 1972. "Ethical Issues in Psychiatric Follow-up Studies." *American Journal of Psychiatry* 128:1358–62.

*Abstract:* "Conducting a follow-up study of 23 wrist-slashers presented an ethical conflict between consideration of the patients' human and medical rights and the investigators' desire for knowledge to improve treatment. The authors feel that many difficulties now encountered in behavioral research can be avoided by improved confidentiality of hospital records, acquisition of patients' consent regarding possible follow-up contact, and well-planned studies in which ethical problems are more fully anticipated beforehand." CONFIDENTIALITY, INFORMED CONSENT

Nettler, G. 1968. "Using our Heads." *American Sociologist* 3:200–07.

Nettler comments on the tension between knowing and doing among sociologists and uses attribution theory to demonstrate that thought and opinion depend on such factors as motive and metaphysics; he suggests that experts are not more knowledgeable than anyone else once outside their narrow framework of expertise. PROFESSIONALISM

Newberry, B. H. 1973. "Truth Telling in Subjects with Information about Experiments: Who is Being Deceived?" *Journal of Personality and Social Psychology* 25:369–74.

*Abstract:* "Two experiments were run in which subjects received information about the experiment from a confederate and were later asked by the experimenter if they had prior information about the experiment. The proportion of subjects who lied about prior information varied from approximately .8 to .3 in various conditions. In both experiments, subjects with information used it to improve task performance. Admission of information on a questionnaire item was more frequent if the item allowed high response latitude; however, verbal questioning produced lower admission rates than did a simple question-naire. Legitimation of the information by the experimenter did not raise admission rates significantly."

In attempting to explain these findings, the author suggests that many subjects wish to remain "hassle-free" and will deny having prior information in order to avoid potential embarrassment. DECEPTION, PSYCHOLOGICAL EXPERIMENTATION

Nikelly, A. G. 1971. "Ethical Issues in Research on Student Protest." *American Psychologist* 26:475–78.

Much has been written about student protest in higher education. The literature reveals two primary themes: that the student is malad-justed, or that society is at fault. All too often the underlying assump-tion in research on student protestors is that the students are maladjusted, while other relevant institutional and societal factors are ignored. The investigator's prejudices, convictions, and values influence the results more than the mechanics and logistics of research. Further-more, impressionistic and clinical descriptions of students are fre-quently based on limited numbers of select and unrepresentative students. Research done in such a fashion often produces unethical and questionable results, results which can be invalid, erroneous, and irrele-vant. Also, research on students is faulted in that the student has no access to results and therefore has no "voice regarding their use or effects on him." COLLECTIVE CONCERN

Nobel, J. H., Jr. 1974. "Peer Review: Quality Control of Applied Social Science." *Science* 185:916–21.

Nobel discusses the shift of federal agency support from outside-initiated basic research to agency-directed applied studies for the theo-retical reason of using the findings of the latter research programs to choose among alternative courses of action. Policy-oriented research, according to Nobel, is characterized by the search for cause-and-effect relationships. Within the framework of quality control, he points out that the internal validity of such research can be threatened by a num-ber of factors, such as intervening historical events, regression artifacts because of the selection of atypical cases, and a differential loss of respondents from comparison groups. The external validity of the re-search, the generalizability of the results, can likewise be threatened by a number of factors, including the interactive effects of testing or treatment, reactive effects of atypical or artificial treatment conditions, confounding of results because of multiple treatments, or responsive-ness to irrelevant components of measures. SOCIAL EXPERIMEN-TATION, SOCIAL POLICY

Orlans, H. 1973. *Contracting for Knowledge.* London: Jossey-Bass.

    The raison d'etre of this book is to make a rational and comprehensive assessment of the worth of applied social science research, an enterprise for which Orlans draws heavily on the work he did in preparation for hearings by the Research and Technical Programs Subcommittee of the Committee on Government Operations (the Reuss hearings, which were never actually held).

    The book is divided into four parts: the professional community and its political and ethical concerns (Orlans points out that only the APA has shown concern both with protecting the rights of research subjects and enforcement procedures); knowledge for hire; location and control of sponsored research; and the uses of social knowledge. PROFESSIONALISM, SOCIAL EXPERIMENTATION, SOCIAL POLICY

————. 1971. "The Political Uses of Social Research." *The Annals* 394: 28–35.

    *Abstract:* "As scientific disciplines, the social sciences are more limited, and hence less useful to government, than either the social science 'establishment' or its radical critics contend. However, as a rationale for political action or inaction, and as a mode of political discourse, they have many demonstrable uses. The social sciences are not 'value free' but a social enterprise of some complexity. At the same time, the federal government is not a conspiracy but a collection of subsystems loosely brought into coherence through the combined policy functions of the President and the Congress. At one level of government, social scientists contribute an orderly collection of facts and information. At another, they contribute to the interpretation of information. But in this interpretive role, their performance cannot be understood in apolitical terms; several kinds of politics influence their behavior: personal, professional, tactical, and party." SOCIAL POLICY

————. 1967. "Ethical Problems in the Relation of Research and Investigators." In *Ethics, Politics, and Social Research,* ed. G. Sjoberg, pp. 3–24. Cambridge, Mass.: Schenkman.

    Orlans argues that only the naive believe that those with viewpoints different from their own are immoral or unethical, and hence "if you disagree with the objectives of an agency, don't decry the morality of its staff but try to change their objective and, in the interim, don't take their money." In his experience most ethical issues arise not in conjunction with the relationship between investigator and sponsor but rather in the relationship with subjects or informants; for instance, is the full disclosure of the purposes of a study practicable or compatible with its purpose? ETHICAL-GENERAL

Panel on Privacy and Behavioral Research, Kenneth E. Clark, Chairman, President's Office of Science and Technology. 1967. "Privacy and Behavioral Research." *Science* 155:535–38.

Concern over threats to the privacy of individuals posed by certain procedures of behavioral research led to the appointment of a panel to investigate the conflicts. The panel restricted its attention to those issues of privacy which arise in the course of behavioral research studies. Although the specific methodology they employed is not detailed, they mention that they reviewed relevant research, examined the attitudes of various segments of the population, and tapped the scientific community's views via professional organizations. The report contains five recommendations based on the panel's findings that behavioral science risks invasion of privacy only on a small scale and that the root of the problem is the conflict between individual civil liberties and the right to know.

Briefly, the panel's suggestions are to devote more attention to the ethics of research; for the federal government to uphold the highest standards for the guidance of all; for primary responsibility to rest with the individual investigator, although the government must be satisfied that the investigator's employing institution is willing to support the activity; to have ethical decisions made by a group, so as to mitigate the investigator's vested interests; and to allow institutions to determine their own ethical review procedures. FREEDOM OF INQUIRY, INSTITUTIONAL REVIEW BOARDS, LEGISLATION AND REGULATION, PRIVACY

Park, L. C., L. Covi, and E. H. Uhlenhuth. 1967. "Effects of Informed Consent on Research Patients and Study Results." *Journal of Nervous and Mental Diseases* 145:349–57.

This study shows that patients, informed of the key conditions of research, manifested positive and beneficial effects; that investigators' guilt was alleviated and doctor-patient relationships were made more comfortable. The authors conclude that informed consent does not appear to limit studies and can be an asset in research design. BIOMEDICAL RESEARCH, INFORMED CONSENT

Parsons, T. 1969. "Research with Human Subjects and the 'Professional Complex.'" *Daedalus* 98:325–60.

In this article Parsons weaves together the three professional functions of research, practice, and teaching; the two focal points concerning research with human subjects of informed consent and the protection of privacy; and a viewpoint of ethics as essentially a matter of social responsibility. He inquires into the legitimation basis of the professional complex and its functions and points out that the university, a network of relationships hallmarked by "collegial" authority, stands at the center of this complex. Both clients and subjects enter into a solidary relation with the professional. In opposition to the usual market relationship where payment is for specific benefits received, this relationship is more akin to marriage in which it is not the *guid pro quo* but the "for better or for worse" principle which operates. Members of solidary groups are committed to help one another and failure does not absolve one from payment. Because of the "competence gap" which makes it impossible for lay persons to judge what the professional does, the client or subject must trust the professional and must believe that the professional operates within the same framework of goals and values as he does. Parsons acknowledges the persistent ambivalence marking the public's attitudes toward professional groups and explains this as a consequence of the time it takes for the worth of the professional function to mature. He touches on some of the difficulties surrounding the use of informed consent, such as offering full information and the impossibility of an exact calculation of risk, and instead would emphasize the mutual obligations of researcher and subject and their receipt of similar rewards, namely awareness of having made a contribution to the advancement of knowledge. INFORMED CONSENT, PRIVACY, PROFESSIONALISM

———. 1968. "Professions." *International Encyclopedia of the Social Sciences* 12:536–47. New York: Macmillan and The Free Press.

Parsons, in tracing the history of professionalization, sees a gradual differentiation of two spheres of development: "the institutionalization of the intellectual disciplines in the societal structure and the practical application of these disciplines," both associated with development and changes in the immunity system. The applied professions, developing within the framework of law and medicine, have answered an increasingly if not dominant significant role in the economic and political activities of modern society, despite the recency of their development. LEGAL, PRIVACY, PROFESSIONALISM

Petersen, N. 1972. "Forbidden Knowledge." In *The Social Contexts of Research*, ed. S. Z. Nagi and R. G. Corwin, pp. 289–322. New York: John Wiley.

In the spring of 1969, Petersen approached relevant professional associations and the administrators at major U.S. universities to inquire into their use and discussion of ethical principles governing research. He found that most believe some limitation ought to be placed on the gathering of new knowledge. He discusses the historical growth of this viewpoint with reference to the U.S. Public Health Service Policy, the Special Committee on Privacy and Behavioral Research assembled under the president's authority which published its report in 1967, and the general attack on the Census Bureau during 1967 and 1968. In addition, he describes the general antiscience attitude which rests on the recognition of the relationship between technological advances, based on the growth of scientific knowledge, and the depletion of natural resources and pollution; the health-field improvements which have kept large numbers alive but suffering; and the fact that the ability to manipulate the environment is no guarantee that the environment will be manipulated for the good of all. Academic freedom is not an absolute right, but rather an institutional norm which, like others, should be weighed to find the ratio most conducive to promoting social welfare. Petersen concludes that "the solution to problems, whatever they are, can only be by the application of informed intelligence. If, because of new political commitments, we set new priorities, that is what politics has always meant. If, however, commitment replaces knowledge, confrontation replaces analysis, and ideology replaces science, then no problem can be solved." FREEDOM OF INQUIRY, LEGISLATION AND REGULATION PROFESSIONALISM, RISK-BENEFIT

Prosser, W. L. 1960. "Privacy." *California Law Review* 48:383–423.
    Prosser, noted legal authority on torts, summarizes the history and the contemporary status in U.S. Law of the "right to privacy" as a legal concept. Beginning with the Brandeis-Warren article of 1890 which dealt with personal annoyance from the press, Prosser reviews the important court decisions, state legislation, and legal literature which have led to the concept's wide acceptance by U.S. courts. He analyzes, on the basis of 300 "right to privacy" cases, the interests involved to the aggrieved and the conduct to be defended against which comprise the "right to privacy," from the point of view of torts theory. Prosser finds "four distinct and only loosely related torts": intrusion, public disclosure of private facts, false light in the public eye, and appropriation of name or likeness for gain. Prosser is concerned that the "right to privacy," as a legal concept, has remained too vague over the 70 years since it was coined as a phrase in a specific context and may be of dubious value to society when its vagueness tends to erode the protection of individual rights already afforded by older, more tested tort theories. His analysis is designed to make lawyers think about the actual offenses and defenses involved when they raise the question of the "right to privacy." LEGAL, PRIVACY

Purcell, K., and K. Brady. 1966. "Adaption to the Invasion of Privacy: Monitoring Behavior with a Miniature Radio Transmitter." *Merrill-Palmer Quarterly* 12:242–54.
    Thirteen young adolescents were fitted with miniature radio transmitters and monitored one hour a day for ten days. After two or four

days the subjects appeared to behave naturally and without regard to the monitoring of their verbal interaction. Normality of behavior was measured by a marked decrease over time in taped references to the research context, the subjective reports of the participants, observations by adult observers, analysis of the amount of talking and interpersonal behavior, and spontaneity and freedom of language and interaction. PRIVACY

Rainwater, L., and D. J. Pittman. 1967. "Ethical Problems in Studying a Politically Sensitive and Deviant Community." *Social Problems* 14:357–65.

   The Pruitt-lgoe Housing Projects were the setting for a research project designed to analyze the pathologies found in urban public housing and to suggest remedies. In the course of the investigation the researchers became deeply involved with the subjects and were confronted with an array of ethical dilemmas. The question of to whom they should be accountable arose early; they decided that since they were conducting a basic social science study, the "client" was the public in general, and the findings could not be prematurely released to anyone in particular but should be equally available to all. Since social science findings can be used to the detriment of subjects in this kind of study with respect to "class-risk," they were concerned about secondary interpretations of the data. Finally, they were forced to confront the issue of confidentiality with respect to the Housing Authority management. This was resolved by the decision not to promise confidentiality to these officials on the principle that sociologists have the right to study and release information about publicly accountable behavior in order to increase knowledge of social systems. COLLECTIVE CONCERN, CONFIDENTIALITY, FREEDOM OF INQUIRY, SOCIAL CONTROL

Record, J. C. 1967. "The Research Institute and the Pressure Group." In *Politics, Ethics and Social Research,* ed. G. Sjoberg, pp. 25–49. Cambridge, Mass.: Schenkman.

   Special interest groups influence the quality of inquiry undertaken by research institutes. This is not usually the case when research is done by an individual, since individuals are not as vulnerable to the dictates of pressure groups as are organizations. Serious ethical questions are raised when a reputable research institute comes into conflict with the inherent needs of a special interest group to avoid objective scholarly inquiry. The very nature of an institute operating in the competitive sphere of a large commercial and political community creates vulnerability: large-scale research requires money, both public and private, most of which is politically sensitive; information sources can be special interest groups; institutes have interest in survival, so they are willing to look for conciliation; responsibility in an organization is unclear; researchers are becoming increasingly sophisticated and therefore demand more of what they perceive and want. Ethical codes have usually dealt more with client-relationship matters than with pressure-group relationships. The 1964 ASA code addressed the issue inadequately when it omitted any statement concerning unethical tampering with findings in response to political pressures. But the question is difficult, and the only hope may lie in morally courageous individuals. "The implicit question becomes whether research can be restructured to reposit final responsibility for the shape and quality of the product in the individual, in an academic environment supportive of integrity." CODES OF ETHICS, COLLECTIVE CONCERN, FREEDOM OF INQUIRY

Reiss, A. J., Jr. 1976(a). "Selected Issues in Informed Consent and Confidentiality With Special Reference to Behavioral/Social Science Research/Inquiry." Yale University. Prepared for the National Commission for the Protection of Human Subjects of Biomedical and Behavioral Research.

Reiss discusses the problems involved in regulating behavioral science inquiry. In the course of such research, conflicts arise between the rights to privacy and the public rights and claims to information. One means of regulating such inquiry is to require informed consent. This in turn raises questions of confidentiality of information and its protection.

In discussing informed consent, Reiss examines such concerns as the problems involved in obtaining it, the methods of obtaining and documenting it, the problem of forecasting what risk/benefits might occur in the course of the research. Also addressed are the advisability of feedback on the procedures of the research as a means of increasing participant satisfaction, and the rights of investigators to information secured on a promise of confidentiality. Situations are discussed in which confidentiality is deemed essential to the research.

Reiss looks at the possibilities for regulating behavioral science inquiry. He notes that "legal regulation carries with it its own consequences that must be investigated by behavioral science inquiry if regulation is to be both enlightened and in keeping with constitutional imperatives." CONFIDENTIALITY, INFORMED CONSENT, LEGISLATION & REGULATION, PRIVACY

————. 1976(b). "Systematic Observation Surveys of Natural Social Phenomena." In *Perspectives on Attitudes Assessment: Surveys and Their Alter-*

*natives,* ed. H. W. Sinaiko and L. H. Broedling, pp. 123–41. Champaign, Ill.: Pendleton Publications.

Reiss compares observation to interview and questionnaire surveys and finds the first superior because of its greater reliability; greater precision, especially with respect to time in the ordering of events; "greater opportunity to reconstruct multiple occurrences within their natural settings and economy in doing so"; and greater accuracy in deriving measures of central tendency. Typical phenomena which can be fruitfully studied by means of systematic observation include interactive processes, the relationship between attitudes and behavior, nonverbal phenomena, language behavior, mass or crowd behavior, and ecological settings. While on the whole there may be less reaction to observations surveys, especially when subjects are unaware of being observed, reactive measurement effects can be caused by the unobserved environment (which may cause more "noise" than for interviews and questionnaires) and by observers. In addition, there are sampling errors.

Reiss notes that systematic observation studies may have difficulties in obtaining access to target populations because of institutional or organizational restrictions. Informed consent requirements may be particularly difficult. Difficulties can also arise if the observation infringes on current conceptions of privacy. This latter would be partially solved if "liability for improper disclosure is coupled with immunity to disclosure." INFORMED CONSENT, OBSERVATION, PRIVACY, SURVEYS

————. 1973. "Social Control of Sociological Knowing." Paper presented at the American Sociological Association Annual Meeting, New York. (Author's permission required for citation.)

This is an extensive and detailed treatment of the problem of protecting human subjects and the limits placed on gaining sociological knowledge. Reiss indicates the difficulty connected with strict adherence to ethical principles as one of distorting social reality. He discusses the major forms of controlling research and some of the difficulties associated with each one. For instance, professional, collegial, and peer relations as a means of applying restrictions to research neglect the rights of corporate bodies; there is some evidence that established sociologists are less liable to censure than others, and there is the possibility that unconventional research would be severely hampered; sponsor-regulation, on the other hand, may lead to the political control of free inquiry. In addition, Reiss indicates some neglected issues in connection with the problem of sociological inquiry. He draws our attention to two distinctively sociological problems: establishing the commensurability of values and examining the effectiveness of regulatory systems. COLLECTIVE CONCERN, LEGISLATION AND REGULA-TION, PROFESSIONALISM, SOCIAL CONTROL

Report of a Working Party. [n.d.] *Survey Research and Privacy*. London: Social and Community Planning Research.

Although modern complex societies need objective information on which to base policy decisions, open societies need to know only a few things about individuals. Since the major emphasis is on seeking answers to such questions as how many, or in what proportion, not on who, attention is given to gaining a wide range of knowledge about the collective characteristics of the population or its subgroupings, not on individuals. Survey research is particularly suited to collecting such information because it is interested in aggregate data, not individual identities. PRIVACY, SOCIAL POLICY, SURVEYS

Resnick, J. H., and T. Schwarz. 1973. "Ethical Standards as an Independent Variable in Psychological Research." *American Psychologist* 28:134–39.

This study reports the conclusion that experimental results can be vitiated when the subjects are provided, in line with new ethical standards, with full knowledge of the experimenter's interest in positive condition. The authors add that it was difficult to find volunteers for the experiment because of subject boredom and disinterest, and that many did not believe the experimental conditions had been fully disclosed. INFORMED CONSENT, PSYCHOLOGICAL EXPERI-MENTATION

Reynolds, P. D. 1976. "The Protection of Human Subjects." An open letter to NIH. *American Sociologist* 9:221–24.

Reynolds lists eight considerations pertaining to the protection of human subjects: the need to maintain scientific productivity; the innocuous nature of most research: the need to minimize disruption of innovation; the need to minimize the demand for formalization of tentative scientific ideas; the need to care for and compensate those few participants damaged by research; recognizing the importance of informed consent; the need to assist and support those investigators cooperating with the procedure; and the need to incorporate trained professionals in reviewing "risky" projects in order to maximize protection for subjects. In addition, he lists six characteristics of an ideal procedure, voices the suspicion that the HEW policy is designed primarily to benefit federal administrators, and describes an alternate procedure used at the University of Minnesota which more closely approximates the ideal. INFORMED CONSENT, LEGISLATION AND REGULATION, PROFESSIONALISM, RISK-BENEFIT

————. 1975. "Value Dilemmas Associated with the Development and Application of Social Science." Report submitted to the International Social Science Council. Paris: UNESCO.

Reynolds, who uses the term "value dilemmas" in preference to "ethics" because of the latter's absolutist overtones and tendency to divide the world into ethical and unethical, identifies two major value dilemmas related to the use of humans in research: the development of scientific knowledge and the degree to which this knowledge is used to benefit mankind. Three elements of the research process are particularly salient to these value dilemmas: that experimental designs provide the best information on causal relationships; that large numbers of people often need to be involved; and that frequently "normal" subjects are needed to establish baseline data. The principle of informed consent is best able to resolve some of these difficult value dilemmas since it enables individuals themselves to decide whether or not they will participate in research; its use, however, assumes that people can give consent if properly informed and that it will not interfere with the ability to draw causal inferences from the data. Reynolds points out that research is always an investigation of the unknown, that the free-will versus determinism controversy remains unresolved, and that humans are reactive agents. Furthermore, he says certain types of research, for example, observational studies or when the focus of research is a collectivity, make obtaining informed consent impracticable. Reynolds goes into considerable detail discussing the problems of measuring the types, extent, and frequency of both negative and positive research effects on individuals and social systems. Negative effects include loss of resources, deception, invasion of privacy, temporary physical or mental distress, and permanent changes in individual attributes. Positive effects can include direct improvement in physical, psychological, or other characteristics of individuals, increase in material goods or services, the sense of "moral goodness" resulting from participation in research, educational benefits, the pleasures associated with novel experiences, and sharing the advantages which may result from research.

In the second major section of the report, on the stated assumption that knowledge can be developed independent of theory and ideology, Reynolds investigates three dilemmas relating to the development of knowledge and its use to benefit mankind: the failure to realize benefits, the attribution of responsibility for such failure, and the ability of scientists to control the application of the knowledge they generate. INFORMED CONSENT, RISK-BENEFIT, SOCIAL EXPERIMENTATION, STRESS

————. 1972. "On the Protection of Human Subjects and Social Science." *International Social Science Journal* 24:693–719.

The major points of this article are as follows: "Damage" to participants in social science research is infrequent; in fact, there is no objective evidence that it occurs at all. As social science becomes more powerful, some research questions may necessitate the taking of "risks" by subjects in order to advance knowledge, much as in medical science. Social scientists cannot expect to develop a potent body of knowledge and at the same time conduct "harmless" research. Any procedure designed to protect human subjects, which at the same time destroys the potential for creating scientific knowledge about social and human phenomena, is patently self-defeating. A major commitment to both the protection of human subjects and the creation of science would suggest that substantial resources be committed to a procedure that attempts to achieve a reasonable balance, for instance, the "approved research protocol-licensed investigator" procedure. Finally, Reynolds warns that if social scientists do not control the conduct of social science research themselves, society will. LEGISLATION AND REGULATION, PROFESSIONALISM, RISK-BENEFIT, STRESS

Riecken, H. W. 1975. "Social Experimentation." *Society* 12:34–41.

Riecken discusses the relative weakness (compared to research) of the development component of research and development in the social sciences, and he points out that "most social inventions (or interventions) are neither systematically developed nor tested in advance of installation." He discusses the many weaknesses of conventional program evaluation and makes a cogent argument in favor of replacing after-the-fact program evaluation by systematic social experimentation or "a cycle of program development, experimental test and modification (or abandonment) based on the outcomes of the experiment." If innovative social intervention is to exist, then deliberately designed variations in treatment, providing a basis for comparisons, must be designed into programs. Riecken perceives this approach as a more humane and efficient method for formulating social policy and developing social programs than simply implementing untested ideas which our history of unsuccessful attempts at and negative results of social reform shows can be unethical and irresponsible. He goes on to discuss the costs, methods, difficulties, and chances of success of social experiments. Because many people are affected by programs resulting from social experiments, such experiments should be open to informed scrutiny. Safeguards should be taken to protect the privacy of respondents or subjects and the confidentiality of the provided information. User services should be established to control the release of information; data repositories should be part of the organizational plan of any social experiment; and there should be review of the quality of analysis of social experiments at or before public release. COLLECTIVE CONCERN, CONFIDENTIALITY, SOCIAL EXPERIMENTATION, SOCIAL POLICY

―――. 1971. "The Federal Government and Social Policy." *The Annals* 394:100–13.

Riecken points out that as far as seeking financial support is concerned, the social sciences have found it beneficial to be allied with the physical sciences. That has meant a focus on quantitative empirical research on politically noncontroversial topics. SOCIAL EXPERIMENTATION, SOCIAL POLICY

―――. [n.d.] "Human Values and Social Experiments." Mimeograph. (Not for circulation or reproduction.)

Riecken points out that it is easier to study the potentially adverse effects of a program subjected to experimental tests than of a program (for instance, Pruitt-Igoe) which goes into effect by administrative action or law. He goes on to discuss the ethical quandaries of control groups failing to receive benefits and those experimental conditions which provide temporary boons to the participants, and the mechanical and legal techniques available for protecting subjects' privacy. PRIVACY, SOCIAL EXPERIMENTATION, SOCIAL POLICY

―――. and R. F. Boruch, eds. 1974. *Social Experimentation: A Method for Planning and Evaluating Social Intervention.* New York: Academic Press.

*Abstract:* "This volume is based on the work of a Social Science Research Council Committee that included Donald Campbell, Nathan Caplan, Thomas Glennan, John Pratt, Albert Reiss, Jr., and Walter Williams, as well as the editors. The committee reviewed the current state of the art of social experimentation as an approach to social program development and evaluation.

"The monograph provides a general orientation to social experimentation for the reader who is interested in the advantages, limitations, and practical possibilities of the method; but it also delves into the major scientific and technical issues of design and measurement. The management of experiments in the field is discussed from a practical point of view; and the decision to experiment as well as the utilization of experimental results in program planning are considered from a political and administrative perspective. The book features numerous illustrative examples drawn from planning and evaluation studies in economics, health rehabilitation, criminal justice, compensatory education, and manpower training. Most important, it is specifically designed for those actively engaged in conducting and managing social intervention programs. It includes a useful annotated bibliography on field experiments."

The last chapter in the book is devoted to examining the topic of "human values and social experimentation," especially the ethics of experimentation and the problem of confidentiality. Social research is especially prone to two major types of ethical problems: unanticipated consequences, for example, the Pruitt-Igoe case, and manipulation. A cardinal point necessary to establish before embarking on a program of research is that the benefits outweigh the risks; this assessment should be made during a process of open debate and discussion. The authors point out that institutional review committees offer substantial but not absolute protection against research risk for subjects. Such committees should include members from outside the research-conducting institution and community representatives when community experiments are being contemplated.

More specific problems, such as the failure to provide benefits for untreated groups (the suggested remedy is to give the controls some treatment condition, too, in order to render the experiments more ethically desirable and also to mitigate such factors as the Hawthorne effect) and "temporary boons," are also considered. With respect to the latter, subjects should be clearly informed and left to decide alone whether or not to participate.

The authors point out that there is widespread adherence to the principle that human experimentation be conducted only under conditions of informed consent but that a controversy exists as to the term's precise meaning. They do not believe it is necessary that controls need to know they are controls, but, if it is decided that such knowledge is necessary, subjects should be told beforehand that they might fall in one of at least two experimental conditions.

Techniques to protect privacy can be mechanical or legal. Legal correctives can involve testimonial privilege or can consist of penalties for unauthorized disclosure. Social science data should be protected by law against disclosure; for instance, a researcher-subject privilege to focus especially on the data. In order to protect confidentiality, access to data must be regulated in some way. A number of techniques are mentioned, for instance, deletion of identifiers, crude report categories for data with public variables, microaggregation, error inoculation, capacity to run analyses for outsiders. In the case of interlinked systems, link file brokerage can be used; direct linkage can be established with statistical safeguards, for example, microaggregation or error inoculation, and file linkages can be mutually insulated. CONFIDENTIALITY, INFORMED CONSENT, RISK-BENEFIT, SOCIAL EXPERIMENTATION

Ring, K., K. Wallston, and M. Corey. 1970. "Mode of Debriefing as a Factor Affecting Subjective Reaction to a Milgram-Type Obedience Experiment: An Ethical Inquiry." *Representative Research in Social Psychology* 1:67–88.

*Abstract:* "Fifty-seven female subjects participated in a Milgram-type obedience experiment conducted to determine the immediate and long-term effects of participation and the effectiveness of modes of debriefing in reducing the emotional tension that this kind of experiment usually generates. It was found that while many of the subjects were upset by the experiment, they regarded it as a positive experience and did not regret being in it. A debriefing which provided a subject with justification for her behavior lowered tension more than one which did not. A follow-up interview of 20 subjects two to five weeks after the experiment failed to disclose any serious negative effects. The results were taken as supporting Milgram's conclusions concerning the effects of participating in obedience experiments."

It is perhaps noteworthy that, although glossed over in the abstract, according to Table 2 in the article, 15 percent of the subjects in the follow-up interview said they regretted taking part in the experiment. DECEPTION, PSYCHOLOGICAL EXPERIMENTATION, STRESS

Rippey, R. M. 1970. "The Researcher in the Community." *School Review* 79:133–40.

The research process of a "federally funded effort to improve education in a small area of Chicago" revealed that the local community can be involved successfully in the process. The development of the research and evaluation component is described. The experiences of the participants in this process suggest that researcher-community relations can remain satisfactory if methods such as the following are used: solicit the opinions and ideas of the community; offer something of yourself to the community; and be prepared to cope with the disappointments and setbacks which will occur in the collection of data. COLLECTIVE CONCERN

Rivlin, A. M. 1974. "Social Experiments: Their Uses and Limitations." *Monthly Labor Review* 97:28–35.

Rivlin states that the idea of social experiments caught on rapidly during the late 1960s because of the desire to rationalize decision making and the failure of traditional data-gathering methods to provide a sufficient basis for this. She distinguishes four types of experiments related to four types of policy questions: estimating the response of microunits, such as individuals and households, to a change in economic incentives; estimating market response to a change in economic incentives; estimating the production function of a public service; changing incentives in order to affect the production of a service which will influence outcomes. She discusses the problems of inference accompanying each of these types and some of the accompanying legal and ethical issues. For instance, informed consent is obtainable when dealing with microunits and since, in most cases, monetary payments have been involved, it would seem that no undue harm can occur. On the other hand, the fourth type of experiment is ethically dubious because of the chance that a major institution such as a public school would be destroyed. In general one of the biggest problems facing social experimentation is the conflict between purely scientific objectives—for example, treatement must be kept constant—and other political and policy objectives, such as the desire to profit from experience, increasing the chances of a successful outcome, and avoiding public criticism. In any case, because social experimentation is slow and costly, other alternatives such as survey research and studying the effects of naturally occurring changes should be explored wherever possible. COLLECTIVE CONCERN, INFORMED CONSENT, SOCIAL EXPERIMENTATION, SOCIAL POLICY

————, and P. M. Timpane, eds. 1975. *Ethical and Legal Issues of Social Experimentation*. Brookings Studies in Social Experimentation. Washington, D.C.: Brookings Institution.

The Brookings Panel on Social Experimentation convened a two-day conference of social scientists, government officials, and others who had devoted attention to the problems of social experimentation, including the planning and execution thereof, and the ethical and legal issues in medical and social research. This book presents the papers and critiques prepared for the conference. It includes articles by Peter G. Brown on "Informed Consent in Social Experimentation: Some Cautionary Notes"; Edward M. Gramlich and Larry L. Orr on "The Ethics of Social Experimentation"; Charles L. Schultze on "Social Experimentation and the Law." INFORMED CONSENT, LEGAL, SOCIAL EXPERIMENTATION

Romano, J. 1974. "Reflection on Informed Consent." *Archives of General Psychiatry* 30:129–35.

*Abstract:* "A current trend in clinical psychiatric research is that of high-risk approach. The ethical problems involved in studies of children at risk for schizophrenia and their parents are principally those of informed consent and of privacy and confidentiality.

"Attention is drawn to the historical evolution of systematic approaches to ethical aspects of experimentation with human subjects and the change in guide rules from the traditional informal ethical principles of medical practice, developed over centuries, toward a civilly enforced body of legal and administrative regulations which will control research projects and the use of humans in human experimentation.

"Those responsible for the establishment of systematic courses in ethics should make sure that they are fully informed about the complex decision making of the clinician in his care of the patient and in his pursuit of new knowledge in human investigation." BIOMEDICAL RESEARCH, INFORMED CONSENT, LEGISLATION AND REGULATION

Rosenthal, R., and R. L. Rosnow. 1975. *The Volunteer Subject*. New York: John Wiley.

Rosenthal and Rosnow offer a systematic review of the available evidence dealing with the nature and status of volunteering subjects. The book has chapters covering the characteristics of volunteer subjects, the situational determinants of volunteering, implications of the interpretation of research findings, including a discussion of the ethical dilemma posed by the normative prescription to have informed voluntary subjects versus the scientific edict that empirical research be as representative and generalizable as possible, empirical research on voluntarism as an artifact, and two concluding chapters, one offering an integrative overview and the other a summary.

"The ethical dilemma results from the likelihood that fully informed voluntarism, while it may satisfy the moral concern of researchers, may be contraindicated for the scientific concern in many cases; and experimenters must weigh the social ethic against the scientific ethic in deciding which violation would constitute the greater moral danger." INFORMED CONSENT, RISK-BENEFIT, VOLUNTARISM

Roth, J. A. 1969. "A Codification of Current Prejudices." *American Sociologist* 4:159.

Roth is critical of all ethical codes because while supposedly designed to protect the larger public, they actually serve to protect the profession. Furthermore, codes are useless without enforcement, yet with enforcement they become a form of scholarly censorship and a mechanism of social control. "At worst, a code of ethics is a codification of current prejudices which can be used to censor deviant ideas. At best, it is a misleading public relations document which has no effect on the development of sociology." CODES OF ETHICS, FREEDOM OF INQUIRY, PROFESSIONALISM, SOCIAL CONTROL

Rubin, Z., and J. C. Moore. 1971. "Assessment of Subjects' Suspicions." *Journal of Personality and Social Psychology* 17:163–70.
This is a report of an experiment on 142 male undergraduate students which found the two variables of self-esteem and number of psychology courses taken linked to subjects' suspicion of experimental deception. It also found a relationship between authoritarianism and subjects following the demand characteristics of the experimenter. Open-ended questionnaires tapping subjects' impressions, not recollections, are best for measuring suspiciousness. DECEPTION, PSYCHOLOGICAL EXPERIMENTATION

Ruebhausen, O. M., and O. G. Brim, Jr. 1966. "Privacy and Behavioral Research." *American Psychologist* 21:423–44.
This is a seminal article addressing the conflict between science and private personality. Recognition of the claim to private personality is relatively recent, but, although in conflict with other valued rights such as that of an informed and effective government, law enforcement, and free dissemination of information, it is nonetheless a "moral imperative" of our times. Privacy has two main facets: the right to be left alone and the right to share and communicate. "Both of these conflicting needs, in mutually supportive interaction, are essential to the well-being of individuals and institutions, and any definition of privacy, or of private personality, must reflect this plastic duality: sharing and concealment." Yet, because persons live in communities, the right to privacy can never be absolute—often it must be set aside to satisfy the community's needs. On the other hand, the growth of science, the technological advances which have given rise to sophisticated surveillance techniques, and the increase in governmental power and control make it necessary to devise some set of rules against unwanted intrusion. According to the authors, the two central concerns are the degree of individual consent and the degree of confidentiality. They point out some of the difficulties surrounding the use of informed consent such as biased sampling, distorted results, and the fact that it is often impossible to describe all aspects of the research beforehand. Similarly they discuss the subpoena risk with respect to keeping data confidential. It is for these reasons that since the community insists on a decent accommodation between the values of privacy and those of behavioral research, the following principles should be incorporated into a general code of ethics: recognition and affirmation of the claim to private personality; positive commitment to respect it in research; obtaining informed and voluntary consent to the fullest extent possible; if impossible because of the subsequent invalida-

tion of research results, responsible officials should judge whether the benefits outweigh the costs; anonymity of respondents should be guaranteed as far as possible; research data should be kept confidential, and research data obtained for one purpose should not be used for another purpose without the respondent's consent, and if that is not obtainable, they should not be used unless the benefits outweigh the potential costs. CONFIDENTIALITY, INFORMED CONSENT, PRIVACY, SOCIAL CONTROL

Rule, J. B. 1974. *Private Lives and Public Surveillance*. New York: Schocken Books.

The theme of this work is "the use, by powerful agencies, of personal data on private individuals in order to control their behavior." It rests on an empirical investigation of five mass-surveillance systems, three in Britain—police surveillance, vehicle and driver licensing, and national insurance—and two in the United States—consumer credit reporting and the BankAmericard system.

Rule examines the link between mass-surveillance systems as a means of social control and changes in modern social structure and identifies a key variable as that of scale, that is, "the extent of interdependence among people in different social units." He is critical of those authors, Westin for instance, who in his opinion have let their fears of mas-surveillance techniques override cool analysis in favor of somewhat unwarranted speculation. Nonetheless, after a careful examination of the internal dynamics of surveillance systems and the role of such systems within the social structure, he concludes in the last chapter, "The Future of Surveillance," that "these practices are sufficiently undesirable in themselves and uncertain in their potential consequences that we would do well to curtail them wherever possible." PRIVACY, SOCIAL CONTROL

Rutstein, D. R. 1969. "The Ethical Design of Human Experiments." *Daedalus* 98:523–41.

Rutstein makes a number of suggestions in connection with the ethical design of experiments using human subjects. Since scientifically unsound experiments are unethical, each research design should be reviewed by at least a (bio)statistician and an expert on ethics; the second line of defense in this connection should be provided by the journals. Second, since research design depends on the investigator's questions, it should be recognized that some questions are ipso facto unethical. Finally, mathematical theory may play a role in solving puzzles which cannot ethically be solved through experimentation. ETHICAL-GENERAL

Sagrin, E. 1973. "The Research Setting and the Right Not To Be Researched." *Social Problems* 21:52–64.

 While agreeing with Rainwater and Pittman (1967) that no public organization has the right to exclude investigators and that every individual is open to scrutiny with respect to those activities for which he or she is publicly accountable, Sagrin insists, using a conflict-based model of society, that every group, unless publicly accountable, has the right to refuse to be researched. In such cases, more indirect methods can be used, for example, documents, public statements, autobiographical accounts, journalistic reports, court proceedings, and so forth. COLLECTIVE CONCERN, PRIVACY

Sanford, N. 1965. "Social Science and Social Reform." *Journal of Social Issues* 21:54–70.

 Sanford's main thesis is that social science cannot be value-free, that it is not possible to make a clear distinction between means and ends, and that social science and social reform thus are closely interrelated.

 He strongly emphasizes the fact that research activity has consequences (for instance, subjects change as a result of being interviewed), and he argues that science itself is a system of ethics which assumes that objective truth exists and that pursuing and communicating it are eminently valuable activities. Sanford distinguishes between scientific method and scientific attitudes and believes there has been an overemphasis on the former and a concomitant neglect of the latter. In the final analysis, he sees science as value and dismisses ethical neutrality as an impossibility. ETHICAL-GENERAL

Sasson, R., and T. M. Nelson. 1969. "The Human Experimental Subject in Context." *Canadian Psychologist* 10:409–37.

 The authors consider the safety, comfort, privacy, and personal dignity of subjects from a psychological perspective. The safety of subjects must be ensured and the responsibility for conducting experiments shared with colleagues. Privacy is very important, and the authors point out that the absence of informed consent constitutes an invasion of privacy. In order to safeguard privacy, data must be kept confidential. Studies which may result in lowered self-esteem on the part of the subjects are especially dangerous; subjects deserve to be treated with dignity and respect.

 Since prior knowledge can be a serious threat to valid experimental results, the true purpose of many experiments is hidden to reduce experimental effects. In this connection, the authors suggest that some of the difficulties surrounding the use of deception result from the unfavorable connotations of the word. "Simulation" is a better word choice. Finally, they indicate that research in educational settings alters the ethical problems since participating as subjects is often part of students' education; in order to minimize negative effects, subjects should be briefed and told that experimental simulation is being used, and then be debriefed. DECEPTION, INFORMED CONSENT, PRIVACY, STRESS

Sawyer, J., and H. Schechter n.d. "Computers, Privacy, and the National Data Center: The Responsibility of Social Scientists." Draft document.

The authors point out that data collection is not new but that vastly improved data retrieval techniques are. The major concern of Congress with respect to a national data center (NDC) has been the protection of privacy. The establishment of such a center would be a great impetus for research because more data would become available at lesser cost from more and better-sampled respondents, data collection would be less redundant, variables would be more comparable and would cover a larger area, and analyses would be easier to verify. The authors acknowledge that although the purpose of an NDC does not include retrieving information about particular individuals, problems of privacy, equity, and accuracy remain. They make a number of recommendations to forestall such difficulties. DATA BANKS, PRIVACY

Schick, A. 1971. "From Analysis to Evaluation." *The Annals* 394:57–71.

Schick detects a switch from analysis of new social-action programs to evaluation of existing ones because of a greater reluctance to innovate, decreased resources, and a decline in confidence that new programs will be effective. He believes that this will lead to greater experimentation in order to pretest the efficacy of new programs. SOCIAL EXPERIMENTATION

Schuler, E. A. 1969. "Toward a Code of Professional Ethics for Sociologists: A Historical Note." *American Sociologist* 4:144–46.

Schuler emphasizes the Camelot experience in explaining the necessity for the ASA to draw up a code of ethics. CODES OF ETHICS

Schultz, D. P. 1969. "The Human Subject in Psychological Research." *Psychology Bulletin* 72:214–28.

Schultz traces changes in the role played by subjects in psychological research from that of observers and "reagents" in the laboratories of Wundt and Titchener to that of "subject-as-object" starting with Watson's work on behaviorism. He comments on the nonrandom and nonrepresentative nature of the typical subject used in psychological research and the attitude-sets and expectations such an individual brings into the laboratory which can influence his or her behavior, and hence the experimental findings.

Schultz speculates on such ethical issues as potential emotional distress, the use of deception per se, the invasion of privacy which results from the failure to elicit a subject's informed consent, or from the failure to hold responses fully confidential.

As remedies he proposes a fostering of awareness of the serious methodological and ethical problems much research is presently prone to, greater insistence on the part of funding agencies and journal editors that subjects be more truly representative of the general population, possible payment of research volunteers by organizations specializing in data collection, and, most important of all, that psychologists cease viewing the people they study in mechanistic terms but rather see them as true participants. "Perhaps ... the best way of investigating the nature of man is to ask him." CONFIDENTIALITY, DECEPTION, INFORMED CONSENT, STRESS

Schwartz, R. D., and S. Orleans. 1967. "On Legal Sanctions." *University of Chicago Law Review* 34:274–300.

In this article the authors examine sanctions, defined as "officially imposed punishments aimed at enforcement of legal obligations," from a sociological perspective. In the first part four common assumptions about the effectiveness of sanctions are examined and found wanting. Contrary to conventional wisdom, sanctions do not necessarily tend to prevent the occurrence of offenses, are not more effective if more severe, can incur great social costs, and are not the best means of social control—there are possibly more viable alternatives to punishment. The second part of the paper offers preliminary results of a field experiment comparing sanction threats with appeals to conscience in terms of efficacy in reducing income tax evasion. "The findings indicate that motivations of various kinds make a difference in tax-paying. They suggest that the two types of appeal affect normative orientation differently according to the status of those subjected to the appeals. Sanction threat increases normative orientation most markedly among the upper class, the better-educated, and non-Catholics. Appeals to conscience change attitues toward tax compliance most among the best and least educated, those employed by others, and Protestants and Jews. As to actual changes in tax compliance, returns currently available for the gross treatment groups suggest that conscience appeals are more effective than sanction threats, though both have some effect." SOCIAL CONTROL

Schwitzgebel, R. K. 1969. Confidentiality of Research Information in Public Health Studies." *Harvard Legal Commentary* 6:187–97.

Schwitzgebel, within the context of public health, investigates two related problems: the circumstances under which the state can take action against an individual on the basis of confidential information, and the circumstances under which an individual can have access to research data. He notes considerable confusion and contradiction in the state laws, especially common law, a difficulty which a statutory approach alleviates to some extent. He concludes: "In general, the statutes granting a confidential status to research information in public health studies appear to be helpful in facilitating research and safeguarding subjects. But more discriminating standards and limits need to be developed to maximize the usefulness of such statutes." CONFIDENTIALITY, LEGAL, LEGISLATION AND REGULATION

―――. 1968. "Ethical Problems in Experimentation with Offenders." *American Journal of Orthopsychiatry* 8:738–48.

Schwitzgebel discusses what he considers three major differences between medical and social science experimentation: importance of the social context (particularly the community's norms and mores), emphasis on the relationships between individuals and groups, and influence of the subject's awareness on the experimental results. Each of these points is relevant when conducting social science research and means that the ethical principles relevant to medical research may be inappropriate for social science research. Schwitzgebel presents a survey of major recommended principles: access to information about the experiment, voluntary consent of the subject, right of the subject to withdraw from participation in the experiment, and avoidance of all unnecessary harmful aftereffects, under which he includes informing subjects about the intended use of the data in order to protect their right to privacy. He goes on to make suggestions for ethically upgrading experimental procedures: obtaining consent, assessing subject attitudes toward the experiment, and establishing subject-competent advisory committees. In discussing the principle of balancing risks against benefits, he suggests that "basic ethical values ... may not be included within the potential scope of risk; in a sense, rights may not be bargained away." BIOMEDICAL RESEARCH, INFORMED CONSENT, RISK-BENEFIT, SOCIAL EXPERIMENTATION

―――. 1967. "Electronic Innovation in the Behavioral Sciences." *American Psychologist* 22:364–70.

Behavioral electronics refer to the application of electronic technology to the understanding, maintenance, and modification of human behavior. The importance of the influence of the social context in shaping the courses of new technological development is discussed, and ethical questions associated with this development are raised. In the use of electronic rehabilitation systems, designed to protect persons from various sorts of danger (location monitoring), the civil liberties of patients are of special concern. Rights not to disclose sensitive information must be safeguarded. Ruebhausen and Brim define privacy as the individual choosing the time, place, and extent of disclosure of his attitudes, behavior, and beliefs. Schwitzgebel adds to this by arguing for postdisclosure rights. Assessment of the possible personal and social hazards of the misuse of electronic rehabilitation equipment is needed.

The use of the community as the laboratory is needed in situations where the object of study cannot be removed from its natural setting. The responsibility for certain uses of electronic innovation in a "community-as-laboratory" study needs formulation prior to testing of the equipment, since otherwise negative social effects can occur: "One cannot drop a bomb on a city to see if it works." It is necessary to understand fully the reciprocal relationship of research formulation by scientists and public conception of the purposes and limits of that research, in order to work out the proper organization arrangements and commitments. CONFIDENTIALITY, ETHICAL-GENERAL, PRIVACY

Science. 1974. "The Continuing Breast Cancer Controversy." *Science* 186:246–47.

A topical report discussing the ethics of a study designed to investigate whether radical or total mastectomy is preferable—the crucial issue is informed consent. BIOMEDICAL RESEARCH, INFORMED CONSENT

Sears, R. R. 1968. "In Defense of Privacy." *School Review* 76:23–33.

In discussing the ethics of educational research, Sears points out that the conflict is not between the rights of children and the rights of researchers (the protagonist fallacy), but rather between the values of privacy and knowledge. He argues that the research relationship cannot be perceived as a *quid pro quo* but is better seen as a voluntary contribution on the part of the subject. He indicates some of the dangers resulting from an external control on science; for instance, how can one judge what will be good and what will be bad for mankind. Great breakthroughs can arise from purely intellectual exercises. "What society wants to know and what it will defend its right to discover, is *anything* that brings order out of the chaos of direct human experience." Although a major function of schools is that of education, it is not the only one; as multipurpose institutions there is no reason why research should not be conducted in the schools provided children give

their informed consent. Furthermore, the threat to privacy which behavioral science poses is minimal. "The blunt fact is that, unless our
scientific understanding of man can be brought to a far higher plane
within the next couple of decades than it has been in the last couple of
millenia, there will be no one left whose privacy can be defended."
FREEDOM OF INQUIRY, INFORMED CONSENT, PRIVACY,
VOLUNTARISM

Sechrest, Lee. 1976. "Another Look at Unobtrusive Measures: An Alterna-
tive to What?" In *Perspectives on Attitudes Assessment: Surveys and Their
Alternatives*, ed. H. W. Sinaiko and L. H. Broedling, Champaign, Ill.:
Pendleton Publications.

In discussing the current status, attitudes, and problems surrounding the use of unobtrusive measures, Sechrest concludes that "unobtrusive, nonreactive measurement is an approach offering many advantages
but serving only as supplementary or complementary to surveys. There
are sufficient problems with unobtrusive measures that they should not
be regarded as substitutes for other measures; rather, they are most
useful and most justified when thought of as providing additional and
often confirmatory data."

He briefly discusses the general ethical issues involved in the use
of unobtrusive measures. He notes that there are those who question the
methodology of unobtrusive measurement and would have the social
sciences avoid it completely. In view of this opposition, Sechrest advises
those who feel unobtrusive measures to be of value to develop systematic ethical rationalizations of these procedures. DECEPTION, IN-
FORMED CONSENT

Secretary's Advisory Committee on Automated Personal Data Systems.
1973. *Records, Computers, and Rights of Citizens.* Department of Health,
Education, and Welfare. Washington, D.C.: U.S. Government Printing
Office.

The committee's task was to analyze the harmful consequences of
automated personal data systems and to make recommendations for
safeguards against such harmful consequences, measures of redress, and
policy and practice related to use of social security numbers. The
impersonality of the processors and the size and accessibility of the
systems are seen as the main problems of computer-based record-keeping. Another important problem is that although improved record-
keeping techniques can have immediate benefits for the public,
organizations see these techniques mainly as attractive technological
solutions to complex social problems, leaving the individual no role in
the development or use of these systems. Such efficiency can become
confused with good social policy endangering personal freedoms.

The rationale for constructing measures to safeguard personal privacy is made explicit on the grounds that there are no statutes establishing individual rights in this area and little evidence to suppose that existing law will evolve to the point of providing such protection. Also, there is the conflict between the right to privacy and the "right to know." What is needed is "mutuality in record-keeping" where there would be disclosure of data and at the same time individual control over the nature and extent of the disclosure.

The committee urged that a Code of Fair Information Practice be established to control the use of administrative personnel data systems and statistical-reporting and research systems. Safeguards should be instituted to prevent the abuse of personal data in record-keeping. The use of social security numbers should be limited to that required by federal law and should not be adopted as a standard universal identifier in the absence of safeguards. CONFIDENTIALITY, DATA BANKS, LEGAL, PRIVACY

Seely, J. R. 1967. "The Making and Taking of Problems: Toward an Ethical Stance." *Social Problems* 14:382–89.

The word "ethics" is etymologically derived from the Greek words for moral and custom, and from the Sanskrit for self-will and strength. For Seely, an ethic "represents a solution and a resolution: a solving of present problems in the form of a strategy for the future" —a dialectic process. He deplores the rigid distinction drawn by some between professional and personal problems. ETHICAL-GENERAL

Seeman, J. 1969. "Deception in Psychological Research." *American Psychologist* 24:1025–28.

Seeman states that deception in experimental design has been increasing and that because subject-set is an extremely important variable, subject suspicion of deception complicates the analysis of results enormously. In terms of public policy, the dilemma surrounding the use of deception centers on the conflict between individual rights and the needs of society. Seeman refers to the Escobedo and Miranda Supreme Court decisions, in which the two guiding principles were that the government must respect the dignity and integrity of its citizens, and that the individual has the right to remain silent unless he freely chooses to do otherwise. The most correct position vis-a-vis the ethics of deception is perhaps the absolutist means-end relationship: "bad" means cannot lead to a "good" end. The use of deception destroys trust, congruence, and reality.

In addition, Seeman attacks the basic assumption of the discipline, namely that the ultimate goal is knowledge. For him the ultimate goal of the scientific enterprise should be wisdom, since "knowledge alone has a neutrality that can be deadly in our time." We must continue asking: knowledge for what, for whom, and at what cost? DE-CEPTION, LEGAL, PSYCHOLOGICAL EXPERIMENTATION, RISK-BENEFIT

Shah, S. T. 1970. "Privileged Communications, Confidentiality and Privacy: Confidentiality." *Professional Psychology* 1:159–64.

The conflicting values of the subject, the experimenter, and society must be carefully balanced. Shah makes a number of points in connection with the confidentiality issue. With the client's waiver of professional confidentiality, the psychologist must still use care and discretion although he cannot strictly refuse to honor his client's wishes. On the other hand he must bear in mind that unauthorized disclosure can lead to lawsuits and censure by the profession and thus must take special precautions to safeguard records against disclosure, including that of subpoena risk. For instance, in cases of conflict of interests between client and employing agencies, the psychologist must decide on his own priorities and then inform all concerned. In legal cases, professional disagreements about the case should be divulged. It should be remembered that the confidentiality of research information is covered by legal privilege only in some states, not in the majority. CONFIDENTIALITY, LEGAL

Sherrill, P. N., and H. D. Field. n.d. "Are Survey Respondents Really Anonymous?" Field Research Corporation Mimeograph.

Although anonymity is routinely promised to respondents in survey research, respondents' information is not so much anonymous as "classified." In order to redress this state of affairs, the authors suggest that in the case of probability samples, respondent identification be kept on a single, detachable sheet in the questionnaire and removed and destroyed immediately after all verification work is completed. In the case of panel studies, the authors suggest a slight modification of this scheme through the use of code numbers on the questionnaire with the actual names filed separately. Both methods, meant only as examples, would be instrumental in protecting informants by establishing de facto confidentiality, necessary so long as we lack de jure confidentiality. CONFIDENTIALITY, SURVEYS

Shils, E. 1966. "Privacy: Its Constitution and Vicissitudes." *Law and Contemporary Problems* 31:281–306.

This is a lengthy discussion of what privacy means, what it entails, and includes an investigation of the concept's historical development.

Privacy is seen as a zero-relationship between two units; it is not separateness because it can exist only within an interactive, communicative framework. Essentially, it refers to a control over information—what goes to whom; voluntariness is an important component. In the present context, privacy refers primarily to legitimate possession over cognitive matters. Shils points out that few live totally in private and that disclosure is often involuntary or inadvertent. He also points to an inescapable fact of authority which needs to have information about subordinates. He traces out the effects of urbanization and modernization in leading to both greater ease in maintaining privacy (for instance, the separation of place of residence and of work) and greater ease in breaking it down with respect to the inroads on privacy made by the press, police, personnel specialists, the growth of empirical social science, the revolution in communications technology, and so on. PRIVACY

———. 1959. "Social Inquiry and the Autonomy of the Individual." In *The Human Meaning of the Social Sciences*, ed. D. Lerner, pp. 114–57. New York: Meridian books.
Modern social science relies heavily on interviewing and observation. Because interviewing is impossible without the subject's consent and cooperation, the ethical problems it causes deal mainly with the interviewer's declaration of his objectives and the confidentiality of the gathered information. Data must be transmitted to others only in a generalized and anonymous form; the giving of consent does not absolve the investigator from future responsibility. While the subject often enjoys being interviewed and can frequently be said to gain in attention and conviviality, the only way in which social science research can directly benefit the subject is through increased self-awareness. This means that the subject must not be deceived and should be given the fullest amount of information possible. Intrusion of privacy can be justified if those intruded upon have given their consent, but intrusion into behavior which the actors believe is private cannot be justified on any grounds except that of maintaining public order. Shils points out that most social science experimentation has been of the small-scale type and does not usually raise acute moral issues because the groups are generally small; the experimental situations are usually brief, nonrecurrent, and quasireal at best; stimuli are rarely of great significance to or leave any lasting impression on the subjects. The little experimentation with large collectivities which does exist has been done mainly under the aegis of the ongoing administrative process, and, "insofar as they are conducted by legitimate governments and do not contravene properly enacted laws or general moral standards, are like any other administrative actions carried out in pursuit of the purposes of a legally constituted government" therefore have an authority quite

different from that of the social scientist. Social science experimentation, according to Shils, however, does not fall into this category. It is more akin to a contractual relationship—the more consensus there is, the fewer ethical problems, and conversely, the less consensus is based on informed consent, the more ethical queries there are. On the whole, Shils sees the record of social science research as clean partly because of the inconsequentiality of social science experimentation: "At present ... much social science experimentation possesses neither the therapeutic nor the genuinely scientific qualification. Even then it might outweigh the objectionability of manipulation as such. Its ethical acceptability therefore rests on the peripheral nature of the stimuli and the transient character of the effects introduced." CONFIDENTIALITY, INFORMED CONSENT, OBSERVATION, SURVEYS

Silverman, I. 1975. "Nonreactive Methods and the Law." *American Psychologist* 30:764–69.

The movement away from the traditional laboratory setting and toward naturalistic experimentation has created ethical problems. Naturalistic experimentation does not use volunteers, informed consent, debriefing, prescreening, or follow-up, and hence presents problems not confronted in traditional research. Silverman is particularly concerned with the legal status of such studies. He prepared ten synopses of experiments using unobtrusive methods, all possibly violating the law, and, therefore, unlike ambiguous ethical quandaries, potentially empirically resolvable. The synopses illustrate how questions of legitimacy, purpose, trespass, harassment, disorderly conduct, fraud, criminal negligence and intent can arise in the course of naturalistic research. Two attorneys were presented with the synopses and asked their interpretations of laws governing such situations. A judge was asked his opinion of similar material. Silverman's discussion of the arguments offered demonstrates that the field of legal specialization (one attorney a practicing criminal law defense lawyer, the other in medicolegal jurisprudence specializing in the legal rights of patients and subjects in medical practice and research) or interpretive slant can determine which situations are seen as violating the law and which not. Silverman doubts that these ambiguities will be resolved until a confrontation by aggrieved parties forces the issue, but he hopes that a discussion of these issues will give researchers reasons to reflect on the feelings and reactions of unwitting subjects. ETHICAL-GENERAL, LEGAL, OBSERVATION

Silverstein, A. J. 1974. "Compensating Those Injured Through Experimentation." *Federal Bar Journal* 33:322–30.

Apropos the general directive to the Kennedy Commission to establish some kind of mechanism whereby individuals who are harmed by biomedical or behavioral science research or their families can receive compensation, Silverstein delineates the problem, discusses types of damage and compensation, presents methods of compensation (for example, common-law action), and finally offers a tentative model of compensation through a federal insurance fund. BIOMEDICAL EX-PERIMENTATION, LEGAL, PSYCHOLOGICAL EXPERIMEN-TATION

Simmel, A. 1968. "Privacy." In *International Encyclopaedia of the Social Sciences,* Vol. 12, ed. D. L. Sills, pp. 480–87. New York: Macmillan and The Free Press.

This article covers some of the determinants and indicators of privacy, the elements of a functional analysis of privacy, and the law of privacy. According to Simmel, "in general, major social changes imply changes in identity boundaries and domains of privacy," and hence he discusses, for example, the effects of urbanization on conceptions of privacy. He suggests, "the right of privacy asserts the sacredness of the person" and that "perhaps the dominant reason for seeking privacy, namely the desire to be insulated from observation, is intimately related to motives of avoiding criticism, punishment, or the discomfort of feeling inhibited." He points out that while a general law of private personality drawn from Roman Law can be found in many continental codes, judges in Anglo-American courts have generally preferred to link privacy rights with property rights, and violations with specific torts such as libel or slander, copyright infringement, breach of contract, trespass, assault and battery. In the United states, common-law jurisprudence in connection with privacy rights was established by the famous article of Warren and Brandeis on this topic in 1890; in the United Kingdom, suit can be brought for invasion of privacy only if property rights have been violated or reputation has been injured. LEGAL, PRIVACY, STRESS

Simmons, D. D. 1968. "Invasion of Privacy and Judged Benefits of Personality-test Inquiry." *Journal of General Psychology* 79:177–81.

This is a study supporting the prediction that protests about personality tests would vary with the judged benefit of the purpose of the inquiry. Thirty-five subjects were asked to rate 37 Minnesota Multiphasic Personality Inventory statements with respect to invasion of privacy and judged benefit for three different role occupancies: job applicant, doctor's patient, and as evidence regarding personal character in a trial. The judged benefits were highest in the medical case, neutral in the personnel case, and negative in the judicial case. The author indicates that we need a "social psychology of personality assessment." PRIVACY, RISK-BENEFIT

Simpson, G. G. 1966. "Naturalistic Ethics and the Social Sciences." *American Psychologist* 21:27–36.

Simpson considers ethics in an evolutionary context and sees a switch from supernaturalistic to naturalistic ethics necessary. The evolutionary functioning of ethics depends on man's ability to predict and foresee the consequences of actions; individual responsibility is seen as the root of the moral sense. ETHICAL-GENERAL

Singer, E. 1977. *Informed Consent: Consequences for Response Rate and Response Quality in Social Surveys.* Paper delivered at the American Sociological Association Meeting, Chicago.

This is a report on a carefully conducted study designed to test the effect on survey outcomes of three elements of informed consent: amount of information provided, assurance of confidentiality, and a signature requirement on the consent form. The study was designed by Singer and carried out by the National Opinion Research Center's field interviewers. Singer found that asking respondents to sign consent forms reduced the response rate and that the promise of confidentiality reduced the nonresponse on a few questionnaire items. Neither the confidentiality assurance nor the signature requirement appeared to affect the quality of the information attained. INFORMED CONSENT, SURVEYS

Sjoberg, G. "Project Camelot: Selected Reactions and Personal Reflections." In *Ethics, Politics, and Social Research,* ed. G. Sjoberg, pp. 141–61. Cambridge, Mass: Schenkman, 1967.

The issue of scientific trust versus social myth is an ever-recurrent one—some hold that scientists ought to stay within normatively defined limits; others say that science recognizes no boundaries. Sjoberg is particularly concerned with establishing the kind of structure which is essential for the effective conduct of social science and discovering the conditions necessary for letting social scientists obtain objective knowledge and maintain their responsibility at the same time. For him it is vital that research be kept separate from administrative control functions. In Nazi Germany and in present-day USSR, social scientists are inseparable from the administrative control functions of the state; even in such a democratic, pluralistic system as the United States, researchers can have problems safeguarding the confidentiality and privacy of their respondents. "The increasing stress in social science upon achieving professional (as opposed to scientific) status serves to rationalize the acceptance of administrative controls emanating from the national level. The professional organizations of social scientists encourage in fact their members to maintain a position of 'respectability' in the eyes of the broader society. And one means of achieving this image is to forge links with the major institutional links in the society, notably those that exert administrative controls over citizen and scientist alike. Here the actual norm stands in sharp contrast to the ideal norm calling upon the scientist to engage in research for truth without regard to the needs and orientations of any particular organization." FREEDOM OF INQUIRY, PROFESSIONALISM, SOCIAL CONTROL

————, and P. J. Miller. 1973. "Social Research on Bureaucracy: Limitations and Opportunities." *Social Problems* 21:129–43.

The authors discuss the difficulties surrounding the study of large bureaucracies, especially the bureaucratic tendency to protect its own interests through secrecy, and point out that a code of ethics should justify studying the powerful as well as studying the powerless. CODES OF ETHICS

Sklair, L. 1969. "Moral Progress and Social Theory." *Ethics* 79:229–34.

This is a philosophical treatment of the relationship between a rational ethic (values which can be rationally defended as holding good for all persons at all times) and social theory. It is clear to Sklair that morality refers to interpersonal relationships. For him, the future of ethics lies with the study of society. ETHICAL-GENERAL

Smith, D., and J. Katz. 1974. "Human Experimentation—A Game Without Rules." *Family Health* 24 (June):46–48.

This is an account in a popular publication of some of the worst excesses committed in the name of biomedical research. Smith comments that if biomedical researchers cannot draw up ethical codes themselves, some kind of governmental regulations will be necessary. The article includes a special report by Jay Katz who suggests the following to *Family Health:* careful design of experiments, extensive animal trials first, followed by a small number of experimental human subjects, informed consent whenever possible, special committee for using prisoners, adequate monitoring, reporting of all results including negative results, careful follow-up of subjects to trace out long-term effects. BIOMEDICAL RESEARCH, ETHICAL-GENERAL

Smith, M. B. 1976. "Some Perspectives on Ethical/Political Issues in Social Science Research." *Personality and Social Psychology Bulletin* 2:445–53.

Abstract: Current principles and regulations concerning the ethics of research on human participants draw on two unrelated frames of reference: informed consent and harm/benefit. Problems involved in informed consent include the inability of some classes of potential participants to give such consent, the incompatibility of some research designs with fully informed consent, and ambiguities about the meaning of "informed." Problems involved in the harm/benefit frame include the impossibility of balancing benefit to science and society against harm to individual, and the question of who is to assess harms and benefits. Two currently proposed extensions of commonly accepted principles are discussed: the possible harm of deceptive procedures to the normative order of society, and the rights of categories of individuals, and of institutions, with respect to consent and harm/benefit. The former is favored, the latter opposed. INFORMED CONSENT, RISK-BENEFIT

————. 1975. "Psychology and Ethics." In *Human Rights and Psychological Research*, ed. E. C. Kennedy, pp. 1–22. New York: Thomas Y. Crowell.
    Brewster Smith describes the work of the American Psychological Association's Cook Committee, of which he was a member, on preparing the document "Ethical Principles in the Conduct of Research with Human Participants." The committee's first draft was attacked for being too strict as well as for being too permissive. Impressed by the lack of ethical consensus, the committee resolved to act as sensitizers only, not law-givers. Smith emphasizes practical issues especially, because ethical considerations in psychological research are closely tied to politics and education. He discusses the ethical responsibilities facing psychologists in their four major role activities of research, human services, public policy, and education. For a discussion on the ethics of research, Smith refers the reader to the Cook Committee report and confines himself to discussing a principle formulated by Rommetweit, that knowledge about individuals should not be sought unless it contributes to those individuals' self-knowledge. Smith prefers to see this negative edict translated into the positive—enhance others' humanity. CODES OF ETHICS, PSYCHOLOGICAL EXPERIMENTATION

————. 1967. "Conflicting Values Affecting Behavioral Research with Children." *Children* 14:53–58.
    The success of behavioral research, as indicated by increased federal support, has led to a demand for greater public accountability and much more emphasis on the ethical principles according to which it is conducted. Congress and the general public are concerned with such issues as violation of privacy, deception, informed consent, and the impact of computer technology on data processing. Many of these issues become even more urgent when the subjects of research are children. However, because the knowledge gained from research is of undoubted utility, ways of recognizing the varying and often compet-

ing values involved are needed, and means of compromising wisely among them must be found. Drawing a distinction between the ethically permissible and the ethically desirable, Smith calls for an upgrading of the normative standards of research: "The predominant cast of much permissible behavioral research falls short of the desirable in too often adopting a manipulative or condescending attitude towards its human subjects rather than a genuinely respectful, collaborative one." DATA BANKS, DECEPTION, INFORMED CONSENT, PRIVACY

Spinrad, W. 1970. *Civil Liberties*. Chicago: Quadrangle Books.
This book deals primarily with civil liberties approached as freedom from restrictions, especially with respect to freedom of expression and association. It traces out the historical development of the topic and devotes considerable space to a detailed analysis of the cases of McCarthyism, although a number of other civil-liberties problems are considered too. Most relevant to the issue of the protection of research subjects is the chapter on academic freedom, defined as "the right of scholars to pursue and impart knowledge as they see fit." Spinrad says that "a society which limits the academics' area of inquiry and expression is hurting itself by reducing its potential for knowledge." It is noteworthy that although the concept of academic freedom is closely linked to the notion of institutional autonomy, actual cases in the United States have usually involved individuals (for example, the famous case where Bertrand Russell was refused an academic appointment because of his antagonism to religion and morality). FREEDOM OF INQUIRY

*Statistical Reporter*. 1977. "Confidentiality of Statistical and Research Data." January: 115–36.
This is an examination of the problems in protecting the confidentiality of statistical and research data. Presented are an identification of the scope of statistical and research data under discussion, an explanation of the basic principles involved in protecting the confidentiality of statistical and research data, and a discussion of the sharing of identifiable data under controlled conditions.
The report includes a useful summary of some current laws affecting confidentiality through the end of 1976. Some laws apply to many or all agencies, some apply only to specific agencies, and some apply to particular types of information wherever maintained.

General laws: General rule on disclosure of confidential information applicable to all agencies; Federal Reports Act; the Freedom of

Information Act; Government in the Sunshine Act; and the Private Act of 1974.

Examples of agency-specific laws are presented from the following agencies: Bureau of the Census, Law Enforcement Assistance Administration, National Center for Health Statistics, Bureau of Economic Analysis, Internal Revenue Service, Social Security Administration, and the Bureau of Mines.

Laws dealing with specific subject matter are listed under the following areas: research privilege, alcohol and drug abuse, protection of identity of human subjects, and international statistics.

The article includes an enumeration of recent developments and activities in the study of privacy and confidentiality issues. It presents a proposal for the protection of confidentiality in federal research and statistics, and it concludes with a call for further developments for the protection of confidentiality of data. CONFIDENTIALITY, LEGIS-LATION AND REGULATIONS

Steiner, I. D. 1972. "The Evils of Research: Or What my Mother Didn't Tell me About the Sins of Academia." *American Psychologist* 27:766–68.

Steiner satirizes the proposed APA code of ethics, which he considers overly restrictive, by promulgating a set of moral principles designed to protect students from such outrageous abuses as the traumatic experience of examinations. He contends that subjects are rarely injured in research studies, and that although a need does exist to protect innocent subjects from overly enthusiastic experimenters, the proposed code will severely limit the majority of scrupulous researchers by attempting to regulate the activities of the abusive few. The most flagrant abuse of human subjects occurs when their time and energy is wasted by studies which are trivial, ill-conceived, or clumsily executed, and this is where he calls for the greatest reform. He wants more responsible research, and less research which is poorly conceptualized, rests on faulty methodology, or tests trivial hypotheses. CODES OF ETHICS, PSYCHOLOGICAL EXPERIMENTATION, STRESS

Storer, N. W. n.d. "Action Concerning the Professional Ethics of Sociologists: An Informal Memorandum on Functions and Forms." Mimeograph.

Formal ethical statements have four major functions: To sustain public trust in the profession (especially true when there is some sign of enforcement); to train new professionals; as a basis for informal sanctions (thus a norm-establishing mechanism); and as a basis for formal sanctions. A fifth potential function of ethical codes is to direct future research. Storer is in favor of a formal ethical statement by the profession, consisting of a general statement plus one or more of the following alternative options: a series of case studies, following the APA model; establishing an advisory group; establishing a committee to facilitate communication between existing institutional review committees; establishing a committee for the purpose of arriving at a general discussion of ethics for teaching graduate students. CODES OF ETHICS, PROFESSIONALISM

Street, H. 1970. "Privacy and the Law." *Queen's Quarterly* 77:318–32.
Street points out that lawyers cannot provide answers unaided but need to be guided by public opinion, especially in connection with how much interference with privacy the public will tolerate. Privacy essentially refers to the right to be left alone, particularly against offensive intrusion and unreasonable publicity, including the passing of information to third parties. He discusses privacy and tort law and points out that thanks to Warren and Brandeis and Prosser there are general tortious principles of privacy in the United States. They have had little impact, however, and in any case, self-controlling institutional arrangements are not enough to guard against infringement on privacy. LEGAL, PRIVACY

Stricker, L. J. 1967. "The True Deceiver." *Psychological Bulletin* 68:13–20.
Stricker notes that 19.3 percent of the studies reported in four major psychological journals in 1964 used deception. He argues that deception has become a prestigious methodological device and finds it noteworthy that only few of the studies reviewed reported on subjects' suspicions of the deception. DECEPTION, PSYCHOLOGICAL EXPERIMENTATION

———, and S. Messick. 1967. "Suspicion of Deception: Implications for Conformity Research." *Journal of Personality and Social Psychology* 5:379-89.
The authors point out that studies of conformity are especially prone to using deception as part of the experimental design, and they report finding a high incidence of suspicion concerning such experimental deception, a surprising finding in view of the fact that the subjects were of high school age and presumably naive. DECEPTION

———, S. Messick, and D. N. Jackson. 1969. "Evaluating Deception in Psychological Research." *Psychological Bulletin* 71:343–51.
While experimental deception is widely used, its efficacy is rarely evaluated. The use of deception is debatable not only because of its dubious ethical status but possibly also because of its limited effectiveness. The authors point out that suspicion can be a useful index for establishing effectiveness. Suspicion of deception can stem from trans-

parency, publicity, communication among subjects, previous experience, generalized suspicion about psychological experiments,
intelligence, sex, Machiavellianism, and so on. Since the effects of suspicion are varied, it is important that deception experiments include a
measure of the extent of suspiciousness, and that the responses of suspicious subjects are measured separately from those of the deceived subjects. DECEPTION

Sullivan, D. S., and T. E. Deiker. 1973. "Subject-Experimenter Perceptions
of Ethical Issues in Human Research." *American Psychologist* 28:587–91.

This is the report of a study in which college undergraduates and
professional psychologists were asked to evaluate the ethical aspects of
experiments. The results indicate that psychologists are more concerned about such issues than undergraduates. It was found that the
students frequently qualified their responses, a finding which suggests
they are using a cost-benefits approach in appraising research. ETHI-
CAL-GENERAL, PSYCHOLOGICAL EXPERIMENTATION,
RISK-BENEFIT

Sykes, G. M. 1967. "Feeling Our Way: A Report on a Conference on Ethical
Issues in the Social Sciences." *American Behavioral Scientist* 10:8–11.

Sykes reports on an NIH-funded conference on ethical issues in
the social sciences. Ethical problems tend to fall into two main categories: the use of deception or coercion, and the possibility of harmful
effects. Most professionals would prefer informal self-regulation to
legislation, but this is offset by growth in funding for social science
research, the concomitant desire that social scientists be held accountable for their products, and the strong streak of antiintellectualism
which suggest that research freedom cannot be taken for granted. In
addition, concern with human subjects can be seen as part of a much
wider movement concerned with individual rights in an "ever more
managed social order." However, the growth of social science knowledge and its usefulness for policy formation means essentially that we
are at the beginning of a long debate. COERCION, DECEPTION,
FREEDOM OF INQUIRY, PROFESSIONALISM

Taeuber, C. 1971. "The Federal Government as a Source of Data." *The
Annals* 394:114–28.

*Abstract:* "The federal government is the source of a large volume
of statistics. Developments have been made in recent years in the timeli-
ness of the release of the data. The growing use of electronic computers
has led to the development of new ways of making data available for
further analysis. Available statistics tend to become used even though
there is not the continuing critical review which would be desirable to

ensure that statistics at all times reflect the situation in the real world they are intended to describe. There are needs for coordination and for the development of ways by which data from different sources can be used without violating the confidentiality of the individual data. Methodological problems in relation to sample surveys have received considerable attention. The development of improved methodology is a promising field for collaboration between federal statistical agencies and the social science community." CONFIDENTIALITY, DATA BANKS, SURVEYS

————. 1967. "Invasion of Privacy." *Eugenics Quarterly* 14:243–46.

Taeuber studies the confidentiality of data within the Census Bureau. The bureau conducts three types of data collection and compilation: the national census, with mandatory replies; more specialized surveys for which replies are voluntary; and surveys conducted for other federal agencies. The bureau is legally enjoined to maintain strict confidentiality—data may not be used for other than statistical purposes, no personally identifiable material may be released. Disclosure is absolutely forbidden and great care is taken to avoid inadvertent disclosure. The bureau attempts to strike a delicate balance between the government's need for information and the individual's right to privacy. Because views on what constitutes an invasion of privacy change, the bureau makes an effort to consult the public on "permissible" and appropriate questions. CONFIDENTIALITY, PRIVACY, SURVEYS

Tybout, A. M., and G. Zaltman. 1974. "Ethics in Marketing Research: Their Practical Relevance." *Journal of Marketing Research* 11:357–68.

As marketing research expands its areas of investigations and increases its use of the experimental method, the significance and frequency of ethical issues will grow. Unfortunately, few ethical guidelines exist for the use of marketing researchers. the American Marketing Association's code of ethics ignores subject rights, and the marketing literature is relatively silent on the issue of ethics. The authors emphasize the necessity for understanding the ethical issues involved in marketing research in order to produce quality data and research. They discuss four basic rights of subjects: the right to choose, the right to safety, the right to be informed, and the right to be heard. Each of the first three, predicated on the basic right of subjects to be heard, is discussed in terms of potential violations, conflicts between the rights of subjects and the rights of clients and the professions, the practical implications of violating subjects' rights and potential data distortion, and possible solutions. The authors close by noting that violating subjects' rights may impair the accuracy of data, may lead to the boycotting of research, and may result in legislation restricting marketing researchers. CODES OF ETHICS, INFORMED CONSENT, SOCIAL EXPERIMENTATION, SURVEYS

*Valparaiso University Law Review.* 1970. "Legal Note: Social Research and Privileged Data." *Valparaiso University Law Review* 4:368–99.

In 1790 the United States became the first modern country to conduct a complete census. According to Price (1962), "social science data became the ultimate basis of sovereign power in the United States." But there is a conflict between the individual's right to privacy and "the social researcher's need to inquire and thereby gain knowledge necessary for informed governmental policy," a conflict sharpened because of the lack of legal protection of the confidentiality of research data. Confidentiality is usually safeguarded by anonymity. The problem arises because not all data can be held in a nonidentifiable form, for instance, for longitudinal studies. When data are personally identifiable, the best protection is confidentiality. An essential ingredient for this is control which is lost when disclosure is required by subpoena.

The writer comments on the essentially mild sanctions, such as expulsion, which are the only possible means of enforcing ethical codes for those professionals who do not require licensing. Reference is made to the 1967 evaluation study of the Woodlawn Organization 1960 manpower training program where two subpoenas were issued by a Senate subcommittee, indicating that assurances of confidentiality and codes of ethics are useless unless the law accords research data privilege either by judicial fiat (very unlikely) or statute. Wigmore identified four criteria necessary to recognize the claim of privilege: communication originated in confidence, confidentiality essential for the giving of information, communication of great importance to society, injury when forced disclosure is more injurious than beneficial to justice. The best way of ensuring privileged status would be by act of Congress to agencies conducting social research: "In effect, the agency would have the authority to privilege any information obtained in the course of a government-sponsored research project. The grant or contract would contain the terms under which disclosure may be made. The agency would assume more responsibility for confidentiality and any outside party desiring to compel disclosure would have to deal directly with the agency." CONFIDENTIALITY, LEGAL, PRIVACY, SOCIAL POLICY

Vargus, B. S. 1971. "On Sociological Exploitation: Why the Guinea Pig Sometimes Bites." *Social Problems* 19:238–48.

Low-income and powerless citizens are beginning to resent their all-too-frequent use as "objects of study" in situations where they do not benefit at all. Often they feel like guinea pigs for researchers who only want to further their own careers. Such strains and problems of researcher-client relationships result from the violation and abuse of respondents' privacy. Research funded by community agencies should serve the goals of the agency and the needs of the community and not the goals of the researcher or university alone. Since the community needs a voice in what researchers do when they conduct community research, a positive step would be to adopt a "trade-off" strategy in which the researcher receives data from the community and in return provides certain specified goods and services. Establishing citizen-faculty advisory committees, paying survey respondents for their time, and reemphasizing ethical training for graduate students may further alleviate some of these problems. COLLECTIVE CONCERN, PRIVACY

Vaughan, T. R. 1967. "Governmental Intervention in Social Research: Political and Ethical Dimensions in the Wichita Jury Recordings." In *Ethics, Politics, and Social Research*, ed. G. Sjoberg, pp. 50-77. Cambridge, Mass.: Schenkman.

"Ethical conflict is potentially present in all social research inasmuch as the values of science may conflict with the values of the social unit being studied." One side maintains that the integrity of scientific knowledge is violated when limits are placed on inquiry; the other, that certain areas fall outside the scope of inquiry and that if they are investigated the autonomy of individuals and the sanctity of institutions are violated. Vaughan's principal point—using the University of Chicago Law School's study of the U.S. jury system, the Wichita Jury Study, as a case study—is that "to accomplish ideological objectives censors interject themselves into the research process via controversy attending ethical conflicts." He goes on to say that the norm dealing with unrestricted freedom of scientific inquiry is based on the value that knowledge is better than ignorance, a viewpoint which generally argues that a scientific end justifies any means, ignoring the fact that the scientific set of values and norms is not paramount but only one of many other sets constituting the social fabric.

Vaughan recommends the adoption of two general procedures by researchers: self-conscious and serious reflection including full appreciation of the other's point of view which may lead to the finding of other methods; and the deliberate courting of counterperspectives. ETHICAL-GENERAL, FREEDOM OF INQUIRY

Venema, A. 1972. *De Databank*. Amsterdam: Paris-Manteau.

This is a strong polemic against computerized storage and retrieval of data in the Netherlands, mainly because of its potential for future misuses under tyrannical government, especially in connection with the persecution of minority groups. COLLECTIVE CONCERN, DATA BANKS, SOCIAL CONTROL

Von Blum, P. 1974. "A Code of Ethics for Teachers." *Chronicle of Higher Education* 9:20.

Von Blum mentions problems concerning authorship, professors neglectful of their teaching duties, sex and race biases, sexual misconduct, and others, and states that we need mechanisms to prevent and redress such wrongs. Coupled with the desire of professions to protect and enhance a favorable public image, this points to the need for a code of ethics which would encourage greater responsibility, especially if it contained adequate enforcement procedures. CODES OF ETHICS, PROFESSIONALISM

Wade, N. 1975. "Genetics: Conference Sets Strict Controls to Replace Moratorium." *Science* 187:931–35.

This is a report in the News and Comment section of *Science* describing the Asilomar Conference. It points out that "the conference decisions were reached in the explicit awareness that science no longer enjoys the automatic favor of governments and society, and that if the scientists present failed to regulate themselves in an evidently disinterested manner, others would do so for them." LEGISLATION AND REGULATION

Waitzkin, H. 1968. "Truth's Search for Power: The Dilemmas of the Social Scientist." *Social Problems* 15:408–19.

Waitzkin discusses the general dilemma facing applied social science researchers, namely, that of encouraging policy makers to use and apply social science knowledge. He points out that, strictly speaking, scientists can only make descriptive statements, and that there is no logical connection between these and normative edicts. However, since truly value-free social research is impossible, the question arises, What is to be done when research duties conflict with those of good citizenry? A dilemma exists between career advancement and social problem-solving. The former often depends on the prestige obtained from publishing scientifically generalizable research results while the latter requires specific data on which to base concrete decisions. He discusses the dilemma of consultation versus cooptation and the danger inherent in the latter because of loss of detachment and critical analysis. Finally he discusses the issue of comprehensive planning versus bargaining— the danger in applying scientific rationality to the large-scale reconstruction of society is that technocracy will replace democracy. ETHICAL-GENERAL, SOCIAL POLICY

Wallwork, E. 1975. "Ethical Issues in Research Involving Human Subjects." In *Human Rights and Psychological Research*, ed. E. C. Kennedy, pp. 69–81. New York: Thomas Y. Crowell.

Wallwork offers a critique of Baumrind (1975), mainly on the basis of her subjectivism and emotionalism. He says that Baumrind is correct in addressing metaethical issues but that her argument contains at least two logical inconsistencies, namely, that ethical disagreements are capable of resolution, a point she refutes herself on grounds of incompatibility among world views (for example, Buddhism versus Christianity), and that rule-utilitarianism can be justified without recourse to metaethics. He disagrees with Baumrind's interpretation of the APA code as resting on act-utilitarianism and instead sees its form of ethical reasoning as closely paralleling Kohlberg's fifth stage of moral development: "Stage 5 moralists believe rules should be established on a social-contract basis, involving democratic group discussion and agreement, such as that involved in formulating the APA code." Nonetheless, he agrees that a "postrelativist" ethics, based on the criterion of "the principle of reversibility" and incorporating two substantive principles, "persons are of unconditional value" and "the right to equal justice," would be superior. From this perspective, he is critical of the APA's cost-benefit analysis and its failure to sufficiently emphasize the importance of informed consent. He suggests that when obtaining informed consent is impracticable, surrogate groups of subjects be used for testing the acceptability of the research; that as a matter of editorial policy APA journals require information regarding compliance with the APA research standards; and that all research projects undergo prior committee review. In general, Wallwork would like to see more emphasis on substantive rights. CODES OF ETHICS, INFORMED CONSENT, PROFESSIONALISM, RISK-BENEFIT

Ware, W. H. 1974. "Computer Privacy and Computer Security." *Bulletin of the American Society for Information Science* 1:3.

According to Ware, privacy is mainly a legal issue, while computer security or access control is primarily a technical or administrative issue. So long as individual data are used only for their primary purpose, no real difficulties result; problems arise mainly with secondary usage. In order to safeguard against misuse, we need public exposure, public discussion of the issues, and an appropriate legislative framework. DATA BANKS

Warwick, D. P. 1975. "Social Scientists Ought to Stop Lying." *Psychology Today* 8:38–40, 105–06.

The author expresses outrage at the deception used in the Rosenthal and Jacobson study of the pygmalion effect in classrooms, the

Black and Reiss police studies, the work of the Piliavins and Milgram, and is critical of covert observation through deliberate misrepresentation. He questions the ethics of those who use deceit to further scientific aims and yet decry deception used to protect the presidency, for instance. He suggests the establishment of truth-in-research laws similar to truth-in-lending ones. DECEPTION, OBSERVATION

———, and J. F. Galliher. 1974. "Who Deserves Protection?" (An exchange between Warwick and Galliher.) *American Sociologist* 9:3, 158–80.

Warwick, in response to Galliher (1973), argues that Galliher's essential point (in social research, the end justifies the means) is a form of Machiavellian ethics of which he wants no part. In his rebuttal, Galliher reiterates the point that public officials are (or should be) publicly accountable and that less-desirable means are sometimes necessary to realize morally superior ends. He is critical of Warwick's perception of sociologists as "detached scientists-scholars" operating from a position of "amoral professionalism." PROFESSIONALISM, RISK-BENEFIT

Wax, Murray L. 1976. "On Fieldworkers and Those Exposed to Fieldwork: Federal Regulations, Moral Issues, Rights of Inquiry." Washington University, St. Louis. Paper.

Wax contends that fieldworkers in social science research should not be subjected to the rigid controls which current HEW regulations on the "Protection of Human Subjects" impose on researchers in general. Biomedical and behavioral researchers conduct experiments in clinical settings, where a lack of informed consent in controlled. research can expose subjects to potential harm. However, the model prevailing here, of "powerful researcher–helpless subject," rightly an area of concern for the regulatory system, does not apply to sociological and anthropological fieldwork.

The relevant features of fieldwork, which distinguish it from behavioral and biomedical research, are discussed: the moral and economic dependency of the fieldworker frequently engendered by his relation to the culture studied; the flexibility demanded by and the impracticality of obtaining prior consent for emergent and changing project conditions; and the ability of a group to easily protect its social secrets and privacy.

In place of prior written and informed consent, Wax advocates a detailed accounting of the fieldwork to be submitted upon its conclusion, subject to review by a committee of academic and professional peers.

The benefit/harm arising from fieldwork studies is discussed. The conclusion is that rarely has harm arisen from such contact.

Wax notes that the regulation of publication of findings is made difficult by constitutional protections. Moreover, those who believe themselves damaged by such studies have legal recourse.

Wax's main conclusion is that the nature of fieldwork prevents it from operating with the rigidity required by bureaucratic norms. FREEDOM OF INQUIRY, OBSERVATION, RISK-BENEFIT

Westin, A. F. 1968. *Privacy and Freedom.* New York: Atheneum.

This is a study of surveillance in our society and its implications for personal privacy. Among a series of topics it addresses the issues of data collection and processing and the threats these pose to individual privacy. Westin observes that the trend of large private and governmental investigative systems to amass personal dossiers on millions of Americans presents a number of dangers—for instance, collected raw data become part of an official file, the contents of which are unknown to an individual and which he cannot challenge creating a "record prison."

Westin recognizes the conflict produced by the need of social decision makers for data and the public's fear of depersonalization and manipulation by the collection and processing of information. As remedies, he suggests distinguishing among three kinds of information: private and noncirculating, confidential with limited circulation, and public and freely circulating. He also urges placing controls on the input, storage, and output of new information systems. However, since the system could be corrupted despite all possible system safeguards, law and ethical restraints mark the final controls. Legally personal information could be defined as a property right and the individual could seek refuge in due process. This would lead to information review by the individual himself and could profoundly affect the information system. Regulatory agencies, legislative review, and criminal penalties should be established. DATA BANKS, LEGAL, LEGISLATION AND REGULATION, PRIVACY

———. 1968. "Social Science Dilemmas in the Data-Collection Age." *Research Symposium: Social Science Research and Individual Rights.* Washington, D.C.: American Society for Public Administration.

Social scientists are using new tools and methods to learn about behavior with the aim of improving society. At the same time, however, increased usage of "electronic instruments of surveillance and data accumulation to meet society's growing needs for greater information" threatens individual claims to privacy. In addition, the need for sophisticated decision making, often processed by technological and managerial elites, can impair our system of participatory democracy. Social scientists find themselves in new roles, analyzing trends and patterns of collective behavior, and passing judgments on to the policy makers. The new instruments of data collection and manipulation mean that citizens can be subjected to experimentation and measurement without their consent. The problem thus is one of providing for dissent and democratic control while retaining the benefits provided by improved information. Westin concedes that self-regulation by the social sciences would be preferable, but he believes that the courts will predominate in settling disputes between the right to privacy versus the obligations of public disclosure. DATA BANKS, PRIVACY, SOCIAL CONTROL, SOCIAL POLICY

————, and M. A. Baker. 1972. *Databanks in a Free Society: Computers, Record-Keeping and Privacy.* Computer Science and Engineering Board, National Academy of Sciences. New York: Quadrangle.

This report, prepared for the National Academy of Science's Project on Computer Databanks, offers an analysis of the impact of computer use on record-keeping processes in the United States. It examines the meaning of large-scale data banks—manual and computerized —for the citizen's constitutional rights to privacy and due process. The authors suggest public policy actions regulating data banks that will strike a balance between society's need for new knowledge and the protection of individual civil liberties.

Appendix B examines public opinion on the related questions of computers, privacy, and record-keeping. Recent opinion polls reveal a solid minority sentiment that individual privacy is being eroded to some extent by record-keeping. However, this concern will vary, depending on the issue, and opinions also differ by the degree to which people consider record-keeping practices necessary and the degree of perceived threat to individual privacy. Also discussed are public attitudes on computers and organizational record-keeping. DATA BANKS, PRIVACY, CONFIDENTIALITY

Wolf, E. P. 1964. "Some Questions about Community Self-Surveys: When Amateurs Conduct Research." *Human Organization* 23:85–89.

Ethical problems can arise when nonprofessionals are involved in the data-gathering processes of social research. The community self-survey, carried out by participant members of the community, often without the assistance of professional social scientists, will frequently, though unwittingly, violate such standards as the right to privacy, informed consent, anonymity, the need to restrict access to files and materials, and to be guarded in private "social" conversations. Dangers of bias-generation, anxiety-production, and overinterviewing are all areas which potentially threaten the good name of social research.

"Violations of privacy and security may create widespread distrust, and unnecessary hostility and resentment created by amateur efforts may endanger valuable research in the future." CONFIDENTIALITY, IN-FORMED CONSENT, PROFESSIONALISM, SURVEYS

Wolfensberg, W. 1967. "Ethical Issues in Research with Human Subjects." *Science* 155:47–51.

This article contains a good description of the state of affairs concerning experimentation on humans before 1967.

Wolfensberg sees the controversy surrounding such research as evidence of the tension between society's needs and individual rights. Ethics codes should be based on clearly stated principles. A key issue is that of informed consent—the ability to be informed is a continuous, not a categorical, variable. Since it is impossible to conduct certain types of research (for example, Milgram's) unless the subject is unaware of certain key features, Wolfensberg holds that informed consent can be said to exist if the subject understands the essential aspects of the research, for instance, his rights, the types of risks involved, both nega-tive and positive consequences, without necessarily being informed of the experimental purpose, although such information is desirable. Wolfensberg discusses five "rights" which research might require a subject to yield: invasion of privacy; donation or sacrifice of personal resources such as time, attention, dignity; surrender of personal auton-omy; exposure to short-term risks; and exposure to long-term risks. He distinguishes three types of research: experimental activities and proce-dures not labeled research, such as psychotherapy; "unnatural" research —risk very small, perhaps less than for the first type; and risky research where the outcomes are unknown, but where real advances in knowl-edge sometimes result. Wolfensberg makes a number of recommenda-tions in connection with the principles on which guidelines should be based: the more potentially harmful the experiment, the more precau-tions are necessary; experimenter responsibility cannot be waived; the more rights to be given up, the more important consent becomes; in cases where little harm results—most second-level experiments—rou-tine release forms are probably sufficient. The latter would inform the subject that there is little likelihood of his receiving direct benefit from the research but that the research is beneficial to society, that participa-tion is voluntary, and that the research will entail no unreasonable discomfort, time, or loss of privacy. CODES OF ETHICS, IN-FORMED CONSENT, RISK-BENEFIT, STRESS

Zeisel, H. 1970. "Reducing the Hazards of Human Experiments Through Modifications in Research Design." *Annals of New York Academy of Sciences* 169:475–86.

Zeisel discusses a number of possible modifications in the design of controlled experiments intended to reduce both risk and the moral and legal objections to certain kinds of research. To minimize risk in experiments where the element of risk is acknowledged to exist, he suggests that such experiments be run only once, that the number of subjects involved be kept to the bare minimum necessary for valid inference, that the experimental condition be one which is expected to give favorable results, that a sequential "play-the-winner" design be used, and that groups of subjects be exposed to experimental treatment at different times so that the last can serve as controls for the first (or instead of control groups, computed baselines be used, as in "regression discontinuity" design, for instance).

In order to reduce legal or moral objections, Zeisel suggests that experiments be moved from the proscribed into the permissible range. For instance, to test the effects of a merit fellowship award, he suggests taking a random sample of those falling just below the eligibility line, exposing half to experimental treatment and using the others as controls. In addition, he recommends the fullest use possible of role-playing, mock trials, and similar techniques; the use of agency-provided aggregate data to test the efficacy of experimental treatments; and the use of indirect experiments—for instance, not obligatory pretrial versus obligatory nonpretrial, but rather obligatory pretrial versus optional pretrial. Finally, he comments on the fact that most subjects are drawn from the underprivileged segments of the population and suggests that the upper strata also be systematically inducted into research. ETHICAL-GENERAL, SOCIAL EXPERIMENTATION, STRESS

Zemach, R. 1969. "Social Surveys and the Responsibilities of Statisticians." *American Statistician* 23:46–48.

Zemach comments on the alarming proliferation of surveys and data-gathering activities and enjoins social scientists to show concern about the ethical and social consequences of this unchecked process. Furthermore, while guidelines have been developed for federal surveys, activities within the private sector remain unchecked. She mentions two popular violations of confidentiality: the practice of drawing samples from lists of survey respondents for follow-up studies which should be discontinued, and the lack of security in handling responses —the promise of confidentiality to respondents should be given greater strength. In addition, she suggests keeping records so that additional data gathering is not necessary, subjecting proposed surveys to cost-benefit analysis, making more use of existing data banks, developing data directories, and supplying aggregated information while keeping individual records confidential. CONFIDENTIALITY, DATA BANKS, SURVEYS

# Name Index

# Subject Index

bibliographies, 85, 103–04, 112, 139–40

biomedical research, text: 3–6, 9, 13–15, 33, 39, 42, 51, 52–53, 57–59; bibliography: 85, 87, 92–93, 94–95, 100–01, 104, 110, 119–21, 122–23, 126, 128, 131–33, 136, 137–38, 140–41, 150–51, 154–55, 165–66, 171–72, 177, 189–90, 196, 197, 202–03, 205

codes of ethics, text: 1–2, 4–5, 23, 30–31, 55–58; bibliography: 85, 94, 95–98, 99–101, 107–08, 112–14, 135–36, 137, 138, 141, 148–49, 151–52, 180–81, 190–91, 194, 205, 206, 208–09, 211–12, 214, 215, 219

coercion, text: 12, 15–17, 35, 40, 47–48; bibliography: 85, 119, 140–41, 156–57, 158, 164, 168, 210

collective concerns, text: 12, 28–31, 34, 41, 48; bibliography: 85, 103, 112, 130–31, 137, 144–47, 148, 149, 150, 151–52, 156–57, 162, 163, 167, 171, 175, 180–81, 182–83, 185–86, 188–89, 193, 212–14

confidentiality, text: 6, 10–12, 14, 19, 23–25, 32, 35, 39, 42, 63; bibliography: 85, 88–89, 91–92, 102, 105, 106, 107, 109–10, 111–14, 115, 118–19, 121, 122–23, 124, 130–31, 133, 135, 138, 144, 146, 147–48, 151, 156, 158–61, 172–74, 180, 181, 185–88, 191–92, 194–95, 196–97, 198–99, 200, 201–02, 207–08, 210–11, 212, 218–19, 220

data banks, text: 9–10, 24–25; bibliography: 85, 89, 91–92, 106, 111–12, 121, 137, 139, 153, 156, 169–70, 194, 198–99, 206–07, 210–11, 213–14, 215, 217–18, 220

deception, text: 12, 17–19, 31, 33, 35, 37, 56, 65–66; bibliography: 85, 88–89, 90–91, 96–98, 104–05, 108, 114, 127–28, 131, 138, 143, 152, 157–58, 166–67, 168, 169, 174–75, 188, 191, 193–95, 198, 199–200, 206–07, 209–10, 215–16

ethical-general, text: 3–4, 9, 13, 16, 23, 29, 36, 41, 47, 55, 64–66; bibliography: 85, 87, 93, 94, 95–96, 101, 103, 106, 109, 119, 125–26, 132–34, 138–39, 142, 143–44, 146–49, 150–51, 154–56, 157, 160, 161, 163, 164–65, 171–72, 176, 192, 193, 196–97, 199, 202, 204, 205, 210, 213, 214, 219–20

field investigations, text: 31, 42, 50, 66, 69; bibliography: 86, 89–91, 95–96, 98–99, 107, 144–46, 152, 162, 166–67

freedom of inquiry, text: 46–47; bibliography: 86, 108–09, 116, 126–27, 128–29, 138–39, 146–47, 148, 177, 178–79, 180–81, 190–91, 197–98, 204–05, 207, 210, 213, 216–17

informed consent, text: 4–8, 10, 29, 36, 43, 56, 63, 66, 68, 69; bibliography: 86, 87, 92, 93–95, 96–97, 100–01, 102–03, 106, 107, 112, 114, 117–19, 123–24, 126, 127–28, 129, 130, 131–32, 140–41, 143, 149, 151, 152, 158–59, 166, 166–67, 168, 171–72, 174, 177–78, 181–82, 183, 184, 186–90, 191–92, 193–95, 196, 197–98, 201–02, 204, 205–07, 211–12, 215, 218–19

institutional review boards, text: 5–9, 52–53, 63, 66–68, 68–69; bibliography: 86, 92–93, 94–95, 110–11, 117–18, 122, 140, 141, 167–68, 177

legal matters, text: 4, 7, 9, 13, 16, 20–21, 24–25; bibliography: 86, 91, 99, 100, 102, 105, 110, 115, 119, 120–21, 130, 133–34, 135, 136, 142, 150, 152–53, 159–60, 170, 172–74, 178, 179, 189, 196, 198–200, 202–03, 209, 212, 217

legislation and regulation, text: 1, 4–5, 8–11, 13, 20, 25, 36, 42, 54, 57–61; bibliography: 86, 88, 89, 93, 94, 106, 107–11, 115–16, 120–21, 122, 123, 126–27, 128–29,

226

# About the Authors

**Robert T. Bower** is Director of the nonprofit Bureau of Social Science Research in Washington, D.C. He was a member of the National Council on the Humanities from 1966 to 1972 and has served as president of the American Association for Public Opinion Research and of the National Council on Public Polls. His last published book was *Television and the Public* (Holt, Rinehart and Winston, 1973).

**Priscilla de Gasparis** was a Research Analyst at the Bureau of Social Science Research while working on this report. Subsequently she was a consultant for the Privacy Protection Study Commission. She is now at the University of Pittsburgh writing her doctoral thesis in sociology, dealing with the impact of informed consent on a number of methods used in the social sciences to gather data. She obtained her B.A. in psychology and moral philosophy from the University of the Witwatersrand and her M.A. in sociology from the University of Pittsburgh.

RELATED TITLES/ *Published by*
*Praeger Special Studies*




NEW METHODS IN SOCIAL SCIENCE RESEARCH: Policy Sciences
and Futures Research

T. Harrell Allen

*SOCIAL SCIENCE AND PUBLIC POLICY IN THE UNITED
STATES

Irving Louis Horowitz
James Everett Katz

---